EA Review

Part 3 Representation

Enrolled Agent Study Guide

2018-2019 Edition

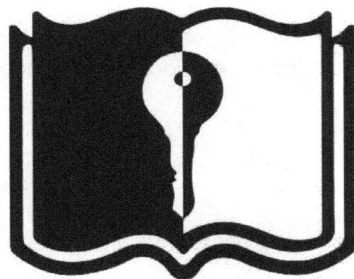

PassKey
Learning Systems

Richard Gramkow, EA
Christy Pinheiro, EA, ABA®
Kolleen Wells, EA
Joel Busch, CPA, JD

Editor: Joel Busch, CPA, JD

This study guide is designed for test-takers who will take their exams in the 2018-2019 EA Exam testing window (May 1, 2018 to February 28, 2019).

PassKey Learning Systems, EA Review Part 3, Representation: Enrolled Agent Study Guide 2018-2019 Edition

ISBN-13: 978-0-9986118-8-4

First Printing. 2018.

PassKey EA Review® is a U.S. Registered Trademark

Official textbook website: *www.PassKeyPublications.com*
Online study: *www.passkeylearningsystems.com*

Table of Contents

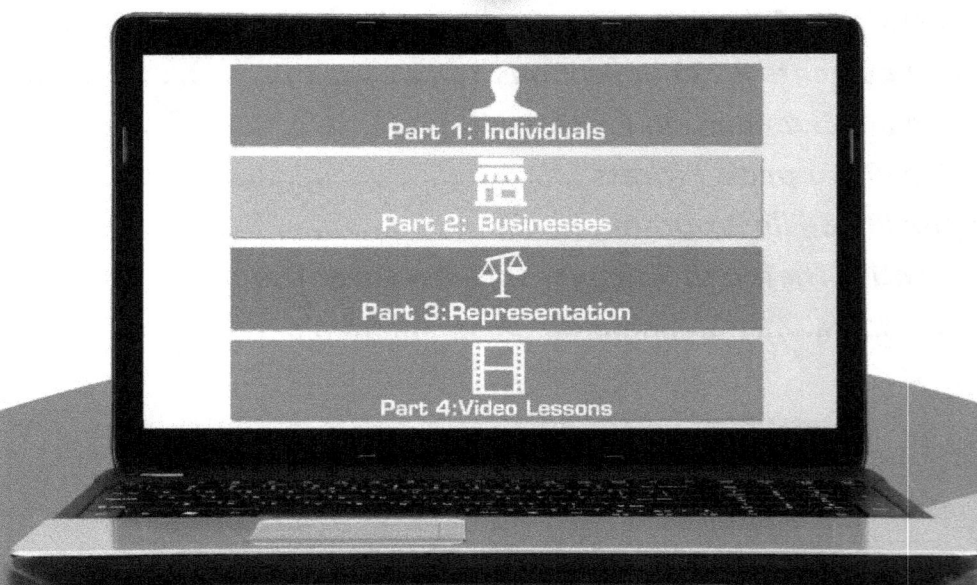

Recent Praise for the PassKey EA Review Series

(Real customers, real names, public testimonials)

This review is the best on the market.

Yaw Asiante-Asamoah

I passed on all three parts on one attempt. The questions in the Review and Workbook are similar to the real exams. I got a big raise, and my bonus went up at my seasonal job. It's worth the money, trust me.

This is the only book you need.

Suika Yutaka

I prefer self-study over any type of course, and I loved this book. Plus, I have a very demanding job, and this made me greatly appreciate the concise style of this book. Also note that this is the most reasonably priced full EA review I know of (i.e., covering all three parts of the exam). Greatest praise!

You can pass using just this book.

Vishnu Kali Osirion

I really rushed studying for this section. These authors make tax law relevant to your day-to-day experiences and understandable. You can pass the exam with just this as a resource. I do recommend purchasing the workbook as well just for question exposure. The questions in the book and in the workbook are pretty indicative of what's on the exam. This is a must buy. Cheers.

Thank you!

Laura Southerland, EA

Thank you for having this course available. I was able to pass each part on the first try by using the online course, study books, my work knowledge, as well as my Bachelor's in Accounting. [PassKey's] practice questions were very similar to the actual EA exam.

I passed all three parts.

Robbie Cantoron

I passed all three parts of the EA exam using [PassKey], which is why I'll give it five stars...There are many tax laws I've learned about by studying this book that I haven't encountered yet preparing returns, so I did end up learning a lot. The trick is to focus (after reading the material) on the multiple-choice questions at the end of each chapter and their solutions: this is how you will apply and practice what you've learned and really learn the details.

This book helped me pass.

Kenichi Mochizukion

I used the PassKey workbook after studying PassKey textbook. The example questions cover all the topics and require good understanding to answer, so it was very helpful to reveal my weak areas prior to the exam.

A Very Easy Read

Jeniz May

This book was very nicely organized, and a very easy read compared to other publications. I passed Part two with PassKey and would definitely recommend using these books.

Wonderful!

Ana Lavallee

PassKey was all I needed to pass the three tests to become an EA in just three months. The books are easy to read and understand. Thank you!

Outstanding!

Derrell L. Chastain

Outstanding! Helped me pass the EA exam...I used all three books!

Highly recommend these materials

Tosha H. Knelangeon

Using only this book and the workbook, I passed all three EA exams on my first try. I highly recommend these materials. As long as you put in the time to read and study all the information provided, you should be well-prepared.

Very useful, I passed 1st and 2nd exams by reading only PassKey!

Shixiong Feng

Very useful; I passed the 1st and 2nd exams by only reading the PassKey EA Review. If you are willing to spend some time to read the whole book thoroughly, then this book is the only thing you need to pass the EA exams.

I passed!

Ismail Osman

The book is excellent to pass the EA exam. I passed Part 1 on my first attempt. These are great study resources. I love PassKey!

Amazing!

Sopio Svanishvilion

PassKey helped me pass all three parts of the Enrolled Agent exam. They are a "must have" if you want to pass your EA exams.

PassKey is the way to go!

Alaina Crowell

I passed all three SEEs on the first try in ten weeks! Each unit is explained so clearly, and I was completely prepared for each SEE. Wonderful books.

Introduction

Congratulations on taking the first step toward becoming an Enrolled Agent, a widely respected professional tax designation. The Internal Revenue Service licenses Enrolled Agents, known as EAs, after candidates pass a competency exam testing their knowledge of federal tax law. As an Enrolled Agent, you will have the same representation rights as a CPA, with the ability to represent taxpayers in IRS audits and appeals—an EA's rights are unlimited before all levels and offices of the IRS.

The PassKey study guide series is designed to help you study for the EA exam, which is formally called the *IRS Special Enrollment Examination* or *"SEE."*

EA Exam Basics

The EA exam consists of three parts, which candidates may schedule separately and take in any order they wish. The computerized exam covers all aspects of federal tax law, with Part 1 testing the taxation of individuals; Part 2 testing the taxation of businesses; and Part 3 testing representation, practice, and procedures.

Each part of the EA exam features 100 multiple choice questions, with no written answers required. The exam may include some experimental questions that are not scored. You will not know which of the questions count toward your score and which do not.

Computerized EA Exam Format
Part 1: Individual Taxation—100 questions
Part 2: Business Taxation—100 questions
Part 3: Representation, Practice, and Procedures—100 questions

You will have 3.5 hours to complete each part of the exam. The actual seat time is four hours, which allows time for a pre-exam tutorial and a postexam survey. An on-screen timer counts down the amount of time you have to finish.

The testing company Prometric exclusively administers the EA exam at thousands of testing centers across the United States and in certain other countries. You can find valuable information and register online at *www.prometric.com/SEE.*

Prometric Testing Center Procedures

The testing center is designed to be a secure environment. The following are procedures you will need to follow on test day:

1. Check in about a half-hour before your appointment time, and bring a current, government-issued ID with a photo and signature. If you do not have a valid ID, you will be turned away and will have to pay for a new exam appointment. Refunds will not be issued by Prometric if you forget to bring proper ID with you.
2. The EA exam is a closed-book test, so you are not allowed to bring any notes or reference materials into the testing room. The center supplies sound-blocking headphones if you want to use them.
3. No food, water, or other beverages are allowed in the testing room.
4. You will be given scratch paper and a pencil to use, which will be collected after the exam.

5. You will be able to use an onscreen calculator during the exam, or Prometric will provide you with a handheld calculator. You cannot bring your own calculator into the examination room.
6. Before entering the testing room, you will be scanned with a metal detector wand.
7. You will need to sign in and out every time you leave the testing room. Bathroom breaks are permitted, but the test timer will continue to count down.
8. You are not allowed to talk or communicate with other test-takers in the exam room. Prometric continuously monitors the testing via video, physical walk-throughs, and an observation window.

> **Important Note:** Violation of any of these procedures may result in the disqualification of your exam. In cases of cheating, the IRS says candidates are subject to consequences that include civil and criminal penalties.

Exam-takers who require special accommodations under the Americans with Disabilities Act (ADA) must contact Prometric directly at 1-800-967-1139 to obtain an accommodation request. The test is administered in English; a language barrier is not considered a disability.

Exam Content

Each May, using questions based on the prior calendar year's tax law, the IRS introduces multiple new versions of each part of the EA exam. If you fail a particular part of the exam and need to retake it, do not expect to see the identical questions the next time.

Prometric's website includes broad content outlines for each exam part. When you study, make sure you are familiar with the items listed, which are covered in detail in your PassKey guides. The IRS no longer releases test questions and answers from prior exams, although questions from older exams (pre-2005) are still available on the IRS website for review. Be aware that tax law changes every year, so be familiar with recent updates and do not rely too heavily on these earlier questions and answers.

Your PassKey study guides present an overview of all the major areas of federal taxation that Enrolled Agents typically encounter in their practices and are likely to appear on the exam. Although our guides are designed to be comprehensive, we suggest you also review IRS publications and try to learn as much as you can about tax law in general, so you are well-equipped to take the exam.

In addition to this study guide, we highly recommend that all exam candidates read:

- **Publication 17,** *Your Federal Income Tax* (for Part 1 of the exam), and
- **Circular 230,** *Regulations Governing the Practice of Attorneys, Certified Public Accountants, Enrolled Agents, Enrolled Actuaries, and Appraisers before the Internal Revenue Service* (for Part 3 of the exam)

You may download these publications for free from the IRS website.

> **Note:** Some exam candidates take *Part 3: Representation, Practice, and Procedures* first rather than taking the tests in order, since the material in Part 3 is considered less complex. However, test-takers should know that several questions pertaining to taxation of *Individuals* (Part 1) and *Businesses* (Part 2) are often included on the Part 3 exam.

Exam Strategy

Each multiple-choice question has four answer choices. There are several different question formats, and examples of each format are featured in your PassKey study guides. During the exam, you should read each question thoroughly to understand exactly what is being asked. Be particularly careful when the question uses language such as "not" or "except."

If you are unsure of an answer, you may mark it for review and return to it later. Try to eliminate clearly wrong answers from the four possible choices to narrow your odds of selecting the right answer. But be sure to answer every question, even if you have to guess, because all answers left incomplete will be marked as incorrect. Each question is weighted equally.

Format One–Direct Question
Which of the following entities are required to file Form 709, *United States Gift Tax Return*? A. An individual B. An estate or trust C. A corporation D. All of the above
Format Two–Incomplete Sentence
Supplemental wages do not include payments for: A. Accumulated sick leave B. Nondeductible moving expenses C. Vacation pay D. Travel reimbursements paid at the federal government's per diem rate
Format Three–All of the Following Except
There are five tests which must be met for you to claim an exemption for a dependent. Which of the following is not a requirement? A. Citizen or Resident Test B. Member of Household or Relationship Test C. Disability Test D. Joint Return Test

There may also be a limited number of questions that have four choices, with three incorrect statements or facts and only one with a correct statement or fact, which you would select as the right answer.

With 3.5 hours allotted for each part of the exam, you have slightly more than two minutes per question. Try to answer the questions you are sure about quickly, so you can devote more time to those that include calculations or that you are unsure about. Remember, the clock does not stop for bathroom breaks, so allocate your time wisely.

To familiarize yourself with the computerized testing format, you may take a tutorial on the Prometric website. However, the tutorial only illustrates what the test screens look like; it does not allow you to revisit questions you have left open or marked for review, as you can do during the actual exam.

Scoring Methods

The EA exam is not graded on a curve, and the IRS does not reveal either a percentage of correct answers needed to pass or a predetermined pass rate. Each question on the exam is worth one point. The IRS determines scaled scores by calculating the number of questions answered correctly from the total number of questions in the exam and converting to a scale that ranges from 40 to 130. The IRS has set the scaled passing score at 105, which corresponds to the minimum level of knowledge deemed acceptable for EAs.

After you finish your exam and submit your answers, you will exit the testing room, and a Prometric staff member will print results showing whether you passed or failed. Test results are automatically shared with the IRS, so you do not need to submit them yourself. Test scores are confidential and will be revealed only to you and the IRS.

If you pass, your printed results will show a passing designation but not your actual score. The printout also will not indicate which specific questions you answered correctly or incorrectly.

If you fail, you will receive a scaled score, so you will be able to see how close you are to the minimum score of 105.

You will also receive the following diagnostic information to help you know which subject areas to concentrate on when studying to retake the exam:

- *Level 1: Area of weakness where additional study is necessary. It is important for you to focus on this domain as you prepare to take the test again. You may want to consider taking a course or participating actively in a study group on this topic.*
- *Level 2: Might need additional study.*
- *Level 3: Clearly demonstrated an understanding of the subject area.*

These diagnostic indicators correspond to various sections of each part of the exam.

If necessary, you may take each part of the exam up to four times during the current testing window. You will need to reregister with Prometric and pay fees each new time you take an exam part.

You may carry over passing scores for individual parts of the exam up to two years from the date you took them.

Pass Rates

The yearly pass rates for the SEE vary by exam. In the prior year testing period, the highest pass rate was for Part 3, with a nearly 90% success rate. Just over 80% of test-takers passed Part 1.

The pass rate for Part 2 was much lower, averaging only about 40%. Prometric notes that it can be misleading to compare pass rates for the various exams because the same individuals do not take each one. The number of candidates who take Part 1 is nearly double the number of candidates taking either Part 2 or Part 3.

Applying for Enrollment

Once you have passed all three parts of the EA exam, you can apply to become an Enrolled Agent. The process includes an IRS review of your tax compliance history. Failure to timely file or pay personal income taxes can be grounds for denial of enrollment. The IRS's Return Preparer Office will review the circumstances of each case and make determinations on an individual basis. You may not practice as an

EA until the IRS approves your application and issues you an enrollment card, a process that takes up to 60 days or more.

Successfully passing the EA exam can launch you into a fulfilling and lucrative new career. The exam requires intense preparation and diligence, but with the help of PassKey's comprehensive *EA Review*, you will have the tools you need to learn how to become an Enrolled Agent.

We wish you much success.

STEP 1: Learn

Learn more about the Enrolled Agent designation, and explore the career opportunities that await you after passing your EA exam. In addition to preparing income tax returns for clients, EAs can represent individuals and businesses before the IRS, just as attorneys and CPAs do. A college degree or professional tax background is not required to take the EA exam. Many people who use the PassKey study guides have had no prior experience preparing tax returns, but go on to rewarding new professional careers.

STEP 2: Gather Information

Gather more information before you launch into your studies. The IRS publishes basic information about becoming an EA on its website (*www.irs.gov/Tax-Professionals/Enrolled-Agents*). You will also find valuable information about the exam itself on the Prometric testing website at www.prometric.com/see. Be sure to download the *Candidate Information Bulletin*, which takes you step-by-step through the registration and testing process.

STEP 3: Obtain a PTIN

PTIN stands for *Preparer Tax Identification Number*. Before you can register for your EA exam, you must obtain a PTIN from the IRS. The PTIN sign-up system can be found at www.irs.gov/ptin. You will need to create an account and provide personal information. Starting in 2017, there is no longer a fee for obtaining or renewing a PTIN. Candidates who choose to use the paper Form W-12, *IRS Paid Preparer Tax Identification Number (PTIN) Application and Renewal*, will have to wait about four to six weeks to have their PTINs processed. Foreign-based candidates without a Social Security number are also required to have a PTIN in order to register to take the exam; they will need to submit additional paperwork with their Form W-12.

STEP 4: Register with Prometric

Once you have your PTIN, you may register for your exam on the Prometric website by creating an account to set up your user ID and password. You must also complete Form 2587, *Application for Special Enrollment Examination*.

STEP 5: Schedule Your Test

After creating an account, you can complete the registration process by clicking on "Scheduling." Your exam appointment must be scheduled within one year from the date of registration. You can choose a test site, time, and date that are convenient for you. Prometric has test centers in most major metropolitan areas of the United States, as well as in many other countries.

You may schedule as little as two days in advance—space permitting—through the website or by calling 800-306-3926 Monday through Friday. Be aware that the website and the phone line show different inventories of available times and dates, so you may want to check both for your preferred testing dates. The testing fee is nonrefundable. Once you have scheduled, you will receive a confirmation number. Keep it for your records because you will need it to reschedule, cancel, or change your appointment.

STEP 6: Adopt a Study Plan

Focus on one exam part at a time, and adopt a study plan that covers each unit of your PassKey guides. You will need to develop your own individualized study program. The period of time you'll need to prepare for each exam is truly unique to you, based on how much prior tax preparation experience you have and your current level of tax knowledge, how well you understand and retain the information you read, and how much time you have to study for each test. For those without prior tax experience, a good rule of thumb is to study at least 60 hours for each of the three exam sections. *Part 2: Businesses* may require additional study preparation, as evidenced by the lower pass rates. One thing is true for all candidates: for each of the tests, start studying well in advance of your scheduled exam date.

STEP 7: Get Plenty of Rest and Good Nutrition

Get plenty of rest, exercise, and good nutrition prior to the EA exam. You'll want to be at your best on exam day.

STEP 8: Test Day

Be sure to arrive early at the test site. Prometric advises arriving at least 30 minutes before your scheduled exam time. If you miss your appointment and are not allowed to take the test, you'll forfeit your fee and have to pay for a new appointment. Remember to bring a government-issued ID with your name, photo, and signature. Your first and last name must exactly match the first and last name you used to register for the exam.

STEP 9: During the Exam

This is when your hard work finally pays off. Focus and don't worry if you don't know the answer to every question, but make sure you use your time well. Give your best answer to every question. All questions left blank will be marked as wrong.

STEP 10: Congratulations. You Passed!

After celebrating your success, you need to apply for your EA designation. The quickest way is by filling out Form 23, *Application for Enrollment to Practice Before the Internal Revenue Service*, on the IRS website. You may also pay online. Once your application is approved, you'll be issued an enrollment card, and you'll officially be a brand new Enrolled Agent!

PART 3: Representation

New Tax Law for Part 3: Representation

Offer in Compromise (OIC) Changes: Any OIC applications received on or after March 27, 2017, when the taxpayer has outstanding unfiled returns, will be rejected without further consideration. Any initial payment required with the OIC application will be applied to reduce the taxpayer's balance. This policy does not apply to current year tax returns if the taxpayer has filed a valid extension.

Steele vs. United States: On June 1, 2017, the U.S. District Court ruled that the IRS may continue to require PTINs but may not charge fees for the issuance or renewal of PTINs. The IRS filed an appeal on September 6, 2017, and has moved to stay the Court's injunction and refund orders. At the time of this book's printing, the case was ongoing and had not yet been resolved. PTINs are still required for tax professionals, but there is no fee to request or renew one's PTIN in 2018.

EA Exam Price Increase and Scheduling Changes: Beginning with the current testing cycle (May 1, 2018 – February 28, 2019), the fee to take the Special Enrollment Exam (SEE) will increase to $181.94 per exam section. Scheduling an exam appointment for the 2018-2019 testing window will be available starting March 1, 2018.

ITIN Expirations: Many Individual Taxpayer Identification Numbers expired on December 31, 2017. This includes any ITIN not used on a tax return at least once in the past three years. Also, any ITIN with middle digits of 70, 71, 72, or 80 is now expired. Affected taxpayers must reapply to renew their ITIN.

Practitioner Priority Line: Taxpayer representatives are now being asked to confirm their Social Security number and date of birth, in addition to their Centralized Authorization File (CAF) number, so that IRS agents can verify their identity when they call the IRS. The new questions result from an updated version of Internal Revenue Manual (IRM) Section, which took effect January 3, 2018.

Form 1023-EZ Changes: This form, updated January 2018, is used by nonprofit entities (generally those with annual gross receipts of $50,000 or less and fair market value of assets of $250,000 or less) to obtain Federal exempt status or reinstate their tax-exempt status for failure-to-file annual returns or notices. The revised form makes the original application or reinstatement process easier than using Form 1023. The updated Form 1023-EZ is only accepted as an e-file. It cannot be filed on paper.

Revised Rules Allow More Taxpayers to Claim the EITC Without a Qualifying Child: The IRS changed its position on who may claim the earned income tax credit (EITC) without a qualifying child in situations in which an individual meets the definition of a qualifying child for more than one taxpayer. The new rule is explained in proposed regulations issued on January 19, 2017.[1] Under the new rules, a taxpayer who may not claim an individual as a qualifying child after applying the tie-breaker rules may now claim the EITC without a qualifying child, if all other requirements are met. For example, this new rule may apply in households with unmarried parents who both work. This change affects all open tax years, including amended returns for prior tax years.

Head of Household Due Diligence: Under the PATH Act, preparer due diligence[2] includes the Earned Income Tax Credit, the Child Tax Credit and Additional Child Tax Credit, and the American Opportunity

---

[1] Federal Register Volume 82, Issue 12 (January 19, 2017), Definition of Dependent
[2] IRC 6695(g)

Tax Credit. Effective for tax years beginning after December 31, 2017, the Tax Cuts and Jobs Act amends the due diligence requirements and any applicable preparer penalties to also apply to head of household filing status.[3] A $510 penalty may be assessed for any preparers where the IRS determines that the due diligence requirements were not met.

New Requirement for Child Tax Credit Beginning in 2018: Beginning with 2018 federal returns, in order for a child to be eligible for the Child Tax Credit, the dependent must have a valid Social Security number. ITINs are no longer sufficient.

Paid Preparer Due Diligence Penalties Increases in 2017: The penalty for each failure to meet due diligence requirements is now adjusted for inflation. The penalty for tax year 2017 is $510. The penalty for failure to meet the due diligence requirements containing EITC, CTC, or AOTC filed in 2017 is $510 per credit *per tax return.* For example, if the preparer fails to meet due diligence for ALL THREE credits on a single return, the preparer's penalty would be $1,530.

Passport Revocations: The IRS has begun implementation of new procedures affecting individuals with delinquent tax debts. These new procedures implement provisions of the *Fixing America's Surface Transportation (FAST) Act*. The FAST Act requires the IRS to notify the U.S. State Department of taxpayers owing a seriously delinquent tax debt. The FAST Act also requires the State Department to deny their passport application or deny renewal of their passport. In some cases, the State Department may revoke their passport. A taxpayer with a seriously delinquent tax debt is generally someone who owes the IRS more than $51,000 in back taxes, penalties, and interest for which the IRS has filed a Notice of Federal Tax Lien, and the period to challenge it has expired, or the IRS has issued a levy. However, there are a number of situations where actions against one's passport will not be taken, including those in bankruptcy and those with a pending installment agreement or OIC with the IRS.

New Centralized Partnership Audit Rules: As result of the Bipartisan Budget Act (BBA) of 2015, Congress enhanced the IRS's ability to audit partnerships. This new "centralized partnership audit" regime is *mandatory* for partnership tax years beginning after December 31, 2017. The new law will allow certain partnerships with 100 or fewer partners to elect out of this new regime. To elect out of the new partnership rules, in addition to the maximum 100-partner requirement, the partnership must only have eligible partners, which are:

- Individuals
- C corporations (and any foreign entity that would be treated as a C corporation if it were a domestic corporation)
- S corporations
- Estates of deceased partners

Note: The IRS is currently rejecting requests to opt out of the new centralized partnership audit regime where they are partners who are disregarded entities and revocable trusts.

---

[3] In 2018, additional questions will be added to the Form 8867, *Preparer's Due Diligence Checklist*, to ensure that tax preparers are performing the required due diligence in determining that the taxpayer is eligible to use the head of household filing status.

IRS Expands W-2 Verification Code for the 2018 Filing Season: The IRS has expanded the W-2 verification code pilot to verify the authenticity taxpayer wage and income data. This initiative is one in a series of steps implemented by the IRS as part of an effort to fight tax-related fraud and identity theft. The IRS has partnered with certain payroll service providers to include a unique sixteen-character verification code on many Forms W-2 provided to employees.

Unit 1: Legal Authority of the IRS

> **More Reading:**
> Circular 230, *Regulations Governing Practice Before the Internal Revenue Service*
> Publication 947, *Practice Before the IRS and Power of Attorney*
> Publication 1, *Your Rights as a Taxpayer*

Overview of SEE Part 3

Part 3 of the EA exam concerns the ethics, laws, and regulations that govern the tax profession: rules that tax practitioners must follow; standards that the tax profession is held to; who may represent taxpayers before the IRS; IRS procedures for assessment, collection, audit, and appeals; and penalties that tax preparers face if they violate the law.

Specifically, Part 3 of the exam is broken down into the following sections and the corresponding percentage of questions:

1. Practices and Procedures – 25 questions
2. Representation before the IRS – 24 questions
3. Specific Types of Representation – 19 questions
4. Completion of the Filing Process – 17 questions[4]

Issues of ethics, practice, and representation are dealt with in detail in Treasury Department Circular No. 230, *Regulations Governing Practice before the Internal Revenue Service.*[5] All practitioners who represent taxpayers before the IRS are subject to the rules and regulations set forth in Circular 230.

Federal Tax Law

The Internal Revenue Code (IRC) is the main body of tax law of the United States. The IRC is enacted by Congress and published as Title 26 of the United States Code. Other tax law is promulgated by individual states, cities, and municipalities. Not all tax law is located in Title 26, however. In 2003, The Financial Crimes and Enforcement Network (FinCEN) delegated enforcement authority regarding the FBAR to the Internal Revenue Service (IRS). FBARs are required under a Bank Secrecy Act provision of Title 31 and not under any provisions of the Internal Revenue Code.

> **Note:** The IRS Enrolled Agent exam deals only with federal laws and not with the laws of any individual state or municipality.

Tax law is determined by all three branches of our federal government, although the legislative branch (Congress) has the primary function of originating tax laws. The executive branch (the president) is responsible for income tax regulations, revenue rulings, and revenue procedures. The president also has veto powers, which means he can stop legislation from becoming law. The judicial branch is responsible for court decisions.

The Internal Revenue Service is the federal agency that enforces tax law. The IRS is the "collection arm" for the U.S. Treasury Department, which is responsible for paying various government expenses.

---

[4] These specifications are listed in the current Enrolled Agent Special Enrollment Examination Candidate Information Bulletin, which is available for download on the official Prometric website.
[5] Regulations governing practice are set forth in Title 31, Code of Federal Regulations, Subtitle A, Part 10, and were published in pamphlet form as Treasury Department Circular No. 230 on June 12, 2014.

The Internal Revenue Service administers the Internal Revenue Code enacted by Congress. The IRS itself does not enact any tax statute—that is the job of the U.S. Congress.

The IRS takes the specifics of the laws ratified by Congress and translates them into the detailed regulations, rules, and procedures of the IRC. The IRS produces several kinds of documents that provide guidance to taxpayers, including the following:

1. Treasury regulations
2. Revenue rulings
3. Revenue procedures
4. Private letter rulings
5. Technical advice memoranda
6. IRS notices

Each of these has "substantial authority," which means the authority to serve as the basis for interpretation of current tax law and to establish precedents for the future.

The Internal Revenue Code defines substantial authority as an "objective standard involving an analysis of the law and application of the law to relevant facts." The weight given an authority depends on its "relevance and persuasiveness," and the type of document providing the authority. For example, a revenue ruling is accorded greater weight than a private letter ruling (other than to whom the private letter ruling was issued to) addressing the same issue. More recent documents also carry greater weight than older ones.

Under IRC §6662, sources of "substantial authority" include the following: provisions of the Internal Revenue Code, temporary and final regulations, court cases, administrative pronouncements, tax treaties, and Congressional intent as reflected in committee reports.

The list was later expanded to include proposed regulations, private letter rulings, technical advice memoranda, IRS information or press releases, notices, and any other similar documents published by the IRS in the Internal Revenue Bulletin.[6]

Treatises and articles in legal periodicals are not considered substantial authority under this statute. An authority no longer remains an authority if it is overruled or modified by a body with the power to overrule or modify it.

Example: Jesse is an Enrolled Agent. He used a decades-old court case as authority to claim a certain deduction on his client's business return. Jesse didn't realize that the case had been overruled by a higher court recently. Therefore, the authority that he used to base his deduction was invalid. Under audit, the deduction was disallowed, and Jesse's client was also assessed an accuracy-related penalty. Jesse could also be assessed a preparer penalty for his negligence.

Treasury Regulations

Treasury regulations are the U.S. Treasury Department's official interpretations of the Internal Revenue Code. The IRC authorizes the Secretary of the Treasury to "prescribe all needful rules and regulations for enforcement" of the code. All regulations are written by the IRS's Office of the Chief Counsel and approved by the U.S. Treasury secretary.

---

[6] The Committee Report for the Revenue Reconciliation Act.

The courts give weight to Treasury regulations and will generally uphold the regulations so long as the IRS's interpretation is reasonable and does not contradict any provisions in the IRC. Treasury regulations are first published in the Federal Register. After publication in the Federal Register, regulations are organized by subject matter and codified in a separate publication called the Code of Federal Regulations (CFR).

The three types of Treasury regulations are:

- **Legislative,**
- **Interpretive, and**
- **Procedural.**

Legislative regulations are created when Congress expressly delegates the authority to the Treasury secretary or the commissioner of the IRS to provide the requirements for a specific provision of the IRC. A legislative regulation has a higher degree of authority than an interpretive regulation. In general, legislative regulations carry the same authority as the law itself. However, a legislative regulation may be overturned if any of the following conflicts apply:

- It is outside the power delegated to the U.S. Treasury.
- It conflicts with a specific statute.
- It is deemed unreasonable by the courts.

Interpretive regulations are issued under the IRS's general authority to interpret the IRC. An interpretive regulation only explains the meaning of a portion of the code. Unlike a legislative regulation, there is no grant of authority for the promulgation of an interpretive regulation, so these regulations may be challenged on the grounds that they do not reflect Congressional intent.

Procedural regulations concern the administrative provisions of the code and are issued by the commissioner of the IRS and not the secretary of the Treasury. They often concern minor issues, such as when notices should be sent to employees or how to file certain IRS forms.

Note: The IRS is bound by its regulations, but the courts are not. Official regulations have the force of law, unless they are overly broad in relation to the statute or are deemed unconstitutional by the courts. U.S. Treasury regulations are authorized by law, but U.S. courts are not obligated to follow any of the IRS's administrative interpretations.

Classification of Treasury Regulations

Regulations are further classified as proposed, temporary, or final:

- **Proposed regulations** are open to commentary from the public. Various versions of proposed regulations may be issued and withdrawn before a final regulation is issued.
- **Temporary regulations** may remain in effect for three years. They are used to provide immediate guidance to the public and IRS employees prior to publishing final regulations.
- **Final regulations** are issued when a regulation becomes an official Treasury decision. They are the highest authority issued by Treasury Department.

Revenue Rulings and Revenue Procedures

The IRS issues revenue rulings and revenue procedures to inform and guide taxpayers. Neither has the force of Treasury Department regulations, but they may be used as precedents. A revenue ruling typically states the IRS position, while a revenue procedure provides instructions concerning that position.

Revenue rulings are intended to promote uniform application of the IRC. The national office of the IRS issues revenue rulings, which are published in the Internal Revenue Bulletin and the Federal Register. A revenue ruling is not binding in Tax Court or any other U.S. court. However, revenue rulings can be used by taxpayers as guidance to avoid certain accuracy-related IRS penalties.

The numbering system for revenue rulings corresponds to the year the ruling was issued. Thus, for example, revenue ruling 2017-1 was the first revenue ruling issued in 2017.

Revenue procedures are official IRS statements of procedure that affect the rights or duties of taxpayers under the IRC. A revenue procedure may be cited as precedent, but it does not have the force of law.

> **Note:** A *revenue ruling* will announce that taxpayers may deduct certain automobile expenses. A *revenue procedure* will then explain how taxpayers must deduct, allocate, or compute these automobile expenses.

IRS Written Determinations

IRS Written Determinations are documents the IRS is required to make open to public inspection. There are many types of official IRS correspondence and determinations. We will discuss the most common types in the following section.

Technical Advice Memorandum (TAM)

A TAM is written guidance furnished by the IRS Office of Chief Counsel upon the request of an IRS director. A TAM is issued in response to a technical or procedural question that develops during:

- The examination of a taxpayer's return
- Consideration of a taxpayer's claim for refund or credit
- A request for a determination letter
- Processing and considering non-docketed cases in an Appeals office

Technical advice memoranda are issued only on closed transactions and provide the interpretation of proper application of tax laws, tax treaties, regulations, revenue rulings, or other precedents.

The advice rendered represents the position of the IRS, but it only relates to the specific case in question. Technical advice memoranda are made public after all the private information has been removed that could identify a particular taxpayer.

Private Letter Ruling (PLR)

A taxpayer who has a specific question regarding tax law may request a private letter ruling (PLR) from the IRS. A PLR is a written statement issued to a taxpayer that interprets and applies tax laws to the taxpayer's specific case. It is issued to communicate the tax consequences of a particular transaction before the transaction is consummated or before the taxpayer's return is filed.

A PLR is legally binding on the IRS, but only if the taxpayer fully and accurately described the proposed transaction in the request and carried out the transaction as described. In addition, it is only binding on the IRS for the particular taxpayer who requested the ruling.

PLRs are made public after the taxpayer's private, identifiable information has been redacted (removed or blacked out). A private letter ruling is not free. Starting in 2016, the minimum fee for a PLR range from $10,000 and up (per request).

> **Example:** Scotty, age 40, decides to roll over his IRA to another financial institution. However, his prior financial institution failed to institute the rollover and instead erroneously distributed the entire amount of his IRA into a regular savings account. By the time Scotty discovered the error, it was past the 60-day required rollover window, and he is subject to IRS penalties and income tax on the distributed amount. Scotty files a private letter ruling request to ask for a waiver to the normal 60-day rollover window. The IRS grants his formal request by issuing a private letter ruling.[7]

IRS Notices

An official IRS notice is a public pronouncement that may contain guidance involving substantive interpretations of the IRC or other provisions of the law. Information commonly published in IRS notices includes:

- Weighted average interest rate updates
- Inflation adjustment factors
- Changes to IRS regulations
- Tax provisions related to presidentially declared disaster areas
- IRS requests for public comments on changes to regulations, rulings, or procedures

Internal Revenue Bulletin

The Internal Revenue Bulletin is the authoritative source of official IRS tax guidance. It is a weekly collection of items of substantial interest to the professional tax community. The IRB announces official IRS rulings and publishes Treasury decisions, executive orders, tax conventions, significant legislation, and court decisions.

Anyone may search the IRS website, www.irs.gov, for past issues of the IRB. Issues are available in both HTML and PDF file formats.

The IRS often releases individual items in advance of their publication in the IRB. Tax professionals may subscribe to the IRS GuideWire service to receive automated email notifications about these items.

Internal Revenue Manual

The Internal Revenue Manual (IRM) is the single official compilation of policies, delegated authorities, procedures, instructions, and guidelines relating to the organization, functions, administration, and operations of the IRS. It is primarily used by IRS employees to guide them in all facets of operations.

The manual currently has 39 separate parts, which include sections on the processing of tax submissions, examinations, collection, and appeals. Criminal investigations, legal advice, and litigation in the courts are also included in the manual. The IRM is public information and can be searched and read directly on the IRS website.

IRS Publications and Forms

The IRS disseminates information to both taxpayers and preparers through its official publications. For example, Publication 17 covers the general rules for filing a federal income tax return for individuals. Publication 17 supplements information contained in the tax form instruction booklet and explains the law in more detail, so it is an important document for taxpayers who prepare their own income tax returns.

---

[7] This example is based on Private Letter Ruling 201204025.

Although the information in publications is drawn from the Internal Revenue Code, Treasury regulations, and other primary sources of authority, publications themselves are not considered to have substantial authority. Taxpayers and preparers may not rely on guidance issued by IRS publications to avoid accuracy-related penalties.

> **Note:** In 2014, a U.S. Tax Court judge declared, "taxpayers rely on IRS guidance at their own peril." [8] Judge Joseph W. Nega ruled against a married couple who used guidance from an IRS publication as the basis for their case disputing penalties imposed after an IRA withdrawal. The judge wrote that IRS guidance was not "binding precedent" or "sufficient authority" to excuse the couple from penalties. The IRS later revised the publication at issue.

> **Study Note:** The Enrolled Agent exam is based largely on IRS publications, and exam candidates will not be tested on court cases unless the law has already made its way into an IRS publication. Similarly, exam candidates will not be tested on any pending tax law or legislation; the exam is based on tax law from the prior year. However, EA candidates must understand the basics of tax law, the court system, and how it relates to the taxpayer and tax professional.

Tax Forms and Schedules

IRS tax forms and schedules are used by taxpayers to report financial information to the IRS and calculate taxes to be paid or disclose other information as required by the Internal Revenue Code.

There are more than 800 forms and schedules in use. Many have accompanying instructions for taxpayers. Forms, schedules, and instructions are updated whenever necessary due to changes in the tax code.

All publications, forms, and instructions are listed and available for download on the IRS website at *www.irs.gov*, usually in both HTML and PDF file formats. Updated versions of publications are listed with the date revisions were made, so taxpayers can know they are using the most current information.

Many libraries and post offices offer free tax forms to taxpayers during the filing season, as do the more than 400 Taxpayer Assistance Centers across the country where the IRS offers face-to-face help to taxpayers. Taxpayers may also call the IRS to order current year tax forms, instructions, and publications by mail.

Due to the growth in electronic filing and the availability of free access to tax forms, the IRS no longer mails paper tax packages to taxpayers.

Written Case Law

Often, taxpayers and tax preparers will disagree with the IRS's interpretation of the IRC. In these cases, it is up to the courts to determine Congressional intent or the constitutionality of the tax law or IRS position that is being challenged. There are many instances where tax laws are disputed or even overturned. Court decisions then serve as guidance for future tax decisions. In most instances, the IRS chooses whether or not to acquiesce to a court decision. This means that the IRS may decide to ignore the ruling of the court and continue with its regular policies regarding the litigated issue.

The IRS is not bound to change its regulations due to a loss in court. The only exception to this rule is the U.S. Supreme Court, whose decisions the IRS is obligated to follow.

---

[8] *Bobrow v. Commissioner of Internal Revenue*

The IRS does not announce acquiescence or non-acquiescence in every case. Sometimes its position is withheld. When it does announce its position, the IRS publishes its acquiescence or non-acquiescence first in the Internal Revenue Bulletin.

Freedom of Information Act Requests (FOIA)

The Freedom of Information Act (FOIA) is a law designed to ensure public access to U.S. government records.[9] Upon written request, federal agencies, including the IRS, are required to disclose requested records, unless they can be withheld under certain exceptions allowed in the FOIA. Under the terms of the act, agencies may charge reasonable fees for searching, reviewing, and copying records that have been requested.

The IRS may withhold a record that falls under one of the FOIA's nine exemptions and three exclusions.

The exemptions protect against the disclosure of information that would harm national security, the privacy of individuals, the proprietary interests of business, the functioning of the government, and other important recognized interests. Exclusions involve especially sensitive law enforcement records related to criminal, FBI, counterintelligence, and international terrorism investigations.

When a record contains some information that qualifies as exempt, the entire record is not necessarily exempt. Instead, the FOIA specifically provides that any portions of a record that can be set apart must be provided to a requester after deletion of the exempt portions.

The IRS generally has 20 business days to say whether it will comply with an FOIA request. When a request is denied, the IRS must give the reason for denial and explain the right to appeal to the head of the agency.

Note: There is a type of FOIA request specific to tax preparers, which is covered in Unit 3, *Authorizations and Disclosures*.

A taxpayer may contest the fees charged in the processing of a records request. The IRS will copy the requested records and send the taxpayer a bill for the fees. In most cases, there is no charge for the first 100 pages, and the fee is 20 cents per page thereafter. A taxpayer may appeal other types of adverse determinations under the FOIA, such as the failure of the IRS to conduct an adequate search for requested documents.

A person whose request was granted in part and denied in part may appeal the part that was denied. If the IRS has agreed to disclose some but not all of the requested documents, the filing of an appeal does not affect the release of the documents that can be disclosed.

Taxpayer Bill of Rights

The IRS has a Taxpayer Bill of Rights. The program is designed to better communicate to taxpayers their existing statutory and administrative protections. The Taxpayer Bill of Rights groups the dozens of rights in the Internal Revenue Code, the IRS *Restructuring and Reform Act of 1998*, and the Internal Revenue Manual into ten fundamental rights to make them clear, understandable, and accessible both to taxpayers and IRS employees. These rights are detailed in IRS Publication 1, *Your Rights as a Taxpayer.* These rights are as follows:

---

[9]For more information, see *The Freedom of Information Act Guide to Treasury Records* at www.treasury.gov and *Freedom of Information Act (FOIA) Guidelines* at www.IRS.gov.

1. **The Right to Be Informed:** Taxpayers have the right to know what they need to do to comply with the tax laws. They are entitled to clear explanations of the laws and IRS procedures in all tax forms, instructions, publications, notices, and correspondence. They have the right to be informed of IRS decisions about their tax accounts and to receive clear explanations of the outcomes.

Note: Certain notices must include the amount (if any) of the tax, interest and certain penalties the taxpayer owes and must explain why he owes these amounts (IRC §7522).[10]

2. **The Right to Quality Service:** Taxpayers have the right to receive prompt, courteous, and professional assistance in their dealings with the IRS, to be spoken to in a way they can easily understand, to receive clear and easily understandable communications from the IRS, and to speak to a supervisor about inadequate service.

Note: When collecting tax, the IRS should treat a taxpayer with courtesy. Generally, the IRS should only contact a taxpayer between 8 a.m. and 9 p.m. The IRS should not contact a taxpayer at his place of employment if the IRS knows, or has reason to know, that his employer does not allow this kind of contact (IRC §6304).

3. **The Right to Pay No More than the Correct Amount of Tax:** Taxpayers have the right to pay only the amount of tax legally due, including interest and penalties, and to have the IRS apply all tax payments properly.

Note: If a taxpayer believes he has overpaid his taxes, he can file a refund claim asking for the money back (IRC §6402).

4. **The Right to Challenge the IRS's Position and Be Heard:** Taxpayers have the right to raise objections and provide additional documentation in response to formal IRS actions or proposed actions; to expect that the IRS will consider their timely objections and documentation promptly and fairly; and to receive a response if the IRS does not agree with their position.

Note: If a taxpayer is notified his return has a mathematical or clerical error, he has 60 days to tell the IRS that he disagrees. If the IRS is not persuaded, it will issue a notice proposing a tax adjustment. The notice provides a taxpayer the right to challenge the proposed adjustment in Tax Court by filing a petition within 90 days of the date of the notice (IRC §6213(b)).

5. **The Right to Appeal an IRS Decision in an Independent Forum:** Taxpayers are entitled to a fair and impartial administrative appeal of most IRS decisions, including many penalties, and have the right to receive a written response regarding the Office of Appeals' decision. Taxpayers generally have the right to take their cases to court.

Note: If the IRS has sent a taxpayer a notice proposing additional tax, he may dispute the proposed adjustment in the U.S. Tax Court before he has to pay the tax (IRC §6213).

6. **The Right to Finality:** Taxpayers have the right to know the maximum amount of time they have to challenge the IRS's position, as well as the maximum amount of time the IRS has to audit a particular tax year or collect a tax debt. Taxpayers have the right to know when the IRS has finished an audit.

Note: The IRS generally has ten years from the assessment date to collect unpaid taxes from a taxpayer (IRC §6502).

---

[10] Examples drawn from the Taxpayer Advocate Service's *What the Taxpayer Bill of Rights Means for You.*

7. **The Right to Privacy:** Taxpayers have the right to expect that any IRS inquiry, examination, or enforcement action will comply with the law and be no more intrusive than necessary, and will respect all due process rights, including search and seizure protections, and will provide, where applicable, a collection due process hearing.

> **Note:** The IRS should not seek intrusive and extraneous information about a taxpayer's lifestyle during an audit if there is no reasonable indication that he has unreported income (IRC §7602(e)).

8. **The Right to Confidentiality:** Taxpayers have the right to expect that any information they provide to the IRS will not be disclosed unless authorized by the taxpayer or by law. Taxpayers have the right to expect appropriate action will be taken against employees, return preparers, and others who wrongfully use or disclose taxpayer return information.

> **Note:** In general, the IRS may not disclose a taxpayer's tax information to third parties unless he gives explicit permission (IRC §6103). There are exceptions for law enforcement and other limited scenarios.

9. **The Right to Retain Representation:** Taxpayers have the right to retain an authorized representative of their choice to represent them in their dealings with the IRS. Taxpayers have the right to seek assistance from a Low-Income Taxpayer Clinic if they cannot afford representation.

> **Note:** A taxpayer may select a qualified representative person to represent him in an interview with the IRS. The IRS cannot force the taxpayer to attend with his representative (IRC §7521(c)) if the representative is qualified to practice before the IRS.

10. **The Right to a Fair and Just Tax System:** Taxpayers have the right to expect the tax system to consider facts and circumstances that might affect their underlying liabilities, ability to pay, or ability to provide information timely. Taxpayers have the right to request assistance from the Taxpayer Advocate Service if they are experiencing financial difficulty or if the IRS has not resolved their tax issues properly and timely through its normal channels.

> **Note:** The IRS cannot levy (seize) all of a taxpayer's wages to collect his unpaid tax. A portion will be exempt from levy to allow payment of basic living expenses (IRC §6334).

IRS Divisions

The IRS has four main operating divisions. These are:

1. **Large Business & International Division:** This division serves corporations, including S corporations, and partnerships, with assets in excess of $10 million. This is the division of the IRS that audits large corporate taxpayers and partnerships, including publicly traded companies like Ford, Apple, Coca-Cola, etc.
2. **Small Business and Self-Employed Division:** This division serves corporations, and partnerships with assets less than $10 million; filers of gift, estate, excise, employment and fiduciary returns; individuals filing an individual Federal income tax return with accompanying Schedule C, Schedule E, Schedule F, Form 2106, *Employee Business Expenses*.[11]
3. **Wage and Investment Division:** This division serves individuals with wage and investment income only (not including international tax returns) filing an individual Federal income tax return without accompanying Schedule C, E, or F, or Form 2106.
4. **Tax Exempt and Government Entities Division:** This division serves three distinct taxpayer segments: employee plans (including IRAs), exempt organizations, and government entities.

---

[11] After the 2017 tax season, the Form 2106 will no longer be applicable, as Employee Business Expenses as a miscellaneous itemized deduction has been eliminated completely under the Tax Cuts and Jobs Act.

Taxpayer Advocate Service

The Taxpayer Advocate Service (TAS) is an independent organization within the IRS whose goal is to help taxpayers resolve problems with the IRS. A taxpayer may be eligible for TAS assistance when he is facing a number of different situations involving economic harm or significant delays in resolving a tax issue.

The Taxpayer Advocate Service is free and confidential, and is available for businesses as well as individuals. TAS has at least one office in every state, the District of Columbia, and Puerto Rico. There are local TAS offices where taxpayers can meet face-to-face with advocates, a video conferencing service for areas where there are no nearby offices, and toll-free telephone service. The quickest contact method is by fax, but a taxpayer may also submit Form 911, *Request for Taxpayer Advocate Service Assistance.* TAS may be able to help a taxpayer who is experiencing a problem with the IRS and:

- The problem with the IRS is causing financial difficulties for the taxpayer, his family, or his business;
- The taxpayer faces (or his business is facing) an immediate threat of adverse action; or
- The taxpayer has repeatedly tried to contact the IRS, but no one has responded, or the IRS has not responded by the date promised.

When the Taxpayer Advocate Service evaluates a taxpayer's request for assistance, it will use the following criteria to determine whether to intervene:

- The taxpayer is experiencing economic harm or is about to suffer economic harm.
- The taxpayer is facing an immediate threat of adverse action.
- The taxpayer will incur significant costs if relief is not granted (including fees for professional representation).
- The taxpayer will suffer irreparable injury or long-term adverse impact if relief is not granted.
- The taxpayer has experienced a delay of more than 30 days to resolve a tax account problem.
- The taxpayer did not receive a response or resolution to his problem or inquiry by the date promised.
- A system or procedure has either failed to operate as intended or failed to resolve the taxpayer's problem or dispute within the IRS.
- The manner in which the tax laws are being administered raise considerations of equity, or have impaired or will impair the taxpayer's rights.
- The National Tax Advocate determines compelling public policy warrants assistance to an individual or group of taxpayers.

The Taxpayer Advocate Service will generally ask the IRS to stop certain collection activities while a taxpayer's request for assistance is pending (such as lien filings, levies, and seizures).

Example: Shirley filed an amended tax return for a prior year. She has an outstanding balance for the prior tax year and has been receiving IRS collection notices. Shirley's expected refund would fully pay her balance due and leave her with a small refund. The official processing time for Form 1040X, *Amended U.S. Individual Tax Return*, is eight to twelve weeks. However, she has been waiting more than four months for her refund to be processed. She has contacted the IRS numerous times but was never given a reason for the delay. Shirley may request intervention from the Taxpayer Advocate Service.

(Test yourself and then check the correct answers at the end of this chapter.)

1. Which branch of government is the main source of tax law in the United States?

A. Legislative.
B. Executive.
C. Judicial.
D. All three branches contribute equally to the creation and adoption of tax law.

2. The IRS generally has _____ to say whether it will comply with an FOIA request.

A. 20 business days
B. Two weeks
C. 30 days
D. 90 Days

3. Of the following situations, which is most likely to warrant intervention by the Taxpayer Advocate Service?

A. A taxpayer is experiencing financial difficulty. His home is in foreclosure, and he is worried he will be unable to pay his federal income tax liability by the due date.
B. A taxpayer has experienced multiple, lengthy delays in trying to contact the IRS by telephone.
C. A taxpayer has waited for weeks for the IRS to discharge the lien on his property, which must be removed immediately or else the sale of the property will fall through.
D. A taxpayer has received an IRS Notice of Federal Tax Lien that his bank account will be subject to levy if he does not pay his federal tax liability.

4. Of the following sources of information, which is not considered "substantial authority" for IRS purposes?

A. Proposed regulations.
B. Legal opinion printed in a law school journal.
C. Congressional intent as reflected in committee reports.
D. Information from an IRS press release.

5. Which of the following statements regarding revenue rulings is correct?

A. Revenue rulings cannot be used to avoid certain IRS penalties.
B. Revenue rulings can be used to avoid certain IRS penalties.
C. Revenue rulings are not official IRS guidance.
D. None of the above.

6. Which of the following would have the highest authority in establishing precedent for tax law for all taxpayers?

A. Private letter ruling.
B. Treasury regulation.
C. IRS publication.
D. Technical advice memorandum.

7. In matters of tax law, the IRS must acquiesce in all decisions rendered by the:

A. U.S. Tax Court.
B. U.S. District Court.
C. U.S. Court of Appeals.
D. U.S. Supreme Court.

8. An IRS revenue officer has a question about a collection procedure involving a taxpayer. He should consult:

A. The Internal Revenue Manual.
B. The Internal Revenue Bulletin.
C. Publication 594, *The IRS Collection Process.*
D. The Congressional Record.

9. A private letter ruling is legally binding on the IRS if:

A. The taxpayer that received the private letter, ruling fully and accurately, described the proposed transaction in his request and carried out the transaction as described.
B. The IRS is notified of any discrepancies on a taxpayer's return.
C. The taxpayer goes to the Tax Court and requests a formal decision.
D. None of the above.

10. Which has the highest level of authority with regards to IRS regulations?

A. Revenue regulations.
B. Procedural regulation.
C. Interpretive regulation.
D. Legislative regulation.

11. Treasury regulations are published in _____.

A. The Congressional Notes.
B. The Federal Register.
C. The Office of Appeals.
D. The IRS Newswire.

1. The answer is A. Although both the judicial and executive branches play important roles in interpreting, implementing, and enforcing tax laws, the legislative branch (Congress) is the main source of tax law in the United States. Congress is responsible for passing tax laws (statutes), which are published as the Internal Revenue Code, issued separately as Title 26 of the United States Code.

2. The answer is A. The IRS has 20 business days to say whether it will comply with an FOIA request. When a request is denied, the IRS must give the reason for denial and explain the right to appeal to the head of the agency.

3. The answer is C. The Taxpayer Advocate Service is designed to attempt to resolve issues when a taxpayer has a serious problem with the IRS or has experienced a serious delay. There are specific criteria used to determine whether taxpayer assistance is warranted, and the example in the correct answer is drawn from an actual case. On Form 911, *Request for Taxpayer Advocate Service Assistance,* a taxpayer must indicate one or more of the following reasons he is asking for help:

- He is experiencing economic harm or is about to suffer economic harm.
- He is facing an immediate threat of adverse action.
- He will incur significant costs if relief is not granted (including fees for professional representation).
- He will suffer irreparable injury or long-term adverse impact if relief is not granted.
- He has experienced a delay of more than 30 days to resolve a tax account problem.
- He has not received a response or resolution to his problem or inquiry by the date promised.
- A system or procedure has either failed to operate as intended, or failed to resolve the taxpayer's problem or dispute with the IRS.
- The manner in which the tax laws are being administered raises concerns of equity, or has impaired or will impair the taxpayer's rights.

4. The answer is B. A legal opinion printed in a law journal does not have substantial authority. Sources of substantial authority are as follows: the Internal Revenue Code, temporary and final regulations, court cases, administrative pronouncements, tax treaties, Congressional intent as reflected in committee reports, proposed regulations, private letter rulings, technical advice memoranda, IRS information or press releases, IRS notices, and any other similar documents published by the IRS in the Internal Revenue Bulletin.

5. The answer is B. Revenue rulings can be used to avoid certain accuracy-related IRS penalties. Taxpayers may rely on revenue rulings as official IRS guidance on an issue to make a decision regarding taxable income, deductions, and how to avoid certain IRS penalties.

6. The answer is B. A Treasury regulation is the Treasury Department's official interpretation of the Internal Revenue Code. It has substantial authority in establishing precedent for tax law.

7. The answer is D. The Internal Revenue Service is required to obey all decisions rendered by the highest court of the land, the U.S. Supreme Court. Although case law helps set precedent and will influence the IRS in its regulations, policies, and procedures, the IRS is not obligated to change its regulations in matters of tax law that are decided by other U.S. courts, including the U.S. Tax Court.

8. The answer is A. The Internal Revenue Manual (IRM) is the single official compilation of policies, delegated authorities, procedures, instructions, and guidelines relating to the organization, functions, administration, and operations of the IRS. It is the resource primarily used by IRS employees to guide them in all facets of operations.

9. The answer is A. A private letter ruling (PLR) is binding on the IRS if the taxpayer fully and accurately described the proposed transaction in his request and carried out the transaction as described.

10. The answer is D. A legislative regulation is authorized by Congress to provide the material requirements of a specific IRC provision. If written correctly, a legislative regulation carries the same authority as the Internal Revenue Code itself. It can only be overturned if it is outside the power delegated to the U.S. Treasury; it conflicts with a specific statute, or it is deemed unreasonable by the courts.

11. The answer is B. Treasury regulations are published in the Federal Register.

Unit 2: Practice Before the IRS

More Reading:
Circular 230, *Regulations Governing Practice Before the Internal Revenue Service*
Publication 947, *Practice Before the IRS and Power of Attorney*
Publication 470, *Limited Practice Without Enrollment*

Practice before the IRS includes all matters connected with a presentation before the IRS, or relating to a taxpayer's rights, privileges, or liabilities under laws or regulations administered by the IRS. Representation, or "practice before the IRS," is defined in Publication 947, *Practice Before the IRS and Power of Attorney.*

Practice before the IRS includes:

- Corresponding and communicating with the IRS
- Representing a taxpayer at conferences, hearings, or meetings with the IRS
- Preparing and filing documents with the IRS
- Providing written advice that has a potential for tax avoidance or evasion

U.S. citizenship is not required to practice before the IRS.

Note: The IRS Office of Professional Responsibility (OPR) has responsibility for matters related to practitioner conduct, discipline, disciplinary proceedings and sanctions. The Return Preparer Office (RPO) is responsible for the issuance of PTINs, acting on applications for enrollment and administering AFSP testing and continuing education for designated groups.

Note: In a significant loss for the IRS, the U.S. Court of Appeals for the District of Columbia upheld a lower court's decision that the IRS did not possess the legal authority to regulate tax return preparers.[12] The issue centered on whether the "practice of representatives" included the mere preparation of tax returns. The appeals court ruled it did not, and the IRS chose not to appeal the decision. This means that tax return preparation, in and of itself, does not constitute "practice before the IRS" under current law.[13]

Enrolled Practitioners

The IRS defines *enrolled practitioners* as attorneys, CPAs, Enrolled Agents, enrolled retirement plan agents, or enrolled actuaries authorized to practice before the IRS. Other individuals may qualify to practice temporarily or engage in limited practice before the IRS. However, they are not referred to as practitioners.

The following individuals may represent taxpayers and practice before the IRS by virtue of their licensing, unless they are currently under suspension or disbarment:

Attorneys: An attorney who is a member in good standing of the bar of any state, possession, territory, commonwealth, or of the District of Columbia.

Certified Public Accountants (CPAs): A CPA who is duly qualified to practice as a CPA in any state, possession, territory, commonwealth, or the District of Columbia.

---

[12] *Loving,* No. 13-5061, D.C. Circuit Court of Appeals.

[13] At the time of this book's printing, the current version of Circular 230 (issued in June 2014) has not yet been updated to reflect the changes necessitated by the *Loving v. IRS* decision, including removal of the RTRP education and competency requirements. However, Publication 947 was more recently revised, and now states that only unenrolled return preparers participating in the Annual Filing Season Record of Completion (AFSP) program may represent a taxpayer before the IRS, and only with respect to returns prepared and signed by the preparer. This rule went into effect in 2016 for all future tax returns.

Enrolled Agents (EAs): An Enrolled Agent in active status may represent clients before any office of the IRS. Like attorneys and CPAs, EAs are unrestricted as to which taxpayers they can represent and what types of tax matters they can handle.

Only attorneys, CPAs, and EAs have unlimited rights to represent taxpayers before the IRS.

Enrolled Actuaries: The practice of an individual enrolled as an actuary by the Joint Board for the Enrollment of Actuaries is limited to certain Internal Revenue Code sections that relate to his area of expertise, principally those sections governing employee retirement plans.

Enrolled Retirement Plan Agents (ERPAs): The practice of an enrolled retirement plan agent is limited to certain Internal Revenue Code sections that relate to his area of expertise, principally those sections governing employee retirement plans.

Annual Filing Season Program (AFSP)

The IRS replaced its now-defunct RTRP program with the voluntary Annual Filing Season Program (AFSP) program. Non-credentialed return preparers can elect to voluntarily demonstrate completion of basic 1040 filing season tax preparation and other tax law training by participating in the program.

The AFSP program is designed to encourage competence and education among unenrolled tax preparers. To receive an annual "record of completion," a preparer must normally have:

- A minimum of 18 hours[14] of continuing education from an IRS-approved continuing education provider, including a six-hour "Annual Federal Tax Refresher" (AFTR) course.[15]
- Passed a knowledge-based comprehension test administered by the CPE provider at the end of the AFTR course.
- A current preparer tax identification number (PTIN).
- Consented to the "duties and restrictions relating to practice before the IRS" in Circular 230. This consent gives the IRS the authority to regulate those individuals who receive the record of completion.

Circular 230 has not yet been updated to include all the information for the IRS's new AFSP program, which is designed to replace the now-defunct RTRP program.

Exempt Individuals

Certain individuals may obtain the AFSP Record of Completion without taking the annual refresher tax course and exam, assuming they took at least fifteen hours of qualifying continuing education courses in 2017. The following unenrolled preparers are exempt from the AFSP "annual refresher" course:

- **State-based return preparer program participants:** Return preparers who are active registrants of the Oregon Board of Tax Practitioners, California Tax Education Council, and/or Maryland State Board of Individual Tax Preparers.
- **SEE Part I Test-Passers:** Tax practitioners who have passed the Special Enrollment Exam Part I within the past two years.

---

[14] Individuals who passed the now-defunct Registered Tax Return Preparer exam are exempt from the six-hour federal tax law refresher course. They only need 15 hours of continuing education each year to obtain an Annual Filing Season Program – Record of Completion.
[15] Individuals will need a total of 18 hours of continuing education hours. An AFTR course does not count toward Enrolled Agent continuing education requirements.

- **VITA/TCPE volunteers:** VITA volunteers who are quality reviewers, instructors, and return preparers with active PTINs.
- **Other accredited tax-focused credential-holders:** The Accreditation Council for Accountancy and Taxation's Accredited Business Accountant/Advisor (ABA) and Accredited Tax Preparer (ATP) programs.

AFSP participants are included in a public, searchable database of tax return preparers on the IRS website.[16] The *Directory of Federal Tax Return Preparers with Credentials and Select Qualifications* includes the name, city, state, zip code, and credentials of attorneys, CPAs, EAs, ERPAs, and enrolled actuaries with a valid PTIN, as well as AFSP Record of Completion holders. An individual may choose to opt out of being listed in the directory.

> **Example:** Anika is a CPA. Her client, Samuel, has a large tax debt. Samuel does not wish to communicate directly with the IRS, but he wants to set up an installment agreement. Anika has Samuel sign Form 2848 giving her power of attorney and calls the IRS on his behalf to set up the installment agreement for him. This action is considered *practice before the IRS*.

> **Note:** Currently, only Annual Filing Season Program participants have limited practice rights before the IRS. AFSP participants may only represent clients whose returns they prepared and signed; and only before revenue agents, customer service representatives and similar IRS employees, including the Taxpayer Advocate Service. Only unenrolled preparers that participate in IRS's Annual Filing Season Program (AFSP) will have limited representation rights. Unenrolled preparers who do not participate in this annual program will no longer have authority to represent clients before the IRS (Publication 947).

Unenrolled Tax Return Preparers

Individuals who prepare tax returns for other taxpayers but who are not EAs, CPAs, attorneys, ERPAs, or enrolled actuaries are called "unenrolled preparers." In general, unenrolled preparers have only limited practice rights before the IRS.

Only unenrolled tax return preparers, that have current AFSP certificates,[17] may represent taxpayers, and only during an IRS examination of the taxable year or period covered by the tax return or claim of refund they prepared and signed.

This representation may occur only before revenue agents, customer service representatives, or similar officers and employees of the IRS, including the Taxpayer Advocate Service. Unenrolled tax return preparers cannot do any of the following:

- Represent taxpayers before appeals officers, revenue officers, counsel, or similar officers or employees of the IRS or Department of Treasury
- Execute closing agreements
- Extend the statutory period for tax assessments or collection of tax
- Execute waivers

---

[16] The Directory of Federal Tax Return Preparers with Credentials and Select Qualifications is located here: *https://irs.treasury.gov/rpo/rpo.jsf*

[17] The IRS believes in a mandatory competency standard for federal tax return preparers. To this end, legislation continues to be their priority. In the interim, however, the AFSP program recognizes the efforts of unenrolled return preparers to improve their professional competency through continuing education. Anyone with a PTIN can prepare a federal tax return, but for those preparers with a PTIN who also work to ready themselves for the filing season through educational efforts, the AFSP program affords them a level of differentiation from the rest of the marketplace.

- Execute claims for refund
- Sign any document on behalf of a taxpayer

Unenrolled preparers who do <u>not</u> have an AFSP certificate are allowed to prepare tax returns for compensation, but they may not represent taxpayers before any level of the IRS, regardless of whether they prepared the return or not.

> **Example:** Wilfred is an unenrolled tax preparer. He does not hold any formal licensing or have an AFSP certificate. The IRS is conducting an audit of Wilfred's client's income tax returns for the years 2014, 2015, and 2016 returns. Wilfred prepared all the tax returns under examination. However, since Wilfred is not an enrolled practitioner, he may not represent his client before the IRS. Wilfred must refer his client to an enrolled practitioner if the client wishes to be represented.

> **Example:** Zelma received her AFSP certificate in 2017. She has always prepared tax returns for her client, Simon. In 2017, Simon receives an audit notice from the IRS for his prior year return. Zelma is able to represent Simon before the IRS as well as respond to the notice, because she has a current AFSP certificate and she prepared the return.[18]

Limited Practice Due to 'Special Relationship'

Other individuals who are not practitioners may represent taxpayers before the IRS because of a special relationship with the taxpayer, without having prepared the tax return in question.

An individual (self-representation): An individual may always represent himself before the IRS, provided he has appropriate identification, such as a driver's license. He does not have to file a written declaration of qualification and authority. Even a disbarred individual may represent himself before the IRS. Disbarred practitioners are also allowed to represent family members, or act as fiduciaries for an estate or trust if they are appointed by the court.

> **Example:** Richard was a tax attorney who was disbarred because of a felony embezzlement conviction. An individual who is disbarred is not eligible to represent other taxpayers before the IRS. Richard was audited by the IRS in 2017. Despite being disbarred, Richard may still represent himself before the IRS during the examination of his own return. Richard may also represent a close family member, like his child or his spouse.

A family member: An individual may represent members of his immediate family. Family members include a spouse, child, parent, brother, or sister of the individual.

> **Example:** Surinder is a 20-year-old accounting student. Surinder lives with her brother, Balwant. Surinder is not an enrolled practitioner. Surinder prepares her brother's tax return. Balwant is later audited. Surinder may represent her brother before the IRS, if Balwant signs a Form 2848, granting his sister representation rights. Surinder will have all the rights that an enrolled practitioner would have, but only with respect to her brother's tax issues.

---

[18] According to current IRS regulations, only unenrolled return preparers who hold a record of completion for BOTH the tax return year under examination and the year the examination is conducted may represent under the following conditions: Unenrolled return preparers may represent taxpayers only before revenue agents, customer service representatives, or similar officers and employees of the Internal Revenue Service (including the Taxpayer Advocate Service) and only during an examination of the taxable year or period covered by the tax returns they prepared and signed. (Publication 947)

Example: Reinaldo's mother is being audited by the IRS. Reinaldo is an accountant who works as a controller for a manufacturing firm. He does not normally prepare tax returns for the public or hold any type of state or federal licensing. Even though Reinaldo is not enrolled to practice before the IRS, he is allowed to represent his mother because of their family relationship.

An officer: A bona fide officer of a corporation (including a parent, subsidiary, or affiliated corporation), association, organized group, or governmental agency may represent its corporation, association, organized group, or governmental agency before the IRS.

A partner: A general partner may represent the partnership before the IRS, but a limited partner may not.

An employee: A regular full-time employee can represent his employer. An employer can be an individual, partnership, corporation, association, trust, receivership, guardianship, estate, or organized group; or a governmental unit, agency, or authority.

Example: Nicolette is a full-time bookkeeper for her employer, Green Lawn Landscaping. The IRS sent her employer a notice regarding some delinquent payroll tax returns. Nicolette may file Form 2848, *Power of Attorney and Declaration of Representative*, and speak with the IRS on her employer's behalf. Even though Nicolette is not an enrolled preparer, she may represent Green Lawn Landscaping before the IRS because of the employee-employer relationship.

A fiduciary: A fiduciary (trustee, executor, personal representative, administrator, receiver, or guardian) is considered to be the taxpayer and not a representative of the taxpayer.

Example: Milton was named the executor of his mother's estate after she passed away. He is allowed to represent his mother's estate before the IRS because he is the fiduciary for the estate.

Authorization for Special Appearances: In rare circumstances, the Commissioner of the IRS or a delegate will authorize a person who is not otherwise eligible to practice before the IRS to represent another person for a particular matter. The request is made to the Office of Professional Responsibility (OPR). If granted, the written consent will detail the specific circumstances related to the appearance.

Persons Ineligible to Practice Before the IRS

Individuals not previously described are generally not eligible to practice before the IRS. Corporations, associations, partnerships, and others that are not individuals also are not eligible to practice before the IRS. Even if named in a power of attorney as a representative, an individual will not be recognized if he has lost his eligibility to practice before the IRS. Reasons for losing eligibility include suspension or disbarment by the OPR, being placed in inactive retirement status, and not meeting the requirements for renewal of enrollment, such as continuing professional education.

Actions That Are Not Practice Before the IRS

"Practice before the IRS" does <u>not</u> include:
- Representation of taxpayers before the U.S. Tax Court: The Tax Court has its own rules of practice and its own rules regarding admission to practice.
- Merely appearing as a witness for the taxpayer: In general, individuals who are not practitioners may appear before the IRS as witnesses—but they may not advocate for the taxpayer.
- The preparation of a tax return.[19]

---

[19] *Sexton v. Hawkins*, U.S. District Court of Nevada, Case No. 2:13-cv-00893.

Example: James and Lina are neighbors and lifelong friends. James is a retired bookkeeper and he prepares Lina's tax return for free. Later, Lina is audited by the IRS. James is not an enrolled practitioner, and he cannot represent Lina before the IRS. However, he is allowed to appear as a witness and provide information on her behalf. He cannot advocate for his friend.

Tax Return Preparers

The IRS defines tax return preparers as individuals who participate in the preparation of tax returns for taxpayers for compensation. This includes preparers who are in business, casual or part-time preparers who receive fees for preparing tax returns, and certain e-file providers. Under Circular 230, the IRS requires the following:

- All paid tax return preparers must register with the IRS and obtain a preparer tax identification number (PTIN). Specifically, Circular 230 states that "any individual who for compensation prepares or assists with the preparation of all, or substantially all of a tax return or claim for refund" must have a PTIN.
- Tax preparers who register for a PTIN must undergo a limited tax compliance check to ensure they have filed their own personal and business tax returns.

PTIN Requirements

The PTIN is a nine-digit number that preparers must use when they prepare and sign a tax return or claim for refund. The use of a PTIN is mandatory on all federal tax returns and claims for refund prepared by paid tax preparers.

The PTIN requirement applies to all Enrolled Agents and many attorneys and CPAs. Attorneys and CPAs do not need to obtain PTINs if they do not prepare federal tax returns.

This is where tax professionals enter their PTIN

Multiple individuals cannot share one PTIN. A PTIN is assigned to a single preparer to identify that he is the preparer of a particular return. A PTIN cannot be transferred to another preparer, even if the practice is later sold. As of the start of the filing season, more than 715,000 tax return preparers had active PTINs for 2017. An applicant must be at least 18 years old to obtain a PTIN. Felony convictions and failure to meet federal tax obligations may affect an individual's ability to obtain a PTIN.

In the past, all paid preparers were required to pay a fee to renew their PTINs online.[20] On June 1, 2017, in a significant loss for the IRS, the U.S. District Court for the District of Columbia ruled that the IRS may continue to require PTINs but may not charge fees for the issuance or renewal of PTINs.[21]

Preparers who fail to list a valid PTIN on tax returns they sign are subject to penalties. Preparers may also be subject to disciplinary action by the Office of Professional Responsibility.[22]

---

[20] As a PTIN expires every December 31, a preparer who renews their PTIN after December 31 may not prepare a tax return in the following year until the PTIN is issued.
[21] *Steele vs. United States.*

Supervised Preparers

Supervised preparers are also required to have PTINs. These are individuals who do not sign tax returns as paid return preparers but are:

- Employed by a law firm, EA office, or CPA practice; and
- Are directly supervised by an attorney, CPA, EA, ERPA, or enrolled actuary who signs the returns prepared by the supervised preparer as the paid tax return preparer.

Supervised preparers may not:

- Sign any tax return they prepare or assist in preparing.
- Represent taxpayers before the IRS in any capacity.
- Identify themselves as Circular 230 practitioners.

When applying for or renewing a PTIN, supervised preparers must provide the PTIN of their supervisor.

Exceptions to PTIN Requirements

An individual who prepares a tax return with no agreement for compensation is not considered a tax return preparer for IRS purposes. This is true even if the individual receives a gift or a favor in return. The agreement for compensation is the deciding factor as to whether the IRS considers an individual a tax return preparer.

Example: Marian is a CPA who does audit and attest work. She works for a CPA firm with a tax division, but she does not prepare tax returns herself. Marian is not required to obtain a PTIN as long as she does not prepare tax returns. Lorene is an Enrolled Agent who works for the same accounting firm. She also does not prepare tax returns. Lorene only does bookkeeping and some occasional tax planning. Unlike her co-worker Marian, Lorene is required to have a PTIN, even though she does not prepare tax returns, because she is an Enrolled Agent. All Enrolled Agents are required to have a PTIN.

Example: Latonya is a retired CPA who only prepares tax returns for her close family members. She does not charge her family to prepare their tax returns. Sometimes, a family member will give Latonya a gift in return. This year, her sister gave her home-baked cookies and her niece gave her a sweater. However, Latonya did not ask for any presents or expect them. She is not a tax return preparer for IRS purposes, and she is not required to obtain a PTIN.

An individual is not considered an income tax return preparer and would not be required to obtain a PTIN in the following instances:

- A person who gives an opinion about events that have not happened (such as tax advice for a business that has not been created).
- A person who furnishes typing, copying, or mechanical assistance.
- A person who prepares the return of his employer (or of an officer or employee of the employer) by whom the person is regularly and continuously employed.
- A fiduciary who prepares a tax return for a trust or estate.
- An unpaid volunteer who provides tax assistance under *Volunteer Income Tax Assistance* (VITA) or *Tax Counseling for the Elderly* (TCPE) programs.

---

[22] The IRS's loss in *Loving v. IRS* does not apply to the requirement that all paid tax preparers obtain PTINs. The judge ruled the PTIN program was valid and could be enforced by the IRS.

- An employee of the IRS who performs official duties by preparing a tax return for a taxpayer who requests it.

Example: Ingrid is a bookkeeper for Creative Candies Corporation. She is a full-time employee, and she prepares the payroll checks and payroll tax returns for all of the employees of Creative Candies. As a full-time employee, Ingrid is not considered a tax return preparer since her employer is ultimately responsible for the accuracy of the company's payroll tax returns.

Example: Quincy is an EA who has a PTIN. He employs an administrative assistant, Madeline, who performs data entry during tax filing season. At times, clients call and provide Madeline with information, which she records in the system. Using the data Madeline has entered, Quincy meets with his clients and provides tax advice as needed. He then prepares and signs their returns. Madeline is not a tax return preparer and is not required to have a PTIN.

Example: Ernie is a retired tax professional. He does not have a PTIN. Ernie volunteers during the tax filing season at a VITA site, where he prepares individual tax returns for lower-income individuals for free. Ernie is not a tax return preparer and is not required to have a PTIN.

Example: Kelsey is a CPA. His neighbor, Jamey, consults with Kelsey about a business he is thinking about starting. Kelsey gives Jamey an opinion regarding the potential business and taxes. In this case, the IRS does not consider Kelsey a tax return preparer. This is because Kelsey is merely giving an opinion about events that have not yet happened.

Note: Do not confuse a PTIN with an EFIN, electronic filing identification number. An EFIN is a number issued by the IRS to individuals who have been approved as authorized IRS e-file providers. Although most tax preparers must use IRS e-file, some preparers are ineligible for the e-file program. Currently, the IRS e-file program does not accept foreign preparers without Social Security numbers who live and work abroad. These preparers must still obtain a PTIN, but they are not required to e-file their clients' returns since they are not eligible for an EFIN.

The "Substantial Portion" Rule

Only the person who prepares all or a "substantial portion" of a tax return is considered the preparer of the return. Preparers of income, estate, and gift tax returns are all subject to rule. With regards to tax preparation firms, only one person in a firm will be deemed the "signing preparer", but both the firm and the person with primary responsibility can be penalized if the return contains an unreasonable position.

A person who merely gives advice on a portion or a single entry on a tax return is considered to have prepared only that portion.

If more than one individual is involved in the preparation of a tax return, the person with the primary responsibility for the overall accuracy of the return is considered the preparer and must sign the return. In order to identify who is responsible for a substantial portion of the return, the following guidelines may be used.

A portion of a tax return is not typically considered to be substantial if it involves only amounts of gross income, amounts of deductions, or amounts on the basis of which credits are determined that are:
- Less than $10,000, or
- Less than $400,000 and less than 20% of the adjusted gross income on the return.

Usually, a single IRS schedule would not be considered a substantial portion of a tax return unless it represents a major portion of the income. One example of this may be a business taxpayer with a Schedule C that represents a majority of the income on the return.

> **Example:** Emilio and Kristy are equal partners in a tax practice, where they both work as Enrolled Agents. In March, Kristy finishes a few tax returns that Emilio had started before he left on vacation. Later, one tax return comes up for audit, and it is determined that the return has a gross valuation misstatement for a large deduction. Emilio prepared Schedule C on the return, and Kristy prepared the rest of the return. Schedule C represents 95% of the income and expenses shown on the return. Therefore, for purposes of any potential preparer penalty, Emilio is considered the preparer of this return, since he completed the schedule that represents the majority of the income and expenses on the return.

Enrolled Agent Licensing

As outlined in Circular 230, there are two tracks to becoming an Enrolled Agent. An individual may receive the designation by passing a three-part exam, or by virtue of past employment with the IRS.

1. Exam Track

For the first track, an EA candidate must apply for a PTIN and register to take the Special Enrollment Examination (SEE), also known as the EA exam, by filling out Form 2587, *Application for Special Enrollment Examination*. An applicant must be at least 18 years old. A candidate then must:

- Achieve passing scores on all three parts of the SEE.
- File Form 23, *Application for Enrollment to Practice before the Internal Revenue Service*, to apply for enrollment within one year from the date of passing the exam.[23] Form 23 can now be submitted online, and the fee can be paid at *www.pay.gov.*
- Pass a background check conducted by the IRS. The tax compliance check makes sure the applicant has filed all necessary tax returns and has no outstanding tax liabilities. The suitability check determines whether an applicant has engaged in any conduct that would justify suspension or disbarment.

2. Previous Experience Track

For the second track, an EA candidate must possess a minimum of five years of past service with the IRS and technical experience as outlined in Circular 230. The application must be made within three years from the date the employee left the IRS. Factors considered with this second track are the length and scope of employment and the recommendation of the superior officer.

The applicant then must:

- Apply for enrollment on Form 23.
- Pass a background check, which includes a tax compliance and suitability check.

Former IRS employees who become Enrolled Agents without taking the EA exam may be granted limited or unlimited representation rights.

---

[23] For successful examination candidates, the IRS goal is to have the application process completed within 90 days of receipt of Form 23. However, the applicant must pass a tax compliance check as well as a background check. The application for enrollment may be delayed if the Office of Professional responsibility finds any problems with either.

The IRS's Return Preparer Office (RPO) makes the determination on applications for enrollment to practice. The RPO provides oversight of competency testing, enrollment, renewal, and continuing education of Enrolled Agents.

Note: Once an individual's application is approved, the RPO will issue an enrollment card, and enrollment becomes effective on that date.

Denial of Enrollment

Any individual who is involved in disreputable or criminal conduct is subject to disciplinary action or denial of enrollment. Disreputable acts alone may be grounds for denial of enrollment, even after the candidate has passed the EA exam. Failure to timely file tax returns or to pay one's taxes may also be grounds for the Return Preparer Office to deny any application for enrollment.

The RPO must inform the applicant of the reason he or she is denied enrollment. The applicant may then file a written appeal to the Office of Professional Responsibility (OPR) within 30 days from the date of the notice. The appeal must be filed along with the candidate's reasoning why the enrollment application should be accepted.

Example: Clint passed all three parts of the EA exam and filed Form 23, requesting enrollment. Because he had failed to file numerous tax returns in the past, his application was denied. Clint filed an appeal with the OPR, explaining he had failed to file on time because he had been seriously injured years ago. He attached supporting evidence, including copies of medical bills and a letter from his doctor. Clint also provided evidence that all his tax returns had been properly filed after his recovery. The OPR accepted Clint's appeal and granted him enrollment.

Renewal of Enrollment

Enrolled agents must renew their enrollment status every three years. To renew, an EA must file Form 8554, *Application for Renewal of Enrollment to Practice before the Internal Revenue Service*, and submit the required nonrefundable fee. If an EA does not renew his enrollment, he may not continue to practice before the IRS.

The three successive enrollment years preceding the effective date of renewal is referred to as the IRS enrollment cycle. Applications for renewal of enrollment must be submitted between November 1 and January 31, prior to April 1 of the year that the next enrollment cycle begins. The last digit of a practitioner's Social Security number determines when he must renew enrollment. If the candidate's SSN ends in:

- 0, 1, 2, or 3 – Their enrollment cycle began April 1, 2016.
- 4, 5, or 6 – Their enrollment cycle began April 1, 2017.
- 7, 8, or 9 – Their next enrollment cycle begins April 1, 2018.

EAs who do not have an SSN (such as foreign preparers who work overseas) must use the "7, 8, or 9" renewal schedule. As part of the renewal process, the IRS will check the practitioner's filing history to verify that he has filed and paid all federal taxes on time. If the Enrolled Agent owns or has an interest in a business, the IRS will also check the tax compliance history of the business. In addition, the IRS will check that the EA has completed all necessary professional continuing education requirements.

The IRS sends a reminder notice when an EA is due for renewal. However, an Enrolled Agent is not excused from the obligation to renew if he does not receive the notice. It is the *practitioner's* sole responsibility to apply for renewal by filing Form 8554.

An EA must inform the Return Preparer Office of an address change within 60 days of a move.

Continuing Education for Enrolled Agents

During each three-year enrollment cycle, an EA must complete 72 hours of continuing education credit. A minimum of 16 hours, including two hours of ethics or professional conduct, must be completed during each enrollment year.

The IRS conducts random CPE audits of EAs by requesting copies of their continuing education certificates of completion for the past three years. Recipients of these letters will be asked to mail or fax the documents within 30 days.

For a new EA, the month of initial enrollment begins the CPE requirement. He must complete two hours of CPE for each month enrolled, and two hours of ethics for the enrollment year. Enrollment for any part of a month is considered enrollment for the entire month.

> **Note:** The initial CPE Requirements for EAs in their *first* enrollment cycle are:
> - 2 hours of CPE for every single month
> - 2 hours of ethics annually (no exceptions)

When an EA's new three-year enrollment cycle begins, the practitioner will be required to satisfy the full 72-hour continuing education credit requirement.

Ethics courses must be taken every year. If a candidate takes more than two hours of ethics courses during a single year, the additional hours may count toward the overall requirements of 16 hours per year and 72 hours per cycle. However, an Enrolled Agent may not take additional ethics courses in the current year and neglect to take them in future years.

> **Example**: Charisse became a new EA on September 30, 2017, which was the third year of the enrollment cycle based on her SSN. She is required to take two hours of CPE for each month before January 1, 2018, which equals eight hours for the period of September through December. Two of those hours must be on the topic of ethics. Since her initial enrollment came during the final year of the enrollment cycle, Charisse must renew her enrollment status in 2018 and will be subject to the full 72-hour CPE requirement during her subsequent renewal periods.

> **Exception:** If an Enrolled Agent retakes and passes the SEE again since his last renewal, he is only required to take 16 hours of CPE, including two hours of ethics, during the last year of his current enrollment cycle.

CPE Providers: Individuals and companies who wish to offer continuing education to EAs must pay a registration fee and apply as providers with the IRS. Providers are issued a provider number and may display a logo that says "IRS Approved Continuing Education Provider". Course providers must renew their status every year.

Approved Programs: Qualifying programs include traditional seminars and conferences, as well as correspondence or individual self-study programs on the Internet, so long as they are approved courses of study by approved providers. In order to qualify as CPE, a course must be designed to enhance professional knowledge in federal taxation or federal tax-related matters. Courses related to state taxation do not meet the IRS requirement unless at least 80% of the program material consists of a comparison of federal and state tax laws.

Contact Hours: Continuing education programs are measured in terms of contact hours. The shortest recognized program is one hour. In order for a course to qualify for CPE credit, it must feature at least 50 minutes of continuous participation. Individual segments at conferences and conventions are considered one total program. For example, two 90-minute segments (180 minutes) at a continuous conference count as three contact hours.

Example: Andreanna is an Enrolled Agent who signs up for a half-day federal tax update class. The instructor starts the class promptly at 8 a.m. and lectures until 9:40 a.m., when the class takes a 20 minute break. The instructor resumes the class at 10 a.m. and it runs until 11:40 a.m., when the class is recessed. Andreanna will receive four CPE credits because she completed four 50-minute segments of instruction, worth one contact hour each.

Instructor Credit: An Enrolled Agent may receive continuing education credit for serving as an instructor, discussion leader, or speaker on federal tax matters for approved educational programs. One hour of CPE credit is awarded for each contact hour completed. Two hours of CPE credit is awarded for actual subject preparation time for each contact hour completed as an instructor, discussion leader, or speaker at such programs. The maximum credit for instruction and preparation may not exceed six hours annually.

Verifying CPE Hours: After completing CPE coursework, an EA will receive a certificate from the course provider. The course provider will also report completed continuing education to the IRS, using the PTINs of the individual participants.

Tax preparers may check their online PTIN accounts to see a display of the CPE programs they have completed, as reported by providers. CPE hours completed prior to 2013 are not included. EAs are required to keep their own records related to continuing education hours for four years following the date of renewal.

CPE Waiver

An EA may request a full or partial waiver of CPE requirements from the RPO. Qualifying circumstances may include:

- Health issues
- Extended active military duty
- Absence from the United States for employment or other reasons
- Other reasons on a case-by-case basis

The request for a waiver must be accompanied by appropriate documentation, such as medical records or military paperwork. If the request is denied, the Enrolled Agent will be placed on the inactive roster. If the request is accepted, the EA will receive an updated enrollment card reflecting his renewal.

Example: Benedict is an EA who is also an Army reservist. He was called to active duty in a combat zone for two years. During his deployment, Benedict was unable to complete his CPE requirements for his Enrolled Agent license. Benedict contacted RPO and requested a waiver based on his current active-duty military service. RPO grants the waiver. Benedict later returns to the United States after an honorable discharge. Benedict is free to begin preparing tax returns as an Enrolled Agent again.

Inactive and Terminated EAs

RPO notifies any EA who fails to comply with the requirements for eligibility for renewal of enrollment. A notice will be sent via first-class mail explaining the reason for noncompliance.

The notice further provides the preparer an opportunity to furnish the requested information, such as missing CPE credits, in writing. An EA has 60 days from the date of the notice to respond to this initial notice. If no response is received, the EA will move to inactive status as of April 1.

To be eligible for renewal after missing one full enrollment cycle, an EA must pay fees for both the prior and current renewal cycles and verify that the required CPE hours have been taken.

To have his termination status reconsidered, an EA must file a written protest within 30 days and provide a valid reason for not renewing on time. Reasons may include serious illness or extended travel out of the country.

Losing the Eligibility to Practice

Practitioners may lose their eligibility to practice before the IRS for the following reasons, among others:

- Failure to meet the annual continuing education requirements for enrollment.
- Failure to renew a PTIN.
- Requesting to be placed on inactive/retirement status.
- Being disciplined by state regulatory agents. An attorney who has been disbarred from practice at the state level or a CPA whose license has been revoked or suspended at the state level is disbarred from practice at the federal level, and cannot practice before the IRS as long as his disbarment, revocation, or suspension is active.

Example: Aileen is an Enrolled Agent. In 2017, the Internal Revenue Service's Office of Professional Responsibility disbarred Aileen for stealing a client's tax payments and preparing tax returns with false deductions for multiple clients. Aileen's Enrolled Agent status is revoked for at least five years.

Unit 2: Study Questions

(Test yourself and then check the correct answers at the end of this chapter.)

1. "Practice before the IRS" does not include:

A. Communicating directly with the IRS on behalf of a taxpayer regarding his rights or liabilities.
B. Representing a taxpayer at an IRS examination.
C. Representing taxpayers before the IRS appeals division.
D. Representation of a taxpayer in the U.S. Tax Court.

2. Cameron is an Enrolled Agent who takes a continuing education class from an approved IRS provider. The class runs continuously from 9 a.m. until 11:45 a.m., when there is a break for lunch. How many CPE credits will Cameron receive for the morning session of the class?

A. One.
B. Two.
C. Three.
D. Four.

3. When does a new EA's enrollment take effect?

A. On the date he applies for enrollment with the IRS.
B. On the date listed on his enrollment card.
C. On the date he receives his enrollment card.
D. On the first day of January after he receives his enrollment card.

4. Denise and Gabriela are best friends. They are not family members. Gabriela must appear before the IRS for an examination. Denise wants to appear before the IRS on her friend's behalf, though she is not a practitioner. Which of the following statements is correct?

A. Denise may represent Gabriela before the IRS without Gabriela being present.
B. Denise may advocate for Gabriela to the best of her ability.
C. Denise may appear before the IRS as a witness and communicate information.
D. Denise may not appear before the IRS in any capacity.

5. Which of the following individuals is required to obtain a PTIN?

A. A CPA who does not prepare any tax returns.
B. An EA who works for a CPA firm, but does not sign any tax returns.
C. A tax attorney who only does representation of clients in the U.S. court system.
D. A retired accountant who prepares tax returns for free for his family.

6. Matthew is a full-time employee for Parkway Partnership. He is not an EA, attorney, or CPA. Parkway requests that Matthew represent the partnership in connection with an IRS audit. Which of the following statements is correct?

A. Matthew is allowed to represent the partnership before the IRS.
B. Matthew is not allowed to represent the partnership before the IRS.
C. Matthew is only allowed to represent individual partners before the IRS.
D. None of the above.

7. What is the enrollment cycle for Enrolled Agents?

A. The enrollment cycle is the year after the effective date of renewal.
B. The enrollment cycle means the three successive enrollment years preceding the effective date of renewal.
C. The enrollment cycle is the method by which the RPO approves EA exam candidates.
D. The enrollment cycle is the method Prometric uses to choose EA exam questions.

8. Which of the following individuals does not qualify as an enrolled practitioner?

A. Certified public accountant.
B. Enrolled actuary.
C. Registered tax return preparer.
D. All of the above are considered enrolled practitioners.

9. All of the following are potential grounds for denial of enrollment except:

A. Failure to timely file tax returns.
B. Failure to pay taxes.
C. Felony convictions.
D. A candidate who is only 18 years old.

10. Everett is an EA with a PTIN. His firm employs a bookkeeper named Fernanda. Fernanda gathers client receipts and invoices and organizes and records all information for Everett. She does not use Everett's professional tax return software, but she does use the firm's bookkeeping software. Everett then uses the information that his bookkeeper has compiled and prepares all the client tax returns. Which of the following statements is correct?

A. Fernanda needs to have a PTIN, and she is required to become an EA because she assists in the preparation of returns.
B. Fernanda needs to have a PTIN, but she is not required to become an EA.
C. Fernanda is not a tax return preparer and is not required to have a PTIN.
D. Fernanda is a supervised preparer and needs to have a PTIN.

11. The IRS's new public directory of tax return preparers includes listings for:

A. Practitioners with a current PTIN.
B. All current PTIN holders.
C. Enrolled agents and CPAs with a current PTIN.
D. All enrolled practitioners with a current PTIN as well as AFSP Record of Completion holders.

12. Which of the following is considered a tax return preparer under Circular 230 regulations?

A. A full-time bookkeeper working for an employer who prepares payroll tax returns.
B. A retired attorney who prepares tax returns under the VITA program.
C. A person who furnishes typing, reproducing, or mechanical assistance.
D. A full-time secretary who also prepares tax returns for pay, part-time from home, during the tax season.

13. Enrolled agents must complete continuing education credits for renewed enrollment. Which of the following describes the credit requirements?

A. A minimum of 72 hours must be completed in each year of an enrollment cycle.
B. A minimum of 24 hours must be completed in each year of an enrollment cycle.
C. A minimum of 80 hours must be completed for the entire enrollment cycle.
D. A minimum of 16 hours must be completed in each year of the enrollment cycle, including two hours of ethics credits.

14. To determine which preparer is responsible for a "substantial portion" of a tax return, each of the following guidelines is used except:

A. Whoever has the primary responsibility for the accuracy of the return.
B. Whoever actually owns or manages the tax practice.
C. Whoever prepares the portion of the return that declares the greatest amount of adjusted gross income.
D. Amounts of gross income, amounts of deductions, or amounts on the basis of which credits are determined that are (1) under $10,000 or less or (2) less than $400,000 and less than 20% of the adjusted gross income on the return will not be considered a substantial portion.

15. Khan is a CPA who employs Amy, an accounting student, to assist in the preparation of tax returns. Khan signs all of the tax returns. Which of the following statements is correct?

A. Amy and Khan can share one PTIN.
B. Amy is required by law to sign the returns that she has prepared.
C. Amy is required to obtain a PTIN.
D. Amy cannot assist with the preparation of tax returns until she becomes a CPA.

16. Barry helps his friend, Jose, who does not speak English fluently. Barry appears before the IRS and translates for Jose at an IRS examination. Which of the following statements is correct?

A. Barry is not considered to be practicing before the IRS.
B. Jose must sign a power of attorney form authorizing Barry to represent him.
C. Barry is practicing before the IRS.
D. The IRS prohibits unrelated persons from being present at an IRS examination.

17. Andrea is an EA. Her records show that she had the following hours of qualified CPE in 2017:
- January 2017, seven hours: Federal tax CPE
- May 2017, one hour: Ethics
- December 2017, nine hours: Federal tax CPE

Has Andrea met her minimum yearly CPE requirements?

A. Yes, Andrea has met her minimum yearly CPE requirements.
B. No, Andrea has met her ethics requirement, but not the overall minimum requirement for the year.
C. No, Andrea has not met her ethics requirement.
D. None of the above.

18. All of the following are permitted to represent the taxpayer before the examination division of the IRS except:

A. The taxpayer's best friend who is an attorney licensed to practice law in the state where the taxpayer lives.
B. The taxpayer's brother who is not an attorney, CPA, or Enrolled Agent.
C. An unenrolled tax return preparer who did not prepare the taxpayer's return.
D. All of the above are permitted to represent the taxpayer before the IRS.

19. What action should an EA take if he chooses to appeal termination from enrollment?

A. Call the Office of Professional Responsibility to complain.
B. File a written protest within 30 days of the date of the notice of termination.
C. File a written protest within 60 days of the date of the notice of termination.
D. File a written protest within 90 days of the date of the notice of termination.

20. Stan is an EA with a PTIN. What must he do to retain his existing PTIN?

A. Nothing. Stan is allowed to retain his PTIN so long as he is current in his enrollment status.
B. Stan must renew his PTIN every three years when he renews his enrollment status.
C. Stan cannot retain his existing PTIN. He must apply for a new PTIN every year.
D. Stan must renew his existing PTIN each year.

21. Enrolled agents who apply for renewal to practice before the IRS must retain information about continuing education hours completed. How long must this documentation be retained?

A. For one year following the enrollment renewal date.
B. For four years following the enrollment renewal date.
C. For five years if it is an initial enrollment.
D. The individual is not required to retain the education information if the CPE provider has agreed to retain it.

22. An Enrolled Agent can represent a taxpayer _____.

A. Before any administrative level of the IRS.
B. Only if the EA prepared the return.
C. At all tax related federal court proceedings.
D. Before collections, examinations and the U.S. Tax Court.

1. The answer is D. "Practice before the IRS" does not include the representation of clients in the U.S. Tax Court. The Tax Court is independent of the IRS and has its own rules of practice and its own regulations regarding admission to practice.

2. The answer is C. Continuing education program credits are measured in terms of contact hours, which must be at least 50 minutes long. The class ran for 165 minutes, which counts as three contact hours. If the class had run *continuously* until 12:20 p.m., it would have lasted 200 minutes, so it would have been worth four CPE hours.

3. The answer is B. An EA's enrollment becomes official on the date listed on his enrollment card, whether he has actually received the card or not.

4. The answer is C. Simply appearing as a witness before the IRS is allowed and not considered practice before the IRS. Individuals who are not practitioners may appear before the IRS as witnesses or communicate to the IRS on a taxpayer's behalf—but they may not advocate for the taxpayer.

5. The answer is B. All EAs are required to obtain PTINs as a condition of their licensing (the PTIN must be included on Form 23, which is the application form to become an Enrolled Agent). Attorneys and CPAs do not need to obtain a PTIN unless they prepare tax returns for compensation. Someone who prepares returns for free is not considered a tax return preparer by the IRS and does not need a PTIN.

6. The answer is A. Matthew is a full-time employee for Parkway Partnership, so in that capacity he may represent his employer before the IRS. A regular full-time employee of an individual employer may represent the employer.

7. The answer is B. The enrollment cycle means the three successive enrollment years preceding the effective date of renewal. After the initial enrollment period, regular renewal enrollments are required every three years. This is known as an enrollment cycle.

8. The answer is C. The registered tax return preparer designation is now defunct due to the IRS's loss in the *Loving v. Commissioner* case. An individual who passed the RTRP exam is considered an unenrolled preparer and not an enrolled practitioner. Unenrolled preparers have limited rights of practice before the IRS. An unenrolled preparer may only represent a taxpayer for the tax return or claim of refund he personally prepared and signed. This representation may occur only before revenue agents and similar employees of the IRS, and not before appeals or revenue officers. An unenrolled preparer also may not sign any document on behalf of a taxpayer.

9. The answer is D. The minimum age for enrollment is 18, so anyone over 17 would not be denied enrollment based on his age. Failure to timely file tax returns or pay taxes, and felony convictions are all potential grounds for denying an application for enrollment. The Return Preparer Office will review all of the facts and circumstances to determine whether a denial of enrollment is warranted.

10. The answer is C. Fernanda is not a tax return preparer and is not required to have a PTIN. An individual who provides only typing, reproduction, or other mechanical assistance but does not actually prepare returns is not considered a tax return preparer by the IRS.

11. The answer is D. The Annual Filing Season Program is the IRS's new voluntary program to replace the registered tax return preparer program. Those who pass the program's education and testing requirements receive an AFSP Record of Completion for the year. Participants will be included in a public, searchable database of tax return preparers on the IRS website. The *Directory of Federal Tax Return Preparers with Credentials and Select Qualifications* includes the name, city, state, zip code, and credentials of all attorneys, CPAs, EAs, ERPAs, and enrolled actuaries with a valid PTIN, as well as all AFSP Record of Completion holders. An individual may opt out of being listed in the directory. Unenrolled preparers with PTINs who are not Record of Completion holders are not listed in the directory.

12. The answer is D. A person who prepares tax returns for compensation is a tax return preparer, even if the activity is only part-time. A person who prepares and signs a tax return without compensation (such as for a family member or as a volunteer) is not considered a tax return preparer for purposes of preparer penalties. An employee who prepares a tax return for his employer or for another employee is not a preparer under Circular 230. The employer (or the individual with supervisory responsibility) has the responsibility for accuracy of the return.

13. The answer is D. A minimum of 16 hours of continuing education credit, including two hours of ethics credits, must be completed in each year of the enrollment cycle. An EA must complete a minimum of 72 hours of continuing education during each three-year period.

14. The answer is B. Ownership or management of a tax practice is immaterial in determining the substantial portion rule. The most important determination is whoever has the primary responsibility for the accuracy of the return. If several people are involved in preparing a return, the person who prepares the part of the return that declares the greatest amount of income would be considered the preparer who must sign the return.

15. The answer is C. Amy must obtain a PTIN. Every individual who prepares or assists in the preparation of a tax return or claim for refund for compensation must have her own PTIN.

16. The answer is A. Simply appearing as a witness or communicating information to the IRS does not constitute practice before the IRS. Barry is merely assisting with the exchange of information and is not advocating on Jose's behalf. An example of an individual assisting with information exchange but not practicing would be a taxpayer's friend serving as a translator when the taxpayer does not speak English.

17. The answer is C. The IRS requires a 16-hour minimum of CE per year, and requires two hours of ethics or professional conduct per year. Andrea has only completed one hour of ethics CE. She has met her annual general CE requirement, but she has not met the ethics requirement for the year, so her minimum requirements have not been met.

18. The answer is C. Unenrolled tax preparers are not permitted to represent a taxpayer except in the examination of a tax return they prepared. Even in that case, the taxpayer must be present during the examination. According to current law, only unenrolled return preparers participating in the Annual Filing Season Record of Completion (AFSP) program may represent a taxpayer, and only with respect to returns prepared and signed by the preparer.

19. The answer is B. An EA who has been terminated from enrollment should file a written protest within 30 days of the date of the notice. The protest must be filed with the Office of Professional Responsibility.

20. The answer is D. The IRS requires all paid preparers to have a preparer tax identification number (PTIN). Stan renew his existing PTIN each year by the December 31 deadline to avoid any lapse in his active PTIN status. He may renew online at the IRS website or by mailing Form W-12.

21. The answer is B. Each individual applying for renewal must retain information about CE hours completed for four years following the enrollment renewal date.

22. The answer D. An Enrolled Agent can represent a taxpayer before any administrative level of the IRS.

Unit 3: Authorizations and Disclosures

> **More Reading:**
> Publication 947, *Practice Before the IRS and Power of Attorney*
> Instructions for Form 2848
> Publication 4019, *Third Party Authorization, Levels of Authority*

Power of Attorney

A power of attorney (POA) is a taxpayer's written authorization for an individual to act on the taxpayer's behalf in tax matters. The power of attorney gives an eligible individual, which includes all practitioners, the ability to represent a taxpayer before the IRS. Often, this occurs when a taxpayer wants to be represented at a conference with the IRS or to have a written response prepared and filed with the IRS.

When a taxpayer wishes to use a representative, he should fill out and sign Form 2848, *Power of Attorney and Declaration of Representative.* In doing so, the taxpayer authorizes a specific individual or individuals to receive confidential tax information and to perform the actions detailed on the form. Up to four representatives can be authorized per form.

Note: In a recent revision to Form 2848, a representative must attest that he is subject to the regulations of Circular 230, governing practice before the IRS. This attestation gives the Office of Professional Responsibility authority to regulate unenrolled tax preparers who use the form.

On Form 2848, the taxpayer describes the tax matters the representative is authorized to handle, the time periods allowed, and the specific acts that are authorized or not authorized. A separate Form 2848 must be completed for each taxpayer who wishes representation; even joint filers must submit separate Forms 2848.

The types of tax and dates of a Form 2848 must be specific. The IRS will reject Forms 2848 with general references such as "all years" or "all taxes." In preparing the form, any tax years or periods that have already ended may be listed under "tax matters." For future tax periods, the period specified is limited to no later than three years after the date the POA is received by the IRS.

A representative must be eligible to practice before the IRS in order to sign Form 2848, and the duty may not be delegated to an employee. A practitioner must provide his PTIN and use his own name as the representative, rather than the name of his business.

Example: Beatriz operates Compass Tax Service Corporation. When she prepares Form 2848, she must represent her client as an individual. Beatriz is granted permission to represent her client, but her corporation and other members of her firm are not.

In filling out Form 2848, a representative must enter the designation under which he is authorized to practice before the IRS, and list the applicable jurisdiction. For example, an Enrolled Agent must list the IRS as the licensing jurisdiction. If a tax practitioner is disbarred or suspended, his power of attorney will not be recognized by the IRS.

Unenrolled individuals may also be authorized to represent a taxpayer under Form 2848, if specifically permitted in very limited circumstances (such as a family member representing a taxpayer, an executor representing an estate, or an unenrolled tax return preparer who prepared the specific tax return at issue).

Example: Christopher is an unenrolled tax preparer. He does not participate in the IRS's Annual Season Filing Program. In most circumstances, Christopher would not be able to represent a taxpayer before the IRS. However, his cousin Dorthea died in 2017, and Christopher is named as the executor of her estate. The estate received an audit notice in 2017. Christopher may file a Form 2848 and represent Dorthea's estate before all levels of the IRS. He will have full representation rights. This is because of the exception for executors representing an estate.

Durable Power of Attorney

The IRS will accept a non-IRS power of attorney, such as a durable power of attorney, but it must contain all of the information included on a standard Form 2848.

A non-IRS power of attorney must contain the following information:

- The taxpayer's name, mailing address, and taxpayer identification number
- The name and mailing address of the representative
- The types of tax involved and the federal tax form number in question
- The specific periods or tax years involved
- For estate tax matters, the decedent's date of death
- A clear expression of the taxpayer's intention concerning the scope of authority granted to the representative
- The taxpayer's signature and date

A signed and dated statement made by the representative should also be attached to the non-IRS power of attorney. The statement is signed under penalties of perjury.

Example: Eleanor signs a durable power of attorney that names her best friend, Fredrick, as her representative. The durable power of attorney grants Fredrick the authority to perform all acts on Eleanor's behalf. However, it does not list specific information such as the types of tax covered. A year after Eleanor signs the power of attorney, she is declared incompetent due to Alzheimer's disease. Later, a tax matter arises concerning a prior year return filed by Eleanor. Fredrick attempts to represent Eleanor before the IRS, but he is rejected because the durable power of attorney does not contain required information. If Fredrick attaches a statement that the durable power of attorney is valid under the laws of the governing jurisdiction, he can sign a completed Form 2848 and submit it on Eleanor's behalf. If Fredrick is eligible to practice before the IRS, he can name himself as the representative on Form 2848.

Note: A durable power of attorney is not subject to a time limit and will continue in force after the incapacitation or incompetency of the individual. It is terminated upon the death of the individual. An ordinary power of attorney is automatically revoked if the person who made it is found to be incompetent, but a durable power of attorney can only be revoked by the person who made it, and while that person is mentally competent.

Unless a particular act is specifically not authorized by the taxpayer, a representative (with the exception of unenrolled tax return preparers) can generally perform the following acts:

- Represent a taxpayer before any office of the IRS
- Record an interview or meeting with the IRS
- Sign an offer or a waiver of restriction on assessment or collection of a tax deficiency, or a waiver of notice of disallowance of claim for credit or refund

- Sign consents to extend the statutory time period for assessment or collection of a tax
- Sign a closing agreement
- Receive (but never endorse or cash) a tax refund check

The rights of unenrolled tax return preparers are limited to representing taxpayers in examinations of the tax returns they prepared and signed.

A qualified representative can represent a taxpayer before the IRS without the taxpayer present, so long as the proper power of attorney is signed and submitted to the IRS.

Example: Geraldine is an Enrolled Agent with a signed Form 2848 for Jeromy, who is being audited by the IRS. Geraldine did not prepare Jeromy's tax return, but she is still eligible to represent him by virtue of her status as an EA. Jeromy does not have to appear at the examination hearing. If Geraldine were an unenrolled preparer, her representation rights would be restricted to the particular tax returns she had prepared for Jeromy that were under examination. She would be able to represent Jeromy only before IRS revenue agents and not revenue officers or appeals officers.

Revocation or Withdrawal of a POA

A power of attorney is valid until revoked by the taxpayer or until the representative withdraws from representation. If the taxpayer is revoking the power of attorney, he must write **"REVOKE"** across the top of the first page with his signature and the date below it. If the representative is withdrawing from representation, he must write **"WITHDRAW"** across the top of the first page with his signature and the date below it. The revocation or withdrawal must be mailed or faxed to the IRS. It must clearly indicate the applicable tax matters and periods.

Example: Karenna is an EA who had a power of attorney for her former client, Lenny. Karenna fired Lenny for nonpayment, but she continued to receive IRS notices on his behalf. Karenna writes "WITHDRAW" on the POA and submits it to the IRS, notifying the IRS that she no longer represents Lenny.

If a taxpayer or representative does not have a copy of the power of attorney, a statement of revocation or withdrawal must be sent to the IRS.

A newly-filed power of attorney concerning the same matter will revoke a previously-filed power of attorney. For example, if a taxpayer switches tax preparers, and the second preparer files a power of attorney on behalf of the taxpayer, the old power of attorney on file will be rescinded. However, the taxpayer can specifically request that the old power of attorney remains active when a newer power of attorney is filed.

An IRS power of attorney is terminated if the taxpayer becomes incapacitated or incompetent.

Updating a Power of Attorney: Any update or modification to a power of attorney must be submitted in writing to the IRS. A recognized representative may substitute or delegate authority if the taxpayer has specifically given him the power to do so. The representative must file the following items with the IRS offices where the power of attorney was filed:

- A written notice of substitution or delegation signed by the recognized representative.
- A written declaration of representation made by the new representative.
- A copy of the power of attorney that specifically authorizes the substitution or delegation.

After a substitution is made, only the newly recognized representative will be considered the taxpayer's representative.

Power of Attorney Not Required: If a third party is not representing a taxpayer before the IRS, a power of attorney is not required. This would include preparation of a taxpayer's income tax return. The following situations also do not require a power of attorney:

- Providing information to the IRS
- Authorizing the disclosure of tax return information through Form 8821, *Tax Information Authorization*, or other written or oral disclosure consent
- Allowing the IRS to discuss return information with a third party via the checkbox provided on a tax return or other document
- Allowing a tax matters partner to perform acts for a partnership
- Allowing the IRS to discuss tax return information with a fiduciary or an executor

Representative Signing in Lieu of the Taxpayer

A representative named under a power of attorney is generally not permitted to sign a personal income tax return unless both of the following conditions are met:

- The signature is permitted under the Internal Revenue Code and the related regulations, and
- The taxpayer specifically grants signature authority on the power of attorney.

For example, IRS regulations permit a representative to sign a taxpayer's return if the taxpayer is unable to sign for any of the following reasons:

- Disease or injury (such as a taxpayer who is completely paralyzed or who has a debilitating injury)
- Continuous absence from the United States (including Puerto Rico) for a period of at least 60 days prior to the date required by law for filing the return
- Other good cause if specific permission is requested of and granted by the IRS

> **Example:** Marc is an EA with a client named Patsy who travels extensively for business. She had signed Form 2848 specifically granting Marc the right to sign her tax returns in her absence. Patsy is currently traveling outside the U.S. for business and will not return until four months after the due date of her returns. Marc is allowed to sign Patsy's return.

When a tax return is signed by a representative, it must be accompanied by a copy of the power of attorney authorizing the representative to sign the return.

Tax Information Authorization, Form 8821

Form 8821, *Tax Information Authorization* (TIA), authorizes any individual, corporation, firm, organization, or partnership to inspect or receive confidential information for the type of tax and periods listed. Any third party may be designated to receive tax information.

Form 8821 is used by tax return preparers, employers, banks, and other institutions to receive financial information on behalf of an individual or a business. It is only a disclosure form, so it does not give an individual authority to represent a taxpayer before the IRS.

Similar to a POA form, Form 8821 requires the taxpayer to list the type of tax, the tax form number, the year or periods the authorization covers, and the specific tax matters that apply. Any prior tax years may be specified, but only future tax periods ending no later than three years after the date Form 8821 is received by the IRS are recognized.

Centralized Authorization File (CAF)

The centralized authorization file (CAF) is the IRS's computer database that contains information regarding the authorizations that taxpayers have given representatives for their accounts.

When a power of attorney or disclosure authorization document is submitted to the IRS, it is processed for inclusion in the CAF. A CAF number is assigned to a tax practitioner or other authorized individual when either a Form 2848 or Form 8821 is filed. It is a unique nine-digit number that is not the same as an individual's SSN, PTIN, or enrollment number.

> **Example:** Matilda is not a tax return preparer. In 2017, Matilda's 21 year-old son, Oscar, is audited by the IRS. Oscar does not wish to speak directly with the IRS. Matilda files a Form 2848 and becomes the authorized representative for her son. She is issued a CAF number.

> **Example:** Rashaan is not an Enrolled Agent or a tax preparer. In 2017, his mother dies, and Rashaan is named as the executor of her estate. He files a Form 2848 and properly lists himself as the executor. He is issued a CAF number, and is allowed to represent his late mother's estate before all levels of the IRS.

Joint filers must complete and submit separate Forms 2848 to have the power of attorney recorded in the CAF. Alternative power of attorney forms, such as a durable power of attorney, will not be recorded in the CAF unless a Form 2848 is also attached.

The issuance of a CAF number does not indicate that a person is either recognized or authorized to practice before the IRS. It merely confirms that a centralized file has been established for the representative under that number.

> **Example:** Salvador is an EA who recently submitted Form 2848 to the IRS on behalf of his client, Tanesha. He later called the IRS to check the status of Tanesha's tax refund. The IRS employee requested Salvador's CAF number, which he provided. The IRS employee found Tanesha's power of attorney information in the CAF system and gave Salvador the information about his client's refund.

Having a CAF number also enables the IRS to automatically send copies of notices and other IRS communications to a representative.

A practitioner may list the current year and any tax years that have already ended. The practitioner may also list future tax years or periods. However, the IRS will not record on the CAF system future tax years or periods listed that exceed *three years* from December 31 of the year that the IRS receives the power of attorney.

> **Note:** The revised Form 2848 instructions include an explanation of how practitioners can receive a list of their powers of attorney recorded on the CAF. A practitioner must make an FOIA request and ask the IRS to provide a copy of his CAF Representative/Client Listing. A sample letter and further instructions, including requirements to prove identity, are available on www.irs.gov by clicking on the "routine access to IRS records" link under the FOIA section.

Third Party Authorizations

A third-party authorization is when a taxpayer authorizes an individual (usually his tax return preparer) to communicate with the IRS on his behalf. This authorization allows the IRS to discuss the processing of a taxpayer's current tax return, including the status of refunds, with whomever the taxpayer specifies. The authorization automatically expires on the due date of the next tax return.

The third-party designee signs here

Third Party Designee	Do you want to allow another person to discuss this return with the IRS (see instructions)? ☑ **Yes.** Complete below. ☐ **No**			
	Designee's name ▶ *John Smith*	Phone no. ▶ *916-111-1111*	Personal identification number (PIN) ▶ 9 5 2 4 0	

Sign Here	Under penalties of perjury, I declare that I have examined this return and accompanying schedules and statements, and to the best of my knowledge and belief, they are true, correct, and complete. Declaration of preparer (other than taxpayer) is based on all information of which preparer has any knowledge.			
Joint return? See instructions.	Your signature	Date	Your occupation	Daytime phone number
Keep a copy for your records.	Spouse's signature. If a joint return, **both** must sign.	Date	Spouse's occupation	If the IRS sent you an Identity Protection PIN, enter it here (see inst.)

A taxpayer can choose a third-party designee by checking the "yes" box on his tax return, which is why it is known as "Check Box" authority. The taxpayer then enters the designee's name and phone number and a self-selected five-digit PIN, which the designee must confirm when requesting information from the IRS.

The designee can exchange verbal information with the IRS on return processing issues and on refunds and payments related to the return. The designee may also receive written account information including transcripts, upon request. A designee cannot receive a tax refund check on a client's behalf.

> **Example:** Tyler named his EA, Vicky, as his third-party designee on his tax return. A few months after filing his return, Tyler still had not received his refund. He asked Vicky if she could check the status of his refund. Vicky called the IRS and was given the information over the phone because she was listed as a third-party designee on Tyler's return. No further authorization was necessary for Vicky to receive this confidential taxpayer information.

The third-party designee authorization is more limited than the authority given by Form 8821, *Tax Information Authorization* (TIA). Form 8821 can be used to allow discussions with third parties and disclosures of information to third parties on matters other than a taxpayer's current return.

Tax Return Copies and Transcripts

If a taxpayer needs an actual copy of his own tax return that has been filed and processed, he may use Form 4506, *Request for Copy of Tax Return.* Copies are generally available for the current year and the past six years. The IRS charges a fee for making the copy.[24]

A taxpayer can often receive all the information he needs by requesting a free transcript of a tax return, which is available immediately online via the IRS's "Get Transcript" tool, or by phone or mail.

Transcripts are available for the current year and the past three years. Form 4506-T, *Request for Transcript of Tax Return,* may be used when a taxpayer wants to authorize an individual or organization to receive or inspect confidential tax return information. This form is often used by financial institutions to verify tax compliance or income, such as when a taxpayer is applying for a mortgage. Form 4506-T does not authorize an individual to represent a taxpayer before the IRS.

The taxpayer must specify on the form what type of information is needed. If a "return transcript" is requested, the IRS will provide most of the line items of a filed tax return. A return transcript also includes items from any accompanying forms and schedules that were filed, but it does not reflect any changes made after the original return was filed.

---

[24] The fee is currently $50 for each return requested and may be waived for taxpayers who live in a presidentially declared disaster area.

If an "account transcript" is requested, the IRS will provide information on the financial status of the account, such as payments made and penalty assessments. Requesting a "record of account" produces the most detailed information as it combines the return transcript and account transcript information.

Privacy of Taxpayer Information (§7216)

The IRS has enacted strict privacy regulations designed to give taxpayers more control over their personal information and tax records. The regulations limit tax professionals' use and disclosure of client information, and explain precise and limited exceptions in which disclosure is permitted.

Tax return preparers must generally obtain written consent from taxpayers before they can disclose information to a third party or use the information for any purpose other than the preparation of tax returns.

The consent form must meet the following guidelines:

- Identify the purpose of the disclosure.
- Identify the recipient and describe the authorized information.
- Include the name of the preparer and the name of the taxpayer.
- Include mandatory language that informs the taxpayer that he is not required to sign the consent, and if he does sign the consent, he can set a time period for the duration of the consent.
- Include mandatory language that refers the taxpayer to the Treasury Inspector General for Tax Administration if he believes that his tax return information has been disclosed or used improperly.
- If applicable, inform the taxpayer that his tax return information may be disclosed to a tax return preparer located outside the U.S.
- Be signed and dated by the taxpayer. Electronic (online) consents must be in the same type as the website's standard text and contain the taxpayer's affirmative consent (as opposed to an opt-out clause).

Unless a specific time period is specified, the consent is valid for one year.

> **Note:** Internal Revenue Code §7216 is a <u>criminal</u> tax provision enacted by Congress that prohibits tax return preparers from knowingly or recklessly disclosing or using tax return information. A preparer may be fined up to $1,000, imprisoned up to one year, or both, for each violation of §7216. There is also an additional civil penalty of $250 for improper disclosure or use of taxpayer information, outlined in IRC §6713. However, unlike §7216, this code section does not require that the disclosure be "knowing or reckless." This means that even an accidental disclosure of sensitive taxpayer information may cause the practitioner to be subject to a civil penalty.

These privacy regulations apply to paid preparers, electronic return originators, tax software developers, and other persons or entities engaged in tax preparation.

The regulations also apply to most volunteer tax return preparers, such as Volunteer Income Tax Assistance (VITA) and Tax Counseling for the Elderly volunteers, and to employees and contractors employed by tax preparation companies in a support role.

Definition: These regulations pertain to the disclosure of **"tax return information,"** which is defined by law and very broad in scope. Tax return information is "all the information tax return preparers obtain from taxpayers or other sources in any form or matter that is used to prepare tax returns or is obtained in connection with the preparation of returns. It also includes all computations, worksheets, and printouts preparers create; correspondence from the IRS during the preparation, filing, and correction of returns; statistical compilations of tax return information; and tax return preparation software registration information."[25]

Allowable Disclosures

In certain circumstances, a preparer may disclose information to a second taxpayer who appears on a tax return. The preparer may disclose return information obtained from the first taxpayer if:

- The second taxpayer is related to the first taxpayer.
- The first taxpayer's interest is not adverse to the second taxpayer's interest.
- The first taxpayer has not prohibited the disclosure.

Example: Xiang is an EA with two married clients, Wendy and Stewart, who file jointly. Wendy works long hours, so she is unavailable when Stewart meets with Xiang to prepare their joint tax return. Later, Wendy comes in alone to sign the return. She also has a question regarding the mortgage interest on the joint tax return. Xiang is allowed to disclose return information to Wendy because it is a joint return. Stewart has not prohibited any disclosures, and both Wendy and Stewart's names are on the return.

A taxpayer is considered related to another taxpayer in any of the following relationships:

- A spouse of another
- Minor child and parent
- Grandchild and grandparent
- General partner in a partnership
- Trust or estate and the beneficiary
- A corporation and shareholder
- Members of a controlled group of corporations

A tax return preparer may also disclose tax return information that was obtained from a first taxpayer in preparing a tax return of the second taxpayer, if the preparer has obtained written consent from the first taxpayer. For example, if an unmarried couple lives together and splits the mortgage interest, the preparer may use or disclose information from the first taxpayer to the second so long as the preparer has written consent.

Affordable Care Act Disclosures

§7216 prohibits tax return preparers, including those who offer services related to the Affordable Care Act, from using tax return information for unauthorized purposes. In addition to criminal penalties, a civil penalty of $250 for each unauthorized disclosure or use of tax return information by a tax return preparer is imposed by § 6713.

---

[25] "Tax return information" also includes the taxpayer's name, mailing address, and taxpayer identification number, including Social Security number or employer identification number; any information extracted from a return, including names of dependents or the location of a business; information on whether a return was, is being, or will be examined or subject to other investigation or processing; information contained on transcripts of accounts; the fact that a return was filed or examined; investigation or collection history; or tax balance due information.

Current regulations allow preparers to use a list of client names, addresses, email addresses, and phone numbers to provide them general educational information, such as that related to the Affordable Care Act. However, a tax preparer must first obtain taxpayer consent before using tax return information to directly solicit clients for health care enrollment services or other services.

> **Example:** Sherry is an Enrolled Agent who is also a health care "navigator" that helps enroll people in qualified ACA health care plans. She wants to contact clients to let them know that she is offering these services. Under the terms of §7216, she must first obtain written consent from her clients before she can solicit them.

This mandate also applies to VITA volunteers. Solicitation to offer health care enrollment services by all tax return preparers, including volunteer preparers, requires prior taxpayer consent.

Disclosure Consent Not Required

A tax return preparer is not required to obtain disclosure consent from a client if the disclosure is made for any of the following reasons:

- A court order or subpoena issued by any court of record, whether at the federal, state, or local level. The required information must be clearly identified in the document (subpoena or court order) in order for a preparer to disclose information.
- An administrative order, demand, summons, or subpoena that is issued by any federal agency (such as the IRS), state agency, or commission charged under the laws of the state with licensing, registration, or regulation of tax return preparers.
- To report a crime to proper authorities. Even if the preparer is mistaken and no crime has occurred, he will not be subject to sanctions if he makes the disclosure in good faith.
- For purposes of peer reviews.

A preparer may disclose private client information to his attorney or to an employee of the IRS, in connection with an IRS investigation of the preparer.

> **Example:** The IRS is investigating a CPA named Adam for possible misconduct. Adam has an attorney who is assisting in his defense. As it turns out, Adam was a victim of embezzlement because his bookkeeper was stealing client checks. He only discovered the embezzlement when the IRS contacted him about client complaints. Adam may disclose confidential client information to his attorney in order to assist with his own defense. Adam may also disclose confidential client information to the IRS during the course of its investigation.

A preparer may disclose tax return information to a tax return processor. For example, if a preparer uses an electronic or tax return processing service, he may disclose tax return information to that service in order to prepare tax returns or compute tax liability.

Tax Practitioner Confidentiality Privilege

Under IRC §7525, enrolled practitioners and their clients are granted limited rights of confidentiality protection.[26] This Federally Authorized Tax Practitioner Confidentiality Privilege (FATP) applies to attorneys, CPAs, Enrolled Agents, enrolled actuaries, and certain other individuals allowed to practice before the IRS.

---

[26] The "federally authorized tax practitioner privilege" is an amendment to the Internal Revenue Code made by the *Internal Revenue Service Restructuring and Reform Act of 1998*.

The confidentiality protection applies to communications that would be considered privileged if they were between the taxpayer and an attorney and that relate to:

- Noncriminal tax matters before the IRS, or
- Noncriminal tax proceedings brought in federal court by or against the United States.

This confidentiality privilege cannot be used with any agency other than the IRS. For example, an Enrolled Agent cannot assert the federal confidentiality privilege with any state taxing agency. The confidentiality privilege does not apply:

- In criminal tax matters
- To any written communications regarding the promotion of a tax shelter
- In state tax proceedings
- To the general preparation of tax returns

There is a long history of court decisions that deny confidentiality of information disclosed to an attorney for purposes of preparing tax returns. In a key 1983 ruling, the court stated that "information transmitted for the purpose of preparation of a tax return," though transmitted to an attorney, is not privileged information.

When information will be transmitted to a third party (in this case, on a tax return) such information is not confidential.[27] This restriction on the confidentiality privilege related to tax preparation applies to other practitioners besides attorneys, including Enrolled Agents and CPAs.

Certified Acceptance Agents

A Certified Acceptance Agent is a person or an entity who, pursuant to a written agreement with the IRS, is authorized to assist individuals and other foreign persons who do not qualify for a Social Security Number but who still need a Taxpayer Identification Number to file a Form 1040. Certified Acceptance agents can authenticate a passport and birth certificate for dependents.

There are four steps that need to be taken by all new and renewing applicants.

- Complete Form 13551, *Application to Participate in the IRS Acceptance Agent Program*, and attach the fingerprint card.
- Complete the Mandatory Acceptance Agent training, print, sign and submit the certification form.
- Attach the certification form for each authorized representative to Form 13551.
- Complete forensic training and submit the certificate of completion to the IRS.

ITIN Expirations: Many Individual Taxpayer Identification Numbers expired on December 31, 2017. This includes any ITIN not used on a tax return at least once in the past three years. Also, any ITIN with middle digits of 70, 71, 72, or 80 is now expired. Starting in 2017, affected taxpayers must reapply to renew their ITIN. Tax professionals can assist taxpayers with the application process by helping to fill out and submit Form W-7, *Application for IRS Individual Taxpayer Identification Number*.

---

[27] *United States v. Lawless*, 709 F.2d 487 (7th Cir. 1983).

Do You Need To Renew Your ITIN?

Follow the steps below to see if you need to renew your ITIN

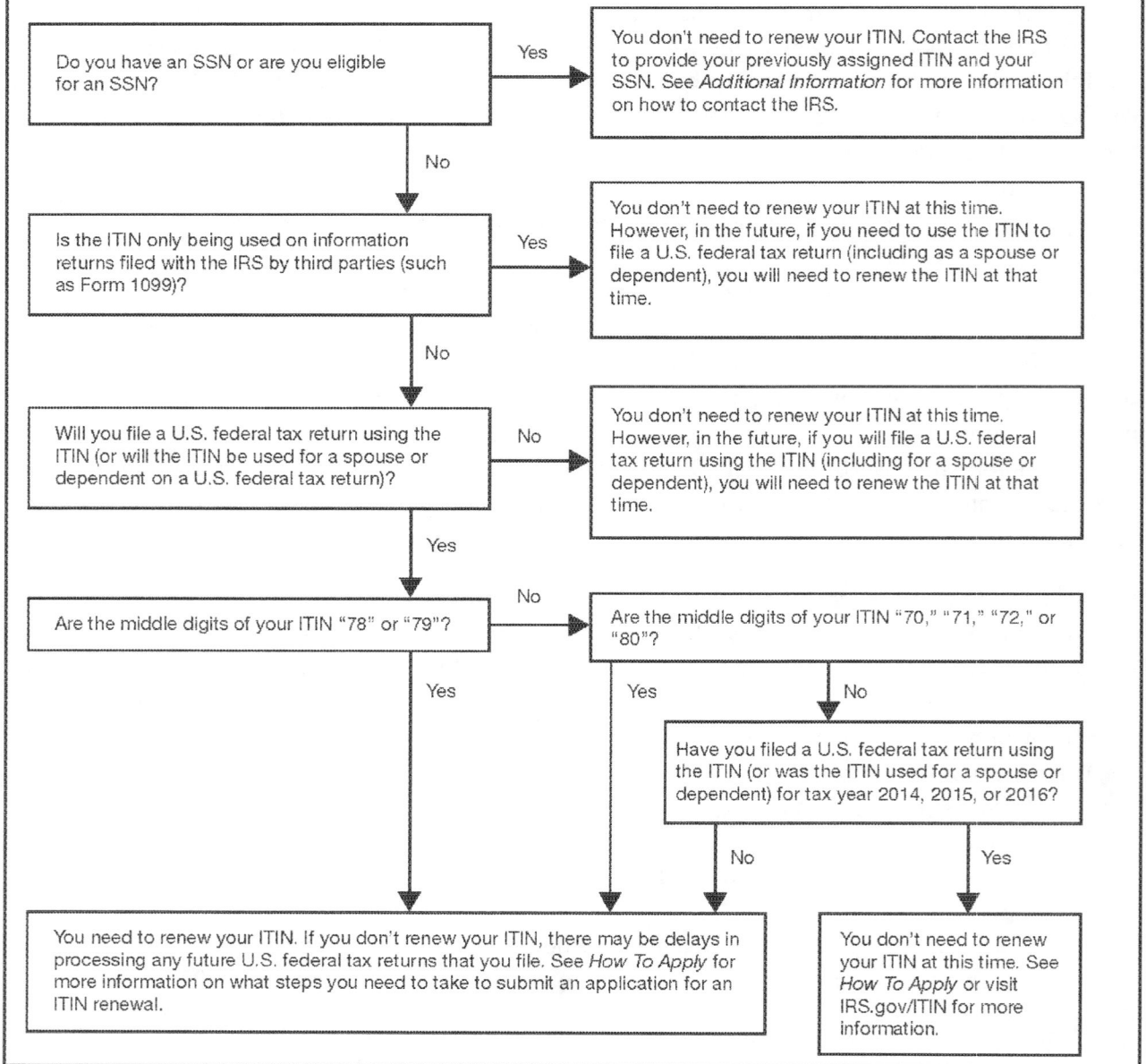

Do you have an SSN or are you eligible for an SSN?

→ Yes → You don't need to renew your ITIN. Contact the IRS to provide your previously assigned ITIN and your SSN. See *Additional Information* for more information on how to contact the IRS.

↓ No

Is the ITIN only being used on information returns filed with the IRS by third parties (such as Form 1099)?

→ Yes → You don't need to renew your ITIN at this time. However, in the future, if you need to use the ITIN to file a U.S. federal tax return (including as a spouse or dependent), you will need to renew the ITIN at that time.

↓ No

Will you file a U.S. federal tax return using the ITIN (or will the ITIN be used for a spouse or dependent on a U.S. federal tax return)?

→ No → You don't need to renew your ITIN at this time. However, in the future, if you will file a U.S. federal tax return using the ITIN (including for a spouse or dependent), you will need to renew the ITIN at that time.

↓ Yes

Are the middle digits of your ITIN "78" or "79"?

→ No → **Are the middle digits of your ITIN "70," "71," "72," or "80"?**

↓ Yes ↓ Yes → No ↓

Have you filed a U.S. federal tax return using the ITIN (or was the ITIN used for a spouse or dependent) for tax year 2014, 2015, or 2016?

↓ No ↓ Yes

You need to renew your ITIN. If you don't renew your ITIN, there may be delays in processing any future U.S. federal tax returns that you file. See *How To Apply* for more information on what steps you need to take to submit an application for an ITIN renewal.

You don't need to renew your ITIN at this time. See *How To Apply* or visit IRS.gov/ITIN for more information.

Instructions for Form W-7 (Rev. October 2017)

(Test yourself and then check the correct answers at the end of this chapter.)

1. Which designation or form gives the appointed person the greatest rights to represent a taxpayer?

A. Third party designee, also known as "Check Box" authority.
B. Form 8821, *Tax Information Authorization.*
C. Form 2848, *Power of Attorney and Declaration of Representative.*
D. Form 4506-T, *Request for Transcript of Tax Return.*

2. For future tax periods, Form 2848 is valid for a period of no later than _____ after the date the POA is received by the IRS.

A. One year.
B. Two years.
C. Three years.
D. Five years.

3. In what situation is a preparer allowed to disclose information without first obtaining written permission from a client?

A. When he is issued a subpoena by a state agency that regulates tax return preparers.
B. When he is contacted by a newspaper reporter investigating a possible crime committed by his client.
C. When the information is requested by his client's uncle who helps support the client financially.
D. When the information is needed by a preparer who volunteers with VITA.

4. All of the following statements regarding the signature requirements for tax returns are correct except:

A. A preparer may sign a taxpayer's return in lieu of the taxpayer, if the taxpayer cannot sign his own tax return due to a physical disability and the preparer is authorized to sign the return through a signed power of attorney.
B. A preparer may sign a taxpayer's return in lieu of the taxpayer, if the taxpayer cannot sign his own tax return due to an extended absence from the United States and the preparer is authorized to sign the return through a signed power of attorney.
C. A preparer is allowed to copy a taxpayer's signature if he has a signed power of attorney.
D. A preparer must have a signed power of attorney in order to potentially sign on the taxpayer's behalf.

5. A durable power of attorney remains in effect until an individual:

A. Gets divorced.
B. Becomes mentally incompetent or incapacitated.
C. Dies.
D. Both B and C.

6. For a taxpayer who wants someone to represent him at an examination by the IRS, all of the following statements are correct except:

A. The taxpayer must furnish that representative with written authorization on Form 2848, *Power of Attorney and Declaration of Representative*, or any other properly written authorization.
B. The representative can be an attorney, CPA, or EA.
C. The representative can potentially be an unenrolled preparer who prepared the taxpayer's current year tax return, but not the year of the return under examination.
D. Even if the taxpayer appointed a representative, the taxpayer may choose to attend the examination or appeals conference and may act on his own behalf.

7. Which statement is correct regarding the privacy regulations of IRC §7216?

A. The regulations do not apply to e-file providers.
B. The improper disclosure must be "knowing or reckless" for criminal provisions to apply.
C. A practitioner may be fined up to $500 and imprisoned for up to one year for each violation of this code.
D. Practitioners must obtain oral consent from taxpayers before they can use information for anything other than the actual preparation of tax returns.

8. Form 8821, *Tax Information Authorization*, may be used to authorize the following:

A. Any individual, corporation, firm, organization, or partnership to receive confidential information for the type of tax and periods listed on Form 8821.
B. Any designated third party to receive tax information.
C. For unenrolled tax return preparers to indicate a representative relationship with a taxpayer and to authorize practice before the IRS.
D. Both A and B.

9. Which of the following is not necessary in connection with Form 2848?

A. For all signatures to be notarized.
B. For the form to be faxed or mailed to the IRS.
C. For the preparer to include his PTIN.
D. All of the above requirements are necessary in connection with Form 2848.

10. How long is a power of attorney authorization valid?

A. One year.
B. Three years.
C. Until it is revoked or superseded.
D. Until the due date of the next tax return.

11. Taxpayers are granted a limited confidentiality privilege with any federally authorized tax practitioner. Confidential communications include all of the following except:

A. Written tax advice.
B. A noncriminal tax proceeding in Federal court.
C. Participation in a tax shelter.
D. Noncriminal tax matters before the IRS.

12. If a practitioner no longer wishes to represent a taxpayer, he should take the following action:

A. Nothing. A taxpayer is the only one who can revoke power of attorney authorization.
B. Write the word "REVOKE" on the POA form and mail or fax it to the IRS.
C. Write the word "WITHDRAW" on the POA form and mail or email it to the IRS.
D. Write the word "WITHDRAW" on the POA form and mail or fax it to the IRS.

13. How many representatives can a taxpayer appoint using a single Form 2848?

A. One per form only.
B. Two.
C. Three.
D. Four.

14. The Centralized Authorization File (CAF) is:

A. An IRS computer database with information regarding the authority of individuals appointed under powers of attorney or designated under tax information authorizations.
B. A public, searchable database of federally authorized practitioners and certain other tax preparers with professional credentials.
C. An automated list of disbarred practitioners.
D. An automated file of taxpayer delinquencies.

15. Floyd is an unenrolled tax return preparer for a married couple. He is also licensed to sell securities. Floyd is not a practitioner. After preparing the couple's joint return, he was concerned that they were not saving adequately for retirement. Using information from their tax return, Floyd created a custom retirement plan for the couple. He had not obtained their consent. Which of the following statements is correct?

A. Because he is not a practitioner, Floyd is not subject to the rules of §7216.
B. Floyd is in violation of §7216.
C. Floyd is not in violation of §7216 because he used information from current clients; therefore, he was not required to obtain their consent.
D. Floyd is not in violation of §7216 because retirement planning is one of the exceptions listed as an allowable use of information.

16. How many years in the future can an authorization on a Form 2848 be recorded to the Centralized Authentication File (CAF)?

A. Current year + 1
B. Current year + 2
C. Current year + 3
D. Current year + 4

1. The answer is C. Only Form 2848, *Power of Attorney and Declaration of Representative,* allows a third party to represent a taxpayer before the IRS. The other consents are much more limited and only allow the third party to receive or inspect tax account information.

2. The answer is C. For future tax periods, the period specified is limited to no later than three years after the date the POA is received by the IRS. The types of tax and dates listed on Form 2848 must be specific. Tax years or periods that have already ended may be listed under "tax matters."

3. The answer is A. A tax return preparer who is issued a subpoena or court order, whether at the federal, state, or local level, is not required to obtain disclosure permission from a client. In all the other cases, disclosure is not allowed unless there has been prior written consent.

4. The answer is C. A tax return preparer is never allowed to copy a taxpayer's signature. A preparer may sign in lieu of the taxpayer in certain situations. For example, rules permit a representative to sign a taxpayer's return if he is unable to do so himself for any of the following reasons:

- Disease or injury
- Continuous absence from the United States for a period of at least 60 days prior to the date required by law for filing the return
- Other good cause if specific permission is requested of and granted by the IRS

When a return is signed by a representative, it must be accompanied by a power of attorney authorizing the representative to sign the return.

5. The answer is C. A durable power of attorney is not subject to a time limit. It remains in effect until the death of the individual, or until the individual revokes it.

6. The answer is C. Only persons eligible to practice before the IRS, including attorneys, CPAs, and EAs, have unlimited rights to represent taxpayers before the IRS. The representation rights of unenrolled preparers are much more limited. An unenrolled preparer who did not prepare and sign the specific tax return under examination would not be allowed to represent the taxpayer. Any unenrolled preparer who is not a participant in the IRS's voluntary Annual Filing Season Program will not be able to represent taxpayers before any level of the IRS.

7. The answer is B. IRC §7216 is a criminal code that limits tax professionals' use and disclosure of private client information. Answer B is correct because criminal penalties will apply only if the improper disclosure is "knowing or reckless," rather than simply negligent. The other answers are incorrect because the regulations do apply to e-file providers; a preparer may be fined up to $1,000, not $500, and imprisoned for up to a year for each violation; and written consent, not oral, is generally required before taxpayer information can be disclosed or used for other purposes.

8. The answer is D. Form 8821, *Tax Information Authorization*, authorizes any individual, corporation, firm, organization, or partnership to receive confidential information for the type of tax and periods listed on the form. Any third party may be designated by the taxpayer to receive confidential tax information. Form 8821 is only a disclosure form, so it will not give an individual any power to represent a taxpayer before the IRS. It may be used only to obtain information, such as copies of tax returns or tax return transcripts.

9. The answer is A. The signatures on Form 2848 are not required to be notarized.

10. The answer is C. A power of attorney is valid until revoked or superseded. It may be revoked by the taxpayer or withdrawn by the representative, or it may be superseded by the filing of a new power of attorney for the same tax and tax period.

11. The answer is C. The confidentiality privilege does not apply in the case of communications regarding the promotion of or participation in a tax shelter. A tax shelter is any entity, plan, or arrangement whose significant purpose is to avoid or evade income tax. Unlike the attorney–client privilege, the federally authorized tax practitioner privilege does not apply in criminal tax matters, and does not apply in state tax proceedings. The privilege may be asserted only in a "noncriminal tax matter before the Internal Revenue Service" and a "noncriminal tax proceeding in Federal court brought by or against the United States." The confidentiality privilege is also not extended to matters related to the general preparation of tax returns.

12. The answer is D. A preparer must write the word "WITHDRAW" on the first page of the POA form, include his signature and the date, and mail or fax the form to the IRS. Email is not an acceptable means of contact. The form must clearly indicate the applicable tax matters and periods. In contrast, if a taxpayer chooses to end a previously authorized power of attorney, he must write the word "REVOKE" on the form, include his signature and the date, and mail or fax the form to the IRS.

13. The answer is D. When a taxpayer wishes to use a representative, he should fill out and sign Form 2848, *Power of Attorney and Declaration of Representative.* By doing so, the taxpayer authorizes a specific individual or individuals to receive confidential tax information and to perform the actions detailed on the form. Up to four representatives can be authorized per form, an increase from the previous Form 2848 that allowed only three representatives to be designated.

14. The answer is A. The Centralized Authorization File, or "CAF," contains information on third parties authorized to represent taxpayers before the IRS and receive and inspect confidential tax information on active tax accounts or those accounts currently under collection or examination by the IRS.

15. The answer is B. All paid tax return preparers are subject to the rules of §7216, a criminal statute. Floyd is in violation of §7216 because he did not obtain written consent from his clients prior to using their private information. A tax return preparer must generally obtain written consent from taxpayers before he can disclose information to a third party or use the information for any purpose other than the preparation of tax returns. Each violation of §7216 could mean a fine of up to $1,000, a prison term of up to one year, or both. There is also a separate civil penalty of $250 for improper disclosure or use of taxpayer information, as outlined in IRC §6713. However, unlike §7216, this code section does not require that the disclosure be "knowing or reckless."

16. The answer is C. An authorization on a Form 2848 be recorded to the Centralized Authentication File (CAF) can be recorded for the current year plus up to 3 years.

Unit 4: Tax Practitioner Responsibilities

> **More Reading:**
> **Circular No. 230**, *Regulations Governing Practice Before the Internal Revenue Service*
> **Publication 947**, *Practice Before the IRS and Power of Attorney*
> **Publication 216**, *Conference and Practice Requirements*

The Treasury Department's Circular 230 sets forth regulations that govern all tax practitioners, including Enrolled Agents, CPAs, attorneys, and others who practice before the IRS. Circular 230 imposes professional standards and codes of conduct for practitioners and tax advisors. It prohibits certain actions, requires other actions, and details penalties for ethical violations and other misconduct by practitioners.

Circular 230 is broken into four subparts:

- Authority to practice
- Duties and restrictions relating to practice
- Sanctions for violations
- Disciplinary procedures

In the next two units, we will look closely at subpart 2 of Circular 230, which describes practitioner responsibilities and standards.

Diligence as to Accuracy §10.22

Central to the Circular 230 regulations is the mandate for practitioners to exercise due diligence when performing the following duties:

- Preparing or assisting in preparing, approving, and filing of returns, documents, affidavits, and other papers relating to IRS matters
- Determining the correctness of oral or written representations made to the Department of the Treasury, including documents that are filed and submitted to the IRS on the taxpayer's behalf
- Determining the correctness of oral or written representations made to clients related to any matter administered by the IRS

§10.22 does not state what due diligence entails, but there is more specific guidance in Circular 230 sections related to standards for written advice.

Reliance on Others: A practitioner will be presumed to have exercised due diligence if he relies on the work product of another person. That is assuming that the practitioner used "reasonable care" when he hired, supervised, trained, and evaluated that person or persons.

Example: Blanca is an Enrolled Agent. During the year, a new client, Clayton, comes to her to prepare his return. Clayton is self-employed. Blanca asks to see his prior year return, which she examines for accuracy. The return was prepared by another tax practitioner, and it includes a depreciation schedule for Clayton's business assets. The schedule appears correct, and the listed items are reasonable. Blanca may use the depreciation schedule as a reference, even though she did not prepare it herself.

Best Practices §10.33

Circular 230 explains the broad concept of *best practices*. Practitioners must provide clients with the highest quality representation concerning federal tax matters by adhering to best practices in providing advice and in preparing documents or information for the IRS.

Practitioners who oversee a firm's practice should take reasonable steps to ensure that the firm's procedures for all employees are consistent with best practices. Best practices include the following:

- Communicating clearly with the client regarding the terms of the engagement.
- Establishing the facts, determining which facts are relevant, evaluating the reasonableness of any assumptions, relating the applicable law to the relevant facts, and arriving at a conclusion supported by the law and the facts.
- Advising the client of the conclusions reached and the impact of the advice rendered; for example, advising whether a taxpayer may avoid accuracy-related penalties if he relies on the advice provided.
- Acting fairly and with integrity in practice before the IRS.

Note: The IRS has issued return preparer best practices related to the Affordable Care Act. Tax preparers are expected to resolve conflicting or contradictory statements from their clients, as they do for other items on a tax return. The IRS issued official guidance on April 7, 2016 to help tax preparers resolve conflicting information between Form 1095-A and Form 1095-B, two common ACA forms.

Competence §10.35

This provision states that a practitioner must be competent to engage in practice before the IRS. "Competence" is defined as having the appropriate level of knowledge, skill, thoroughness, and preparation for the specific matter related to a client's engagement.

Circular 230 says a practitioner can become competent in various ways, including consulting with experts in the relevant area or studying the relevant law.

Example: Chantelle is an Enrolled Agent who has many years of experience in preparing partnership tax returns. In 2017, she takes continuing education classes related to changes in partnership law, and consults with another tax professional in her office on a particularly complex partnership return. Also in 2017, a longtime client whose mother has died asks Chantelle to handle the estate tax returns for him. Chantelle rarely handles estate tax matters and does not have time to research the law sufficiently to handle this case, so she refers the estate return to a tax attorney who specializes in estate tax law. Chantelle has fulfilled her Circular 230 obligations related to §10.35.

Knowledge of Client's Omission §10.21

A practitioner who knows that his client has not complied with the revenue laws or who has made an error or omission on his tax return has the responsibility to advise the client promptly of the noncompliance, error, or omission, as well as its consequences.

The practitioner is not responsible for correcting the noncompliance once he has notified the client of the issue, or for notifying the IRS of a client's noncompliance.

Example: Daniel is an EA with a new client, Cristal, who has prepared her own returns in the past. Daniel notices that Cristal has been claiming head of household status on her tax returns, but she does not qualify for this status, because she does not have a qualifying dependent. Daniel is required to promptly notify Cristal of the error and tell her the consequences of not correcting the error. However, Daniel is not required to amend Cristal's prior year tax returns to correct the error. Nor is he required to notify the IRS of Cristal's claim of incorrect status.

The §10.21 obligations are not limited to practitioners preparing returns, so the discovery of an error in the course of a tax consulting or advisory engagement will also trigger its requirements.

Example: Cynthia is an EA who takes over another tax return preparer's practice. She discovers that the previous preparer has been taking section 179 deductions on assets that do not qualify for this treatment. Cynthia must notify her clients of the errors and the consequences of not correcting the errors. She is not required to correct the errors.

Conflicts of Interest §10.29

Conflicts of interest are common, especially when it comes to divorce. There are special rules that apply to tax practitioners with regards to conflicts of interest between two clients. If there is a potential conflict of interest, the practitioner must disclose the conflict and be given the opportunity to disclose all material facts. A practitioner will have a conflict of interest if:

- The representation of one client will be directly adverse to another client; or
- There is a significant risk that the representation of one or more clients will be materially limited by the practitioner's responsibilities to another client, a former client, a third person, or by a personal interest of the practitioner.

A practitioner may represent a client when a conflict of interest exists if:

- The practitioner reasonably believes that he will be able to provide competent and diligent representation to each affected client;
- The representation is not prohibited by law; and
- Each affected client waives the conflict of interest and gives informed consent, confirmed in writing, within 30 days after giving any non-written informed consent to the tax practitioner.

IRS regulations allow the written consent to be made within a reasonable period after the informed consent, but not later than 30 days after the date on which the conflict is known by the practitioner.

Example: Arturo and Damian are business partners. Carlene is an Enrolled Agent who prepares both their partnership return, as well as their individual returns. In 2017, Arturo and Damian have a major argument about the direction of the business. Arturo calls Carlene and tells her that he is going to dissolve the partnership. Carlene must prepare a conflict of interest waiver for Arturo and Damian, as well as the partnership itself, if she plans to keep them both as her clients.

The written consent must be retained for at least 36 months from the date representation ends, and must be given to any officer or employee of the IRS, if requested. At minimum, the consent should adequately describe the nature of the conflict and the parties the practitioner represents.

Example: Janessa is an EA who prepares tax returns for Darla and Elmer, a married couple. In 2017, Darla and Elmer go through a contentious divorce, and Janessa believes there is potential for conflict of interest relating to the services she would provide each of them. She prepares a written statement explaining the potential conflict of interest and reviews it with her clients. Darla and Elmer still want Janessa to prepare their returns, and Janessa determines that she will be able to represent each fairly and competently. She has both Darla and Elmer sign the statement that waives the conflict and gives their consent for her to prepare their individual tax returns. Janessa must retain the record of their consent for at least 36 months after she last represents either party.

IRS Information Requests §10.20

Under Circular 230, §10.20, when the IRS requests information, a practitioner must comply and submit records promptly.

If the requested information or records are not in the practitioner's possession, he must promptly advise the requesting IRS officer and provide any information he has regarding the identity of the person who may have possession or control of the requested information or records. The practitioner must also make a "reasonable inquiry" of his client regarding the location of the requested records.

However, the practitioner is not required to make inquiry of any other person or to independently verify any information furnished by his client. Further, the practitioner is not required to contact any third party who might be in possession of the records.

A practitioner may not interfere with any lawful effort by the IRS to obtain any record or information unless he believes in good faith and on reasonable grounds that the record or information is privileged under IRC §7525. A practitioner can also be exempted from these rules if he believes in good faith that the request is of doubtful legality.

If the IRS's Office of Professional Responsibility requests information concerning possible violations of the regulations by other parties, such as other preparers, the practitioner must furnish the information and be prepared to testify in disbarment or suspension proceedings.

Example: An IRS revenue agent submitted a lawful records request to Howell, an EA, for accounting records relating to a former client who was under IRS investigation. However, earlier in the year, Howell had fired his client for nonpayment and returned his records. Howell promptly notified the IRS officer that he no longer had the records. He also attempted to contact his former client, but the phone number was disconnected. Howell is not required to contact any third parties to discover the location of the requested records. Therefore, Howell has fulfilled his obligations under §10.20.

Return of Client Records §10.28

A practitioner is required to return a client's original records upon request, whether or not his fees have been paid. Client records include:

- All documents a client provided to a practitioner that pre-existed their business engagement.
- Any materials that were prepared by the client or a third party that were provided to the practitioner relating to the subject matter of the representation.
- Any document prepared by the practitioner that was presented to the client relating to a prior representation if such document is necessary for the taxpayer to comply with his current federal tax obligations.

The practitioner must, at the request of a client, promptly return any and all records that are necessary for the client to comply with his federal tax obligations. Client records generally do not include the practitioner's work product. However, they may include any work product that the client has already paid for, such as a completed copy of a tax return. Client records do not include any return, claim for refund, schedule, affidavit, appraisal, or any other document prepared by the practitioner if he is withholding these documents pending the client's payment of fees.

A client must be given reasonable access to review and copy any additional records retained by the practitioner that are necessary for the client to comply with his federal tax obligations. The practitioner may retain copies of all the records returned to a client.

Example: Karolyn's client, Alpine Corporation, has been slow to pay in the past, so she asks the owners to pay for the tax returns when they pick them up. The president of Alpine Corporation refuses to pay and demands the tax returns anyway. Karolyn must return the corporation's original records, but she is not required to give away any work product that the owners have not yet paid for.

Example: Jamison is an EA with a client, Kathrine, who becomes upset after he tells her she owes money to the IRS. Kathrine wants to get a second opinion, and she does not want to pay Jamison for his time. Jamison is required to hand over Kathrine's original tax records, including copies of her W-2 forms and any other information she brought to his office. Jamison returns her original records, but he is not forced to give her a copy of the tax return he prepared, since she did not pay his fee for the return.

Copies of Tax Returns

Under IRC §6107, tax return preparers are required to give a completed copy of a tax return or claim for refund no later than the time the return or claim is presented for the taxpayer's signature. The copy can be in any media, including electronic media.

Preparers are required to keep copies of all returns they have prepared or retain a list of clients and tax returns prepared. At a minimum, the list must contain the taxpayer's name, taxpayer identification number, tax year, and the type of return prepared. The copies of tax returns or the lists must be retained for at least three years after the close of the return period. [28]

Note: In practice, most preparers keep scanned, digital, or hard copies of client tax returns rather than simply a list of the returns prepared.

Tax Return Preparer Employer Records (IRC §6060): The employer of tax return preparers must keep a record of all those employed and make it available for IRS inspection upon request. The records must include the name, taxpayer identification number, and place of work of each tax return preparer employed. Records must be retained for at least three years following the close of the return period.

Practitioner Fees §10.27

The IRS prohibits practitioners from charging "unconscionable fees." Although that term has not been defined, it is generally believed to refer to fees that the courts would consider grossly disproportionate in relation to the services provided.

The IRS has traditionally held that a practitioner may not charge a contingent fee (for example, a fee determined as a percentage of the taxpayer's refund) for preparing an original tax return. A contingent fee might also include a fee that is based on a percentage of the taxes saved or one that depends on a specific result. However, in 2014, a U.S. district court ruled that the IRS lacked statutory authority to regulate contingent fee arrangements for the preparation and filing of ordinary refund claims (refund claims after the taxpayer has filed a return but before the IRS has started an audit of the return).[29]

The IRS chose not to appeal the decision, so this part of the Circular 230 prohibition on contingent fees is no longer in effect.

---

[28] Under Section 6060(c) the term "return period" means the 12-month period beginning on July 1 of each year. The close of the return period is defined as June 30, meaning the three-year period to retain records begins July 1 of each year.

[29] The opinion in *Ridgely v. Lew* was issued in July 2014. Late in 2015, the IRS Advisory Council (IRSAC) issued a report recommending that legislation be enacted to overturn the results in Loving and Ridgely by expressly affirming the Treasury Department's authority under 31 U.S.C. §330 to regulate paid tax return preparers. At the time of this book's printing, no such legislation had been introduced. The IRS does not plan to appeal the decision, but they have not acquiesced to the case, either.

It should also be noted that certain practitioners, such as certified public accountants, may still be subject to prohibitions against charging contingent fees under applicable state regulations.

Notwithstanding the general limitation that has applied to charging contingent fees, a practitioner has been allowed to charge a contingent fee in limited circumstances, including:

- Representation during the examination of an original tax return, or during the examination of an amended return or claim for refund, if the amended return or claim for refund was filed within 120 days of the taxpayer receiving a written notice of examination or a written challenge to the original tax return.
- Services rendered in connection with a refund claim for credit or a refund filed in conjunction with a penalty or interest charge assessed by the IRS.
- Services rendered in connection with any judicial proceeding arising under the IRC.

Advertising Restrictions §10.30

A practitioner may not use any form of advertising that contains false, deceptive, or coercive information, or that is in violation of IRS regulations. Practitioners who are authorized e-Service providers may use the IRS e-file logo.

Note: Tax practitioners are **specifically prohibited** from using official IRS insignia, including the following logos (below):

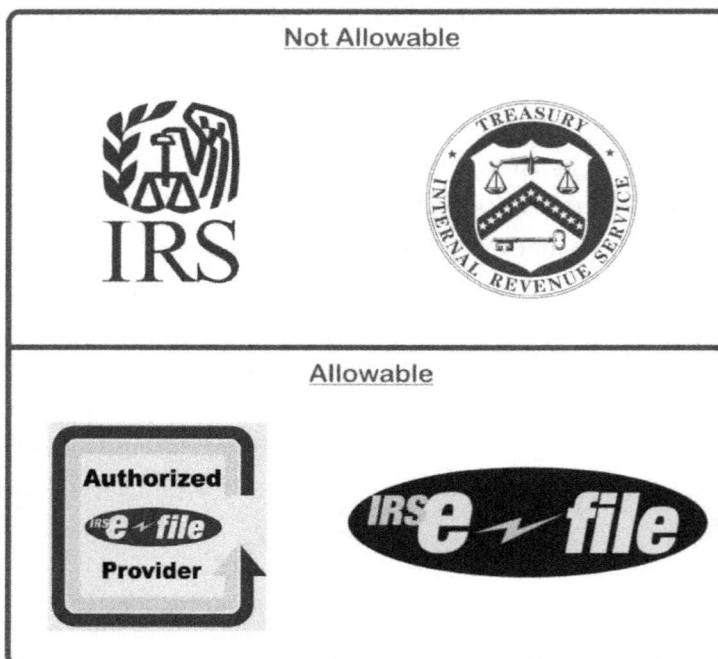

Advertising Standards: Permissible Logos

Acceptable Designation Terms

In describing their professional designation, Enrolled Agents may not use the term "certified" or imply any type of employment relationship with the IRS. Examples of acceptable descriptions for EAs are "enrolled to represent taxpayers before the Internal Revenue Service," "enrolled to practice before the Internal Revenue Service," and "admitted to practice before the Internal Revenue Service."

Solicitation Restrictions

A practitioner may, in certain circumstances, solicit his professional services. The solicitation may not violate federal or state law, or other applicable rules (such as attorneys who are bound to conduct guidelines in their particular states). A practitioner may not continue to contact a prospective client who has communicated that he does not wish to be solicited.

Mail Advertising: Mail advertising is allowed, but a solicitation must be clearly labeled as such and, if applicable, the source of information used in choosing the recipient must be identified. In the case of direct mail and e-commerce communications, the practitioner must retain a copy of the communication, along with a list of persons to whom the communication was mailed or distributed, for at least 36 months.

Practitioners may also send solicitations to other practitioners indicating their availability to provide professional services (such as bookkeeping or payroll services). The advertising and communications must not be misleading, deceptive, or in violation of IRS regulations.

Fee Information: A practitioner may publish and advertise a fee schedule. A practitioner must adhere to the published fee schedule for at least 30 calendar days after it is last published. Fee information may be published in newspapers, mailings, websites, email, or by any other method. A practitioner may charge based on the following:

- Fixed fees for specific routine services
- Hourly rates
- A range of fees for particular services
- A fee for an initial consultation

When advertising fees on radio or television, the broadcast must be recorded, and the practitioner must retain a copy of the recording for at least 36 months from the date of the last transmission or use.

> **Example:** Lorene is an EA who publishes an advertisement in her local newspaper. The ad includes a published fee schedule for preparing certain tax return forms at deeply discounted rates. Lorene is inundated with calls and decides that the ad was a mistake. Regardless, she must adhere to the published fee schedule for at least 30 days after it was published.

> **Example:** Markus is an EA who pays for a radio commercial about his services. He also mentions average prices for tax preparation. The advertisement plays for four months during tax season. Markus is required to keep a copy of the radio commercial for at least 36 months from the last date that the commercial aired.

Negotiation of Taxpayer Refund Checks §10.31

A practitioner must not endorse or negotiate (cash) a refund check issued to the taxpayer. For example, a practitioner cannot use Form 8888, *Allocation of Refund (Including Savings Bond Purchases),* to enter his own bank account in order to obtain payment for his tax preparation fee. Form 8888 instructions state that entering an account in someone else's name, such as a preparer's, will cause the direct deposit request to be rejected and the taxpayer to be sent a paper check instead. A preparer could also be subject to a penalty under IRC §6695(f).

In the latest Circular 230 revision, §10.31 clarifies that this provision applies to any practitioner, not just to one who prepares tax returns.

It also expands the scope of "endorse or otherwise negotiate any check" to state that negotiation of a taxpayer check includes accepting or directing payment by any method, including electronically or via direct deposit or wire transfer.

> **Example:** McKinley is an Enrolled Agent with a new client who will receive a $500 refund on her tax return. The client has not yet paid McKinley's tax return preparation fee, so he enters his own bank account number, rather than his client's, on Form 8888. McKinley plans to take his $200 fee from the refund and give his client the remaining $300. However, directing a taxpayer's refund into the preparer's bank account is expressly forbidden, and McKinley could be subject to a preparer penalty for improper negotiation of a client's refund.

Other Duties and Prohibited Acts in Circular 230

No Delay Tactics Allowed §10.23: A practitioner must not unreasonably delay the prompt disposition of any matter before the IRS.

> **Example:** Patricio is an Enrolled Agent who is representing a client in an IRS examination. Patricio has repeatedly rescheduled appointments with an IRS revenue agent in an attempt to delay proceedings. He has also delayed furnishing certain documents that the IRS has requested, and when he does provide them, the records are incomplete. Patricio's actions are in violation of Circular 230.

No Employment of Disbarred or Suspended Persons §10.24: A practitioner may not knowingly employ a person or accept assistance from a person who has been disbarred or suspended from practice. This restriction applies even if the duties of the disbarred or suspended person would not include actual preparation of tax returns.

In addition, a practitioner may not accept assistance from a former government employee in matters in which the former employee personally and substantially participated in the particular matter while employed by the government.

Practice by Former Government Employees §10.25: A former government employee (and his partners and associates) cannot represent or knowingly assist a taxpayer if the representation would violate any law of the United States.

A government employee who personally and substantially participated in a particular matter cannot represent or assist a taxpayer in the same particular matter after leaving his government position. §10.25 also places other restrictions on former government employees, including former IRS workers, in order to avoid conflicts of interest during representation.

Performance as a Notary §10.26: A practitioner who is a notary public and is employed as counsel, attorney, or agent in a matter before the IRS or who has a material interest in the matter cannot engage in any notary activities related to that matter.

Signature Requirements for Tax Returns

Signature requirements for the preparation of tax returns are not spelled out in Circular 230, but instead are based on Treasury regulations. The requirements are as follows:

1. **Preparer Signature and PTIN:** A preparer is required by law to sign the tax return, include his PTIN, and fill out the preparer areas of the form. The preparer's declaration on signing the return states that the information contained in the return is true, correct, and complete based on all information he has. This statement is signed under penalties of perjury. The preparer must sign the return after it is completed but before it is presented to the taxpayer for signature. The preparer can sign original returns, amended returns, or requests for filing extensions by rubber stamp, mechanical device (such as a signature pen), or computer software program.[30]
2. **Taxpayer Signature:** Regardless of whether a paid preparer or someone else has prepared a return, a taxpayer must sign his own return, affirming it is correct under penalties of perjury. A taxpayer is legally responsible for the accuracy of every item on the return. [31]
3. **More Than One Preparer:** If the original preparer is unavailable for signature, another preparer must review the entire preparation of the return or claim and then must manually sign it. For purposes of the signature requirement, the preparer with primary responsibility for the overall accuracy of the return or claim is considered the preparer, if more than one preparer is involved. The other preparers do not have to be disclosed on the return.

A preparer may sign on behalf of the taxpayer in the client's signature area only if certain standards are met (see Unit 3, under the section: *Representative Signing in Lieu of the Taxpayer*).

---

[30] Use of electronic signatures is optional for tax professionals. The e-signature option helps reduce office expenses like paper, postage and physical storage space and time-consuming efforts spent obtaining a physically signed authorization form. A taxpayer may always choose to sign their return or e-file forms using a handwritten signature instead of an electronic one.

[31] Although the taxpayer is ultimately responsible for the items reported on the tax return, when a preparer e-files a taxpayer's return, the Form 8879 (IRS e-file Signature Authorization) must be completed by the preparer and signed by both the preparer and the taxpayer. The Form 8897 is signed under penalty of perjury by both parties.

(Test yourself and then check the correct answers at the end of this chapter.)

1. Circular 230 §10.35 states that a practitioner must be _____ to engage in practice before the IRS.

A. Honest.
B. Diligent.
C. Ethical.
D. Competent.

2. Under IRC §6107, what is a tax return preparer required to keep for at least three years after the close of the return period?

A. A list of clients/tax returns prepared.
B. Copies of all tax returns prepared.
C. Both a list of clients/tax returns prepared and copies of all tax returns prepared.
D. Either A or B.

3. An employee of a tax accounting firm has spent hours constructing a spreadsheet used to determine a client's estimated tax payments. The client has yet to pay the firm for fees charged in connection with his tax return. Which of the following best describes the firm's responsibility regarding the client's request for a copy of the spreadsheet?

A. The firm is under no obligation to hand over the spreadsheet. It is also not required to give the client access to view or copy it.
B. The firm is required to hand over the spreadsheet.
C. The firm is not required to hand over the spreadsheet, but is required to allow the client access to view or copy it.
D. None of the above.

4. With the taxpayer's properly signed power of attorney, a practitioner may:

A. Receive a taxpayer's refund check, but not endorse or cash the check.
B. Receive and endorse a taxpayer's refund check and invest the proceeds in the taxpayer's own mutual fund.
C. Receive a taxpayer's refund check and endorse it, but only to pay tax preparation fees.
D. None of the above.

5. Which of the following statements is correct regarding a client's request for his original records in order to comply with his federal tax obligations?

A. The practitioner may choose not to return client records if there is a fee dispute.
B. A legal case relieves the practitioner of his responsibility to return a client's records.
C. The practitioner must, at the request of the client, promptly return a client's records, regardless of fee disputes.
D. The practitioner must, at the request of the client, return client records within one month of payment.

6. Dennis, an Enrolled Agent, wants to hire his friend, Brandon, who is also an Enrolled Agent. Brandon has been disbarred from practice by the IRS for misconduct. Brandon has appealed the disbarment, and it is currently under review. Which of the following statements is correct?

A. Dennis can still hire Brandon as a tax return preparer, provided Brandon does not represent any taxpayers.
B. Dennis can still hire Brandon, provided Brandon does not prepare or sign any tax returns.
C. Dennis cannot hire Brandon.
D. Dennis can hire Brandon while his appeal is pending.

7. An Enrolled Agent represented both a taxpayer and a former business partner of the taxpayer before the Internal Revenue Service with regard to a specific tax matter. Due to the potential conflict of interest, the EA obtained a written consent from each of the clients waiving the conflict of interest and giving informed consent. The EA must keep those written consents for how long after the conclusion of representation?

A. 24 Months
B. 36 Months
C. 48 Months
D. 72 Months

8. If more than one tax return preparer is involved in preparing a return, who is required to sign?

A. All preparers involved in the preparation of the return.
B. Only the preparer with primary responsibility for the accuracy of the return; however, the other preparers must be disclosed on the return.
C. Only the preparer with primary responsibility for the accuracy of the return; the other preparers do not need to be disclosed on the return.
D. Only the taxpayer.

9. All of the following statements regarding a practitioner's responsibility to provide information requested by the IRS are correct except:

A. He must promptly turn over all records relating to the IRS request, no matter what the circumstances.
B. If the records are not in his possession, he must make a "reasonable inquiry" of his client about their whereabouts.
C. He is not legally obligated to contact any third party who might possess the requested records.
D. If he believes in good faith and on reasonable grounds that the requested material is legally privileged information, a practitioner may choose to decline a records request.

10. Sara, an Enrolled Agent, buys a practice owned by Mark, an EA who is retiring. As she reviews the records from Mark's practice, she learns he has been incorrectly claiming dependents for certain taxpayer clients. What should Sara do?

A. Notify the clients of the error and the consequences of not correcting the error.
B. Inform the clients that she will refuse to prepare their taxes if they do not file amended returns.
C. Contact the IRS to alert agents about the error and to request audits of those clients' prior year returns.
D. Inform Mark that he made mistakes on his clients' returns and advise him to notify them.

11. Whit is an EA who decides to advertise his fee schedule in the local newspaper. Which of the following fee arrangements is prohibited?

A. Hourly fee rates.
B. Fixed fees for tax preparation.
C. Contingent fees for original returns.
D. Flat fees for initial consultations.

12. Which of the following statements is correct?

A. Conflicts of interest apply only to attorneys and not to other tax professionals.
B. A practitioner may represent clients who have a conflict of interest under certain circumstances, but waivers to the conflict must be signed by both parties.
C. A practitioner may represent clients who have a conflict of interest if the practitioner receives a written confirmation of a waiver of the conflict of interest from the clients within 45 days of receiving any non-written, informed consent from the clients.
D. A practitioner may not represent clients who have a conflict of interest.

13. If a practitioner knows that a client has filed an erroneous tax return, he is required to:

A. Correct the error.
B. Advise the client about the error and the consequences of not correcting the error.
C. Do nothing if he was not the one who prepared the erroneous return.
D. Inform the IRS about the error.

14. Which does not constitute a "best practice" for practitioners under Circular 230?

A. Consulting other professionals when questions arise about a particular tax issue.
B. Acting fairly and with integrity in practice before the IRS.
C. Communicating clearly with the client regarding the terms of the engagement.
D. Advising the client regarding the consequences of advice rendered.

15. Which of the following statements is correct regarding practitioners?

A. Practitioners cannot notarize documents of the clients they represent before the IRS.
B. Practitioners cannot be notaries.
C. Practitioners are required to be notaries.
D. A notary who is also a practitioner will not be eligible for the e-file program.

16. Melanie is an EA who submits her clients' returns via IRS e-file. In order to save paper, she does not give a copy of the prepared tax return to her clients if they do not request it. Melanie allows her clients to have a copy of the return, so long as they pay a small fee. Which of the following statements is correct?

A. Melanie is not in violation of Circular 230.
B. Melanie is in violation of Circular 230.
C. Melanie is not in violation of Circular 230 if she gives clients the option of receiving a copy of their return for a small fee.
D. Melanie cannot offer a copy of the return to a client unless the client requests it.

17. Mark is an Enrolled Agent in the process of representing Arthur, his client, before the Internal Revenue Service for an old tax matter on a jointly-filed return. Arthur's ex-wife, Michelle, also asked the Mark to represent her for the same matter. Which of the following is required for Mark to represent them both?

A. Both taxpayers must sit down together and discuss the matter before a mediator.
B. Both taxpayers must waive the conflict of interest and give informed consent in writing to the EA.
C. Mark must charge both parties the same amount.
D. This representation is prohibited by law.

1. The answer is D. Circular 230 §10.35 replaces the previous section detailing the covered opinion rules. It states that a practitioner must be competent to engage in practice before the IRS. "Competence" is defined as having the appropriate level of knowledge, skill, thoroughness, and preparation for the specific matter related to a client's engagement.

2. The answer is D. Under IRC §6107, a tax return preparer must keep copies of all returns he has prepared or a list of clients and tax returns prepared. The list must include the taxpayer's name, taxpayer identification number, tax year, and the type of tax return prepared. The copies or list must be kept for at least three years after the close of the return period.

3. The answer is A. The firm is under no obligation to hand over its own work product to a client who has not paid his fees. A tax return preparer is required only to return a client's original records. The client must also be given reasonable access to review and copy any additional records retained by the preparer that are necessary for the client to comply with his federal tax obligations. The spreadsheet is not necessary for the client to comply with his federal tax obligations.

4. The answer is A. With proper authorization, a practitioner may receive a refund check issued to the taxpayer. A practitioner is not allowed to negotiate taxpayer refunds under any circumstances, regardless of whether the client has given permission.

5. The answer is C. Client records must generally be returned promptly upon client demand, regardless of fee disputes. Client records are defined as any original records belonging to the client, including any work product that he has already paid for, such as a completed copy of a tax return. However, the practitioner is allowed to withhold the return of his own work papers or work product until the client has resolved any outstanding payment issues.

6. The answer is C. Dennis cannot knowingly hire a disbarred practitioner, regardless of whether that person would prepare tax returns. A practitioner may not knowingly employ a person or accept employment from a person who has been disbarred or suspended by the Office of Professional Responsibility, even if that person's case is under appeal.

7. The answer is B. In conflict of interest cases, a preparer must obtain a written consent signed by each party and retain the records for at least 36 months (three years) from the date representation ends.

8. The answer is C. Only the preparer with primary responsibility for the accuracy of the return is considered the preparer and is thus required to sign the return under penalties of perjury. The other preparers do not need to be disclosed on the return. The taxpayer is also required to sign the return, whether prepared by a preparer or not. The taxpayer is legally responsible for the accuracy of every item on his tax return.

9. The answer is A. Although Circular 230 dictates that a practitioner comply promptly with information and record requests, there are limited circumstances when records do not have to be turned over. A practitioner may decline to do so if he believes in good faith that the request is not legal or that the information is privileged. A practitioner also does not have to contact any third party to inquire about the records; he must simply make a reasonable inquiry of his client.

10. The answer is A. Under the rules of Circular 230, a practitioner has a duty to advise a client about issues of noncompliance, errors, or omissions, in addition to the consequences of the errors. However, the practitioner is not obligated to correct the error, inform the IRS of the error, or insist the client file an amended return. The duty to advise also applies when a practitioner discovers an error or omission in the course of tax consulting or an advisory engagement.

11. The answer is C. Circular 230 prohibits a practitioner from charging a contingent fee based on the refund amount for an original return. A practitioner may publish and advertise a fee schedule. All the other fee structures are acceptable (please note that the IRS currently lacks authority to regulate contingent fee arrangements for preparation of returns and refund claims due to the outcome of the Ridgely case in 2014, however, Circular 230 has not yet been updated to reflect this important court case).

12. The answer is B. Under certain circumstances, a practitioner can represent clients who have a conflict of interest. The practitioner must reasonably believe he will be able to provide competent and diligent representation to each affected client; the representation cannot be prohibited by law; and each affected client must be fully notified and sign a consent waiving the conflict of interest in writing. A practitioner must receive a written confirmation of a waiver of the conflict of interest from the clients within 30 days of receiving any non-written, informed consent from the clients.

13. The answer is B. If a practitioner knows that a client has filed an erroneous tax return, he must advise the client to correct the error. The practitioner is not required to amend the return, but he must advise the client about the error and the consequences of not correcting the error. He is not required to notify the IRS about his client's error.

14. The answer is A. Although it may be a good idea to consult with other tax professionals when particular tax questions arise, this is not listed as one of the "best practices" in Circular 230.

15. The answer is A. Practitioners cannot notarize documents of the clients they represent before the IRS. However, they are not prohibited from performing notary services for clients in connection with other financial or personal matters.

16. The answer is B. Melanie is in violation of Circular 230. Tax return preparers must furnish copies of completed returns and claims for refund to all their clients. This must be done no later than when clients sign the original documents.

17. The answer is B. In order for Mark to represent them, both taxpayers must waive the conflict of interest and give informed consent in writing to the EA.

Unit 5: Practitioner Standards and Tax Advice

More Reading:
Circular 230, *Regulations Governing Practice Before the Internal Revenue Service*

Circular 230 outlines broad standards for practitioners when it comes to tax positions taken on income tax returns, as well as other forms of written advice they provide clients. Practitioners who fail to meet these standards are subject to penalties and other sanctions.

Requirements for Written Advice §10.37

§10.37 was extensively revised in the most recent version of Circular 230. It presents the due diligence requirements for practitioners to exercise when issuing written advice. The definition of "written advice" has been expanded to encompass almost anything in writing, including email, text, or any other type of electronic communication, on any federal tax matter.[32]

A practitioner must:

- Base the written advice on reasonable factual and legal assumptions.
- Consider all relevant facts and circumstances that he knows or reasonably should know.
- Use reasonable efforts to identify and ascertain the facts relevant to written advice on each federal tax matter.
- Not rely upon representations, statements, findings, or agreements of the taxpayer or any other person if reliance on them would be unreasonable.
- Relate applicable law and authority to facts.

In addition, when issuing written advice, a practitioner cannot take into consideration the chances that a tax return may or may not be audited, or that a particular matter may or may not be raised on audit.

> **Example:** Randy is an Enrolled Agent. Randy's client, Paulette, asks him what the odds are that the IRS will audit certain deductions she wants to claim on her Schedule C. Randy responds that the IRS audits only about two percent of these types of tax returns, so the risk is worth taking, although the law is unsettled about whether the deductions are allowable. In the tax return he prepares, Randy includes the questionable deductions. Randy is playing "audit lottery," which is in violation of Circular 230. This type of practitioner advice is specifically prohibited by the IRS.

Similar to the provisions in §10.22, §10.37 has a paragraph that allows a practitioner to rely on the advice of another person, so long as the advice is reasonable and the reliance is in good faith. However, the section specifies that reliance is not reasonable when the practitioner knows or reasonably should know that:

- The opinion of the other person should not be relied on;
- The other person is not competent or lacks the necessary qualifications to provide the advice; or
- The other person has a conflict of interest in violation of the rules described in this part.

A "standard of review" paragraph was added that establishes the basis by which the IRS will evaluate whether a practitioner has complied with the written advice rules of §10.37. It applies a

---

[32] There are two exceptions to what is considered written advice under §10.37: (1) continuing education presentations on federal tax matters and (2) government submissions on general policy, are excluded.

"reasonable practitioner" standard, with all facts and circumstances taken into account. The scope of the engagement and the type and specificity of the advice sought by the client are also to be considered.

Standards for Tax Returns and Documents (§10.34)

In addition to §10.37, Circular 230's §10.34 is vital to understanding a practitioner's responsibilities when it comes to providing written advice to a client.

The section directly ties back to IRC §6694, which describes tax return preparer penalties. §10.34 has four parts: positions taken on tax returns, positions taken on other documents or affidavits submitted to the IRS, advising clients on potential penalties, and relying on information furnished by clients.

Standards for Tax Returns: A practitioner may not willfully sign a tax return or claim for refund that he knows (or reasonably should know) contains a position that:

- Lacks a reasonable basis.
- Is an unreasonable position as described in IRC §6694(a)(2). [33]
- Is a willful attempt by the practitioner to understate the liability for tax or reflects a reckless or intentional disregard of rules or regulations.

In determining potential penalties, the IRS will take into account a pattern of conduct to assess whether a practitioner acted willfully, recklessly, or through gross incompetence. In addition to civil penalties, criminal penalties may also apply to tax return preparers who file fraudulent returns with unreasonable positions.

Tax Position Definitions
More Likely Than Not: There is a *greater than* 50% likelihood that the tax treatment will be upheld if the IRS challenges it. If a preparer is unsure that a position meets this standard, he may generally avoid penalties by disclosing the position on the return. However, a disclosure statement will not protect the preparer if the position is patently frivolous.[34] The "more likely than not" standard must be used for tax shelters and reportable transactions.
Reasonable Basis: This is the minimum standard for all tax advice and preparation of tax returns. The IRS defines it this way: "*Reasonable basis* is a relatively high standard of tax reporting that is significantly higher than not frivolous or not patently improper. The reasonable basis standard is not satisfied by a return position that is merely arguable". The precise likelihood that a reasonable basis position will be upheld on its merits is not defined in Circular 230. For purposes of avoiding §6694 penalties, the reasonable-basis standard applies only if the relevant tax position is disclosed on the return or document so that the IRS is aware of a potential issue.
Unreasonable Position: In general, this is an undisclosed position with no substantial authority.

Adequate and appropriate disclosure can be made by using Form 8275, *Disclosure Statement,* which allows a preparer to disclose positions that do not have substantial authority, but still have a reasonable basis, assuming the position is not otherwise already disclosed on the return.

---

[33]Section 6694(a) imposes penalties on paid preparers who prepare returns reflecting an understatement of liability due to an unreasonable position if the preparer knew (or reasonably should have known) of the position. No penalty is imposed, however, if it is shown that there is reasonable cause for the understatement and the preparer acted in good faith.
[34] See Regulation 1.6694-2(a)(1) for more information.

Disclosure Statements

Circular 230 §10.34 specifies the use of disclosure statements in certain instances. A tax return that requires a disclosure to the IRS must include Form 8275, *Disclosure Statement*, or Form 8275-R, *Regulation Disclosure Statement*.

Form 8275 is used by taxpayers and preparers to disclose items or positions on a tax return that are not otherwise adequately disclosed. It is primarily used to avoid accuracy-related penalties so long as the return position has a reasonable basis and the taxpayer (and preparer) acted in good faith in taking the position. Form 8275 cannot be used to avoid the portion of the accuracy-related penalty attributable to certain types of misconduct, including the following:

- Negligence
- Disregard of regulations
- Any substantial understatement of income tax on a tax shelter item

A disclosure statement cannot be used by a preparer to avoid penalties if the position has no reasonable basis.

Form 8275 is used for most disclosure matters. Form 8275-R is only used in limited circumstances when a taxpayer takes a position that runs contrary to Treasury regulations.

Example: Hazel is an EA with a client who has a very complex tax situation. She notices that the IRS publications reflect one position, but there is a recent court case that may allow a more favorable position for her client. There are also two other similar cases being litigated, but the outcome of those cases is currently unknown. Hazel believes that the position has a 30% chance of prevailing on its merits. Hazel thinks that the client's position has a reasonable basis and decides to disclose the position on the tax return. Even though the position is contrary to the IRS's current position, Hazel may take the position on the return, so long as it is disclosed. She must file Form 8275 along with the tax return stating the position and referencing the court case or any other basis she has for the position.

Example: Rochelle is an Enrolled Agent. She prepares a tax return for a self-employed client. A large deduction on the return did not have a reasonable basis and was not disclosed. Rochelle can be liable for a substantial preparer penalty, and her client may be liable for an accuracy-related penalty.

Example: Frank, a CPA, prepares a final tax return for a deceased individual. He receives a question from the executor about the deductibility of a particular expense. The IRS has no applicable guidance for the deduction, but there has been a recent court case where the taxpayer was allowed to claim a similar deduction. Thus, prior law supports a position favorable to the taxpayer. However, Frank's client is now deceased and the executor's records are incomplete. The executor is certain that the expense can be ultimately deducted, but Frank believes that the deductibility of the expense is uncertain. Frank uses Form 8275, *Disclosure Statement*, to properly disclose the taxpayer's position. By filing Form 8275, Frank and his client can avoid the accuracy-related penalty if the expense is later disallowed by the IRS.

Standards for Submission of Documents to the IRS: A practitioner may not advise a client to submit a document, affidavit, or other paper to the IRS:

- The purpose of which is to delay or impede the administration of the federal tax laws,
- That is frivolous, or

- That contains or omits information in a manner that demonstrates an intentional disregard of a rule or regulation, unless the practitioner also advises the client to submit a document that evidences a good faith challenge to the rule or regulation (such as a disclosure statement).

A practitioner must not knowingly sign a frivolous return. A frivolous position is defined as one that the practitioner knows is in bad faith and is improper. A practitioner may sign a return with a tax position that meets at least one of two standards:

- The position is "more likely than not" to be sustained on its merits, or
- The position has a "reasonable basis."

Advising Clients on Potential Penalties

A practitioner is required to inform a client of any penalties that are reasonably likely to apply to a position taken on a tax return if:

- The practitioner advised the client with respect to the position, or
- The practitioner prepared or signed the tax return.

The practitioner also must inform the client of any opportunity to avoid penalties by disclosure of the position and of the requirements for adequate disclosure. This rule applies even if the practitioner is not subject to an IRC penalty related to the position, or to the document or tax return submitted.

Reliance on Information from Clients: When preparing income tax returns, a practitioner is not required to verify all the information furnished by his clients. In general, a practitioner:

- May rely in good faith without verification of information that a client provides.
- Should not ignore the implications of the information.
- Should make reasonable inquiries if the information appears to be incorrect, inconsistent, or incomplete.

Example: Shayne is an EA who conducts an interview with his client, Tameka. She states she made a $50,000 charitable contribution of real estate during 2017. However, this is not true, and Shayne fails to make reasonable inquiries to Tameka about the contribution. He does not ask about the existence of a qualified appraisal and he does not complete an IRS-required substantiation form. Shayne includes the deduction for the charitable contribution on Tameka's tax return, which results in an understatement of tax liability. Tameka's return is later audited, and the charitable deduction is disallowed. Shayne is in violation of §10.34 and would be subject to a preparer penalty for his negligence.

Example: Jennie is an EA with a client who says he paid $19,000 of alimony during 2017. However, from his statement alone, Jennie cannot know whether the $19,000 is indeed alimony. All or a portion of payments to a former spouse may be child support or family support, which are treated differently than alimony for federal tax purposes. It is Janie's responsibility to ask pertinent questions of her client in order to make the correct determination of whether or not the payment is actually alimony.

Reporting Requirements for Tax Shelter Activities

There are certain types of tax shelter activities that must be reported to the IRS. A *reportable transaction*, also called a *listed transaction*, is one that the IRS has determined has the potential for tax avoidance or evasion.

The rules for reportable transactions apply to all individuals and entities (including trusts, estates, partnerships, and corporations). Form 8886, *Reportable Transaction Disclosure Statement*, must be attached to a taxpayer's return for any year that he participates in this type of tax shelter. A separate statement must be filed for each reportable transaction.

The fact that a tax shelter transaction must be reported on this form does not necessarily mean the IRS will disallow its tax benefits. If a reportable transaction is not disclosed and results in an understatement of tax, an additional penalty equal to 30% of the understatement may be assessed.

A taxpayer may request a ruling from the IRS to determine whether a transaction must be disclosed. In addition to the 30% understatement of tax penalty, a civil penalty of 75% of the reduction of tax associated with the reportable transaction may be imposed, with a minimum penalty of $10,000 ($5,000 if the taxpayer is an individual) and a maximum penalty as high as $200,000 ($100,000 if the taxpayer is an individual), pursuant to IRC section 6707A(b).[35]

> **Note about Covered Opinions:** One of the most significant changes in the latest revision to Circular 230 was the elimination of the complex "covered opinion" rules in §10.35.[36] These rules led many practitioners to use blanket disclaimer statements on almost every piece of written communication, including emails. With the deletion of the covered opinion requirements, the IRS stated that practitioners remove all such disclaimers that state they are required by the IRS, OPR, or Circular 230.

Firm Compliance Procedures §10.36

§10.36 has been rewritten to address the measures a firm must take to ensure compliance with all provisions of Circular 230. A practitioner (or practitioners, if the duty is shared) who oversees a firm's practice must ensure adequate procedures are in place for every member, associate, or employee to comply with the requirements specified in Circular 230.

If a firm has not identified an individual with principal authority over the practice, the IRS may identify one or more practitioners who will be considered responsible for the §10.36 compliance requirements.

A practitioner who does not take reasonable steps to ensure the firm has adequate procedures in place to comply with Circular 230 requirements may face disciplinary action. He may also be subject to sanctions if he knows of other members of the firm who are engaging in a pattern of noncompliance, and he fails to take prompt action to correct the noncompliance.

> **Example:** Evonne is an Enrolled Agent working for a tax practice. Evonne knows that her coworker is filing fraudulent EITC claims, but does nothing. Evonne can be subject to sanctions, because she knew that other members of the firm were committing EITC fraud, and she did not report the illegal activity.

---

[35] In previous years, Form 8271, *Investor Reporting of Tax Shelter Registration Number*, was a required form. Before the enactment of the AJCA (the American Jobs Creation Act of 2004), section 6111 provided that tax shelter organizers were required to provide investors in tax shelters the registration number for the tax shelter. Form 8271 is no longer required. Because only a few investors must still file Form 8271 (for pre-AJCA section 6111 tax shelters) and because the IRS already is aware of these transactions, the Treasury Department has decided that investors are no longer required to file Forms 8271. As such, Form 8271 will be obsolete. However, these final regulations continue to require that material advisors must provide the reportable transaction number to all taxpayers and material advisors. See Internal Revenue Bulletin: 2007-38
[36] Now replaced by the general "competence" standard.

(Test yourself and then check the correct answers at the end of this chapter.)

1. In the "standard of review" section of Circular 230, the IRS will evaluate whether a practitioner has complied with the written advice rules of §10.37 by applying a _____ standard:

A. "More likely than not"
B. "Substantial authority"
C. "Reasonable person"
D. "Reasonable practitioner"

2. Glen is a CPA who prepares income tax returns for his clients. One of his clients submits a list of expenses to be claimed on Schedule C of the return. Glen is required to do which one of the following?

A. Glen is required to independently verify the client's information.
B. Glen can ignore the implications of information known by him.
C. Glen does not have to make inquiry if the information appears to be incorrect or incomplete.
D. Glen must make appropriate inquiries to determine whether the client has substantiation for his Schedule C expenses.

3. When should a practitioner not rely on the advice of another person?

A. When the advice is reasonable and the reliance is in good faith.
B. When the person is competent in providing the advice.
C. When the person has a conflict of interest in the tax matter.
D. When the practitioner has a professional relationship with the other person.

4. Under Circular 230, what is the responsibility of a practitioner who oversees a firm's tax practice?

A. To ensure the firm has adequate procedures in place to ensure compliance with all provisions of Circular 230.
B. To appoint another practitioner in the firm to monitor compliance of other employees.
C. To review the personal tax filings of all employees of the firm to make sure they comply with Circular 230.
D. All of the above.

5. A practitioner is required to inform a client of penalties that are reasonably likely to apply to a position taken on a tax return if:

A. The taxpayer decides to self-prepare a return.
B. The practitioner gave the client professional advice on the position.
C. The IRS has the taxpayer under examination.
D. The taxpayer is deceased.

6. Ryan is an EA with a client named Hannah who has had significant income from a partnership for the past five years. However, Ryan did not see a Schedule K-1 from the partnership among the information Hannah provided to him this year. What do Circular 230 due diligence provisions require Ryan to do?

A. Attempt to estimate the taxable amount that would be reported as income on the Schedule K-1 based on last year's Schedule K-1 and include that amount on Hannah's return.
B. Call Hannah's financial advisor and ask him about Hannah's investments.
C. Nothing, because Ryan is required to rely only on the information provided by his client, even if he has reason to believe the information may not be accurate.
D. Ask Hannah why she did not provide him with the partnership's Schedule K-1, as she had in previous years.

7. All of the following statements are correct about section §10.37 of Circular 230 on written advice except:

A. An email to a client about a federal tax matter would be included in the definition of written advice.
B. A practitioner should advise a client of the chances his tax return will be chosen for audit.
C. A practitioner should base his written advice on reasonable factual and legal assumptions.
D. A practitioner should relate the applicable law and authority to the facts relevant to written advice issued on a federal tax matter.

8. A practitioner cannot sign:

A. A tax return for a family member.
B. A tax return that he prepares for free.
C. A tax return with a properly disclosed tax shelter position.
D. A frivolous tax return with a disclosure.

9. Bethany is an EA with a client, Dylan, who wishes to claim a deduction for a large business expense. However, there is a question about whether the expense is "ordinary and necessary" for his business. If the deduction were disallowed, there would be a substantial understatement of tax (over 10%). Bethany researches the issue and tells Dylan that the position should be disclosed. Dylan does not want to disclose the position on the return, because he is afraid that the IRS will disallow it. What are the repercussions for Bethany?

A. None. All the penalties apply to the client.
B. Bethany may be liable for preparer penalties.
C. Bethany will not be liable for preparer penalties so long as she explains the potential penalties to the client.
D. None of the above.

10. Which type of transaction must always be reported to the IRS?

A. Listed transaction.
B. Reliance opinion.
C. A loss from a Ponzi scheme.
D. A position with a more likely than not chance of being upheld.

Unit 5: Quiz Answers

1. The answer is D. In the most recent revision of Circular 230, a "standard of review" paragraph was added that establishes the basis that the IRS will use to evaluate whether a practitioner has complied with the written advice rules of §10.37. It applies a "reasonable practitioner" standard, with all facts and circumstances taken into account. The scope of the engagement and the type and specificity of the advice sought by the client will also be considered.

2. The answer is D. A practitioner is not required to independently examine evidence of deductions. He may rely in good faith, without verification, upon information furnished by the taxpayer if it does not appear to be incorrect or incomplete. However, the practitioner must make reasonable inquiries about the validity of the information.

3. The answer is C. The revised §10.37 details the current standards for written tax advice. Similar to the provisions in §10.22, §10.37 says a practitioner may rely on the advice of another person, so long as the advice is reasonable and the reliance is in good faith. However, reliance is not reasonable when the practitioner knows, or reasonably should know, that:
- The opinion of the other person should not be relied on,
- The other person is not competent, or lacks the necessary qualifications to provide the advice, or
- The other person has a conflict of interest in violation of the rules.

4. The answer is A. Under §10.36, a practitioner (or practitioners, if the duty is shared) who oversees a firm's practice must ensure adequate procedures are in place for every member, associate, or employee to comply with the requirements specified in Circular 230. A practitioner(s) who does not take reasonable steps to ensure the firm has adequate procedures in place may face disciplinary action or sanctions if he knows of other members of the firm who are engaging in a pattern of noncompliance, and he fails to take prompt action to correct the noncompliance.

5. The answer is B. A practitioner is required to inform a client of any penalties that are reasonably likely to apply to a position taken on a tax return if:
- The practitioner advised the client with respect to the position, or
- The practitioner prepared or signed the tax return.

6. The answer is D. Ryan must ask Hannah about the missing Schedule K-1 and ask pertinent questions to understand the facts of the situation. A practitioner who has reason to believe his client has not complied with the revenue laws or has made an error in or omission from any return, document, affidavit, or other required paper has the responsibility to advise the client promptly of the noncompliance, error, or omission.

7. The answer is B. §10.37 has been expanded to define written advice as almost anything in writing, including electronic communications, on any federal tax matter. When issuing written advice, a practitioner is expressly prohibited from taking into consideration the chances that a tax return may or may not be audited, or that a particular matter may or may not be raised on audit. A practitioner must:
- Base the written advice on reasonable factual and legal assumptions.
- Consider all relevant facts and circumstances that he knows or reasonably should know.

- Use reasonable efforts to identify and ascertain the facts relevant to written advice on each federal tax matter.
- Not rely upon representations, statements, findings, or agreements of the taxpayer or any other person if reliance on them would be unreasonable.
- Relate applicable law and authority to facts.

8. The answer is D. A tax return preparer cannot sign a frivolous tax return, even if the return has a disclosure. A frivolous position is defined as one that the preparer knows is in bad faith or is improper.

9. The answer is B. If the return does not adequately disclose the position and it is later examined by the IRS, Bethany may be subject to a preparer penalty. The disclosure form is filed to avoid the potential for penalties due to disregard of rules regarding the substantial understatement of income tax.

10. The answer is A. A listed transaction, also called a reportable transaction, is a type of tax shelter activity that must be reported to the IRS. Form 8886, *Reportable Transaction Disclosure Statement*, must be attached to a taxpayer's return for any year he participates in this type of tax shelter.

Unit 6: Due Diligence for Refundable Credits

> **More Reading:**
>
> ***www.eitc.irs.gov***
>
> **Publication 596,** ***Earned Income Credit***
>
> **Publication 4687,** ***Refundable Credits Due Diligence***
>
> **Publication 3524,** ***EITC Eligibility Checklist***

Each year, tax preparers complete more than half of the tax returns claiming the Child Tax Credit (CTC), Additional Child Tax Credit (ACTC), Earned Income Credit (EITC) and/or the American Opportunity Tax Credit (AOTC). The IRS estimates that one in four of these claims is incorrect, which results in billions of dollars paid out in erroneous refunds each year.

The IRS recently updated their due diligence requirements to include the Child Tax Credit as well as the American Opportunity Credit.

The due diligence rules for these refundable credits are more stringent than they were in previous years. This is because both the number of individuals claiming these refundable credits and the number of erroneous claims is high. Paid preparers must meet four additional due diligence requirements on returns with these claims or face possible penalties. Employers may also be penalized for an employee's failure to exercise due diligence.

New "Knowledge Requirement" for EITC, CTC/ACTC, and AOTC Returns

IRS regulations specify these due diligence requirements and set a performance standard for the *knowledge requirement:* what a reasonable and well-informed tax return preparer, knowledgeable in the law, would do. The IRS assesses more than 90% of all EITC due diligence penalties for failure to comply with the knowledge requirement of IRC § 6695. Under the "knowledge requirement," a preparer must:

- Apply a common-sense standard to the information provided by the client.
- Evaluate whether the information is complete and gather any missing facts.
- Determine if the information is consistent; recognize contradictory statements and statements the preparer knows are not true.
- Conduct a thorough, in-depth interview with every client, *every year.*
- Ask enough questions to reasonably know the return is correct and complete.
- Document in the file any questions he asked and his client's responses.

Example: Cordell is an EA. His client, Ayanna, states that she is separated from her spouse. Her dependent son is 12 years old and lives with her. Ayanna wants to claim the EITC and file as head of household. In reviewing his client's records, Cordell notes that Ayanna earns a minimal income, which appears insufficient to support a household. As the preparer, Cordell must ask appropriate questions to determine Ayanna's correct filing status, determine how long the child lived with each parent during the year, and probe for any additional sources of income. He must interview her thoroughly and document her answers. He must also fill out Form 8867, *Paid Preparer's Earned Income Credit Checklist*, and complete the EITC worksheet. After asking various questions, Ayanna discloses that she receives substantial child support, which is not taxable or reportable on the return. She also receives food stamps and other public benefits, which also help support her son. Food stamps are also not taxable. Cordell notes this information in his work papers and is now more confident that he can prepare Ayanna's return accurately.

Example: Amanda is an EA. A new 28-year-old client, Bernie, wants to claim two sons, ages 14 and 15, as qualifying children for the EITC. Amanda is concerned about the age of the children since Bernie's age seems inconsistent with the ages of the children. Amanda asks additional questions and discovers the boys are both adopted, which explains the age inconsistency. She completes the EITC Worksheet and Form 8867, and submits Form 8867 to the IRS. She retains copies of these records, as well as the adoption records that Bernie provides her and notes of her client interview, for a period of three years. Amanda has complied with her due diligence requirements.

Preparer Compliance Requirements

There are four mandatory "requirements" with regards to compliance. For the EA exam, you should memorize these four compliance requirements. It is possible that you will be asked several questions about this topic.

- **Requirement 1:** Completion and submission of Form 8867, *Paid Preparer's Due Diligence Checklist*
- **Requirement 2:** Completion of worksheet(s) and computation of the credit(s)
- **Requirement 3:** Knowledge
- **Requirement 4:** Record retention

The new due diligence requirements for preparers related are explained as follows:

1. **Complete and Submit Form 8867:** The preparer must complete Form 8867, *Paid Preparer's Due Diligence Checklist,* and submit this completed form to the IRS with every return with an EITC, CTC or AOTC. At the time of the interview, the preparer must document in their files the questions asked and the client's answers.
2. **Complete the worksheets and compute the Credit:** Most tax preparation software will compute these credits automatically on worksheets within the actual software program, but the IRS emphasizes that using software is not a substitute for knowledge of the law.
3. **Knowledge:** A preparer must not know (or have reason to know) that the information used to determine eligibility or to compute the amount of the credit is incorrect. A preparer must ask his client additional questions if the information furnished seems incorrect or incomplete.
4. **Retain Records:** A preparer must retain the following records for each claim:
   - Form 8867, *Paid Preparer's Due Diligence Checklist*
   - The applicable worksheet(s) for EITC, CTC/ACTC and AOTC claimed on the return
   - Any documents or other written proof relied on to complete the Form 8867 or to determine eligibility
   - A record of how, when, and from whom the information the preparer obtained to prepare the tax return as well a record of any additional questions the preparer asked to determine eligibility for and the amount of the credits and the client's answers.
   - All records should be kept for *three years* from the latest of:
     - The due date of the tax return.
     - The date the tax return was electronically filed.
     - For a paper return, the date the return was presented to the client for signature.

o The date you gave the part of the return for which you are responsible to the signing tax return preparer, (if you are a non-signing tax return preparer).

The records must be retained in either paper or electronic format, and they must be produced on-demand if an IRS field auditor asks for them.

Form 8867 Documentation Requirements

Form 8867 includes several mandatory questions that preparers must ask taxpayers in order to comply with due diligence requirements.

Form 8867 is also used by a preparer to identify the documents that the taxpayer provided and that the preparer used to determine credit eligibility. In determining the residency of qualifying children, a preparer must specify whether he relied upon documents such as school, medical, or social service records. In determining the disability of a qualifying child, a preparer must indicate whether he relied upon documents such as a statement from a doctor, other health care provider, or social services agency.

Example: Collin is an EA. His new client, Delia, 62, wants to take a dependency exemption for her son, Ernest, who is 32. She also wants to claim the Earned Income Tax Credit and the Dependent Care Credit for her son. Since Ernest is beyond the normal age limit for these credits, Collin makes reasonable inquiries and Delia produces a doctor's statement that says Ernest is severely disabled and incapable of self-care. Therefore, Delia may claim her son as a dependent, and the credits will be allowed regardless of Ernest's age. Collin has fulfilled his due diligence requirements by conducting a thorough interview with his client, including asking enough questions to understand an individual tax situation, documenting the answers, and seeking appropriate supporting evidence. He completes his due diligence requirements by submitting Form 8867 to the IRS.

If Schedule C is included with the tax return, the preparer must specify whether he determined credit eligibility by relying upon any documents the taxpayer provided in connection with the business. These documents may include a business license, Forms 1099, records of gross receipts and expenses, or bank statements.

Example: Ezekiel is an EA. Geneva is his new client. Geneva wants to claim the EITC as well as the AOTC. She has two qualifying children who both attend a local community college. Geneva tells Ezekiel she had a Schedule C business and earned $12,500 in income, but had no expenses. This information appears incomplete because it would be unusual that someone who is self-employed has no business expenses. Ezekiel is required to ask reasonable questions to determine if the business exists and if the information about Geneva's income and expenses is correct. Ezekiel must submit Form 8867 to the IRS and keep copies of any documents Geneva provides for at least three years.

Common Errors on Refund Claims

There are certain types of errors that the IRS sees commonly on refund claims. Errors can delay the taxpayer's refund or can lead to a rejection of the credits listed on the return.

Note: Preparers are not always required to ask for documents to prove the relationship and residency of a qualifying child before completing a claim for a refundable credit, although a paid preparer may request those documents if the information provided by the client appears to be incorrect, inconsistent, or incomplete.

Most Common EITC Errors

The three issues that account for most EITC errors are:

- Claiming EITC for a child who does not meet the qualifying child requirements
- Filing as single or head of household when married.
- Incorrectly reporting institution income or expenses.

A common method of EITC fraud is the "borrowing" of dependents. Unscrupulous tax preparers will "share" one taxpayer's qualifying child or children with another taxpayer in order to allow both to claim the EITC. Any taxpayer who is claiming the EITC must have a Social Security number that is valid for employment purposes. Any qualifying child who is listed on an EITC return must also have a valid SSN (an ITIN or ATIN is not sufficient).

Example: Herbert has four children, but he only needs the first three children to receive the maximum EITC amount. The preparer lists the first three children on Herbert's return and lists the other child on another return. The preparer and Herbert are "selling" the dependents and will then split a fee or split the refund. This is an example of tax fraud that involves both the preparer and the taxpayer.

Most Common AOTC Errors

- **Claiming AOTC for a student who didn't attend an eligible educational institution.** The AOTC is for post-secondary education only, which may include education at a college, university or technical school. The AOTC can only be claimed for the first four years of post-secondary education.
- **Claiming AOTC for a student who didn't pay qualifying college expenses.** Educational expenses must be paid or considered paid by the client, the client's spouse or the dependent student claimed on the tax return.
- **Claiming AOTC for a student for too many years.** The AOTC is only available for the first four years of post-secondary education and your client can only claim it for four tax years per eligible student. This limitation includes any past years that the client may have claimed the Hope Credit.

Example: Janice is an Enrolled Agent. She interviews Jared, a 26-year-old client who states that he's a full-time college student and would like to claim the AOTC. He provides a Form 1098-T, Tuition Statement, showing $6,000 paid for tuition at a qualifying institution. The Form 1098-T is a good indicator that Jared is eligible for the AOTC but Janice must ask more questions to determine eligibility. Jared states that he does not have a bachelor's degree yet, because he switched majors last year. He has been an undergraduate student for five years. Since a taxpayer can only claim the AOTC for four tax years, this means that Jared is ineligible to take the American Opportunity Credit on his 2017 return. He may still be eligible for the Lifetime Learning Credit.

The Most Common Child Tax Credit Errors

- **Claiming a child who does not meet the age requirement:** The child must be under the age of 17 at the end of the tax year. There are no exceptions to this rule.
- **Claiming a child who does not meet dependency requirements:** The child must be claimed as a dependent on your client's return and meet all the eligibility rules for a dependent.

- **Claiming the credit for a child who does not meet the residency requirement:** The child must be a U.S. citizen, U.S. national or a U.S. resident alien and the child must have lived with your client for more than half the year.
- **Children with an ITIN:** If the qualifying child uses an ITIN, *Individual Taxpayer Identification Number,* the child must meet the substantial presence test to qualify.

Since tax professionals prepare more than half of all returns claiming refundable credits, the quality of their work has a significant impact on reducing erroneous claims. Preparers who file high percentages of questionable claims or returns with a high risk of error may be subject to on-site audits. IRS agents will review preparer records to verify due diligence compliance, including whether they are meeting the knowledge requirement. Penalties may be assessed when noncompliance is identified.

In the previous year, the IRS sent more than 7,000 letters to preparers suspected of filing questionable refund claims. The letters detailed the critical issues identified on the returns and explained the consequences of filing inaccurate claims. The IRS warned these preparers that their future refund claims would be monitored closely and that their clients' returns may be audited.

The IRS says many of the claims were prepared using "do-it-yourself" tax software rather than professional tax software that requires Form 8867 to be submitted along with each applicable refund claim.

Penalties for Failure to Exercise Due Diligence

The penalties for preparers failing to exercise due diligence with refund claims can be severe. Taxpayers also face consequences for not complying with the due diligence rules. If the IRS examines a taxpayer's return and disallows all or part of an EITC, AOTC, or CTC/ACTC claim on a return, the taxpayer:

- Must pay back the amount in error with interest,
- May need to file Form 8862, *Information to Claim Earned Income Credit after Disallowance*, for the Earned Income Tax Credit, Child Tax Credit, Additional Child Tax Credit, or American Opportunity Tax Credit[37]
- Cannot claim the credit for the next two years if the IRS determines the error is because of reckless or intentional disregard of the rules, or
- Cannot claim the credits for the next ten years if the IRS determines the error is because of fraud.

For 2017, tax preparers face a penalty of $510 for each failure to comply with due diligence requirements. This penalty applies per credit. For example, if IRS finds a tax practitioner who has prepared 25 returns that fail to meet the EITC due diligence requirements, the penalty for tax year 2017 is $12,750. If those same returns also failed to meet the AOTC due diligence requirements, the penalty is increased to $38,250. There is no maximum dollar penalty amount.

Further, if the IRS examines a taxpayer's claim and it is determined that the preparer did not meet all four due diligence requirements, the preparer can be subject to penalties even beyond the usual penalty for each failure to comply. If a preparer receives a return-related penalty, he may also face:

- Disciplinary action by the OPR
- Suspension or expulsion from IRS e-file

---

[37] In October 2017, Form 8862 was revised to include the Child Tax Credit, Additional Child Tax Credit, and American Opportunity Tax Credit.

- Injunctions barring him from preparing tax returns

The IRS has streamlined procedures for faster referrals to the U.S. Department of Justice to try to prevent preparers from making fraudulent refund claims. These preparers could be permanently or temporarily barred from all types of federal tax preparation.

1. Austin is an Enrolled Agent who submits a return for his client. The return claims the Earned Income Tax Credit, but Austin fails to submit Form 8867 for the return. What penalty does Austin potentially face?

A. None. Austin must keep a copy of each Form 8867, but the forms are not required to be submitted to the IRS.
B. $400
C. $510
D. $1,000

2. A client tells a tax return preparer:
- She has no Form 1099.
- She was self-employed cleaning houses.
- She earned $12,000.
- She had no expenses related to the cleaning business.
- She has three children who live with her, all three are under the age of 3.

The client says she would like to claim the Earned Income Tax Credit. What is the best course of action for the preparer in this case?

A. Refuse to prepare the return based on the client's information.
B. Ask probing questions to determine the correct facts and ask for proof of income or any expenses.
C. Accept the taxpayer's word so long as she fills out a legal liability release form.
D. Make the client swear to the truthfulness of her statements before an IRS officer.

3. All of the following are potential penalties for a preparer who files fraudulent refund claims *except*:

A. Suspension or expulsion from IRS e-file.
B. Criminal prosecution by the OPR.
C. A ban from preparing tax returns.
D. A preparer penalty.

4. When must a tax return preparer complete a client checklist for a client claiming the AOTC?

A. Every year.
B. For the first year preparing a return for a new client.
C. Every other year.
D. The client checklist is recommended, but is not required.

5. All of the following are due diligence requirements except:

A. To evaluate the information received from the client.
B. To apply a consistency and reasonableness standard to the information.
C. To verify the taxpayer's information with the appropriate third parties.
D. To make additional reasonable inquiries when the information appears to be incorrect, inconsistent, or incomplete.

6. The IRS can impose the following ban related to the AOTC, EITC, and/or CTC:

A. Ten-year ban for fraud.
B. Two-year ban for fraud.
C. Permanent ban for fraud.
D. The IRS cannot ban a taxpayer from claiming credits on future returns if the taxpayer otherwise qualifies for them.

7. Mack and Judy have valid ITINs. They have two children, both of whom have valid SSNs. Assuming they meet the income requirements, can Mack and Judy claim the EITC in 2017?

A. They can claim the EITC for themselves and their children.
B. They can claim the EITC for their children, but not for themselves.
C. They cannot claim the EITC, regardless of whether their children have valid SSNs.
D. Their children can claim the EITC, but only if they file separate returns.

8. All of the following are common errors taxpayers make in claiming the EITC except:

A. Incorrectly reporting income or expenses.
B. Incorrectly claiming a child who does not meet the specific EITC requirements.
C. Filing as head of household when married.
D. Listing earned income for the year.

9. Which of the following is not one of the requirements for AOTC claims?

A. Reviewing the client's Social Security Card.
B. Making sure the client has qualifying educational expenses.
C. Completing and submitting the Form 8867.
D. Following the knowledge requirement.

10. All of the following are common errors taxpayers make in claiming the Child Tax Credit or Additional Child Tax Credit except:

A. Claiming the CTC/ACTC for a child who does not meet the age requirement.
B. Claiming the CTC/ACTC for a child who does not meet the dependency requirements.
C. Claiming the CTC/ACTC for a child who does not meet the educational requirements.
D. Claiming the CTC/ACTC for a child who does not meet the residency requirement.

11. In preparing an Earned Income Credit Worksheet and Form 8867, how long should a return preparer retain copies?

A. One year from the filing of the return.
B. Two years from the filing of the return.
C. Three years from the filing of the return.
D. Six years from the filing of the return.

1. The answer is C. Form 8867, *Paid Preparer's Earned Income Credit Checklist,* must be submitted for each client's return that claims the Earned Income Tax Credit, or the preparer will be in violation of his due diligence requirements. For tax year 2017, each failure can result in a penalty of $510.

2. The answer is B. The best course of action would be to ask probing questions and ask for proof of income and expenses. The tax return preparer must document the client's answers as part of his due diligence requirements. During the interview, a preparer must ask additional questions if the information appears incorrect, inconsistent, or incomplete.

3. The answer is B. The OPR may take disciplinary action against tax return preparers who violate rules related to fraudulent claims. However, the OPR never prosecutes criminal cases. Criminal cases are referred out to the proper authorities (the U.S. Justice Department).

4. The answer is A. For any client claiming the AOTC, a preparer must complete Form 8867 every year, even if the client is an existing client who has claimed the credit in the past. The preparer is required to keep a copy of the form in his records for at least three years.

5. The answer is C. A tax return preparer is not required to verify a taxpayer's answers with third parties. Due diligence requires a preparer to:

- Evaluate the information received from the client,
- Apply a consistency and reasonableness standard to the information,
- Make additional reasonable inquiries when the information appears to be incorrect, inconsistent, or incomplete, and
- Document additional inquiries and the client's response.

6. The answer is A. The IRS can impose the following types of bans related to refund claims of the AOTC, EITC, or CTC:
- Two-year ban for reckless or intentional disregard of due diligence rules, or
- Ten-year ban for fraud.

7. The answer is C. If a primary taxpayer, the spouse, or both have ITINs, they are ineligible to claim the Earned Income Tax Credit, even if their dependents have valid SSNs. A taxpayer (and his or her spouse, if married) must have valid Social Security numbers in order to claim the EITC. Qualifying children also must have valid SSNs.

8. The answer is D. To qualify for the EITC, a taxpayer must have earned income during the tax period. Assuming it is reported correctly, listing earned income is not an error made in claiming the EITC. The IRS cites the other three errors as common issues it sees with EITC claims.

9. The answer is A. Reviewing a client's Social Security cards is not a requirement but is a best practice, and recommended by the IRS. If you do review a Social Security card, make sure you keep a copy of the card for your records.

10. The answer is C. The Child Tax Credit does not have an "educational" requirement. The IRS cites the other three errors as common issues with CTC/AOTC claims. For more information on this subject, see detailed instructions in Publication 4687, *Refundable Credits Due Diligence.*

11. The answer is C. In preparing an Earned Income Credit Worksheet and Form 8867, the tax preparer a return should retain copies for at least three years from the filing of the return.

Unit 7: Recordkeeping and Penalties

> **More Reading:**
> Publication 583, *Starting a Business and Keeping Records*
> Publication 535, *Business Expenses*
> Publication 552, *Recordkeeping for Individuals*
> Publication 947, *Practice Before the IRS and Power of Attorney*

There are basic recordkeeping requirements for U.S. taxpayers that tax professionals need to be familiar with and make sure their clients understand. Recordkeeping requirements may be tested on all three parts of the EA exam, with Part 3 focusing primarily on substantiation and record retention for preparers.

Records that clearly demonstrate income, expenses, and basis should be retained, but tax law generally does not require that specific types of records to be kept. Taxpayers may scan records and retain them electronically, as the IRS does not require a taxpayer to keep original paper records. A taxpayer must be able to store, preserve, retrieve, and reproduce electronic records when needed.

Supporting Documents

As an essential part of due diligence, it is a preparer's responsibility to request appropriate documentation from clients in order to prepare an accurate tax return. A preparer should review prior year tax returns to identify relevant issues, such as items that need to be carried forward to the current year and tax years going forward.

In addition, depending on the type of tax return being prepared, a preparer may need to see the following types of supporting documentation:

- **Financial documents:** Canceled checks, bank statements, credit card statements, receipts, brokerage records.
- **Legal documents:** Birth certificates, divorce decrees, lawsuit settlements.
- **Business entity supporting documents:** Partnership agreement, corporate bylaws, corporate minutes.
- **Expense records:** Mileage logs; receipts for business expenses such as travel, meals, entertainment, and lodging; and receipts and written acknowledgements from charitable organizations, particularly for non-cash contributions and expenses of $250 or more.

For a taxpayer to deduct travel, entertainment, gift, transportation, charitable, employee, and other expenses, he must be able to substantiate those expenses. A taxpayer cannot deduct amounts that are estimates. A written record, including one prepared on a computer, generally is required to be considered adequate.

Example: A teacher tells her tax return preparer she had $23,000 in unreimbursed employee business expenses during the tax year. She provides no documentation, and her preparer does not ask to see any receipts. The IRS audits her return and disallows the expenses, which include an improper deduction for an $8,000 Mediterranean cruise. The preparer's failure to request receipts from his client shows a lack of due diligence.

Example: A taxpayer claims numerous deductions for her volunteer work in caring for feral cats. The U.S. Tax Court disallows expenses that were $250 or more because she failed to meet the substantiation requirement that required acknowledgement from the charitable organization. Even though the cat rescue organization is a qualifying charity, the taxpayer did not obtain a contemporaneous, written acknowledgement from the organization, so her deduction was disallowed, even though she had proof of her expenses.

Business expenses claimed on a taxpayer's Schedule C must be both "ordinary and necessary." An ordinary expense is one that is common in the taxpayer's particular trade or business. A necessary expense is one that is helpful and appropriate in the taxpayer's trade or business, but it does not have to be indispensable in order for it to be deductible.

A taxpayer generally cannot deduct personal, family, or living expenses. If an expense is used partly for business and partly for personal purposes, only the business portion is deductible.

Example: Erin is a self-employed architect who uses her van to visit clients and meet with suppliers and other subcontractors. She and her family also use the van for personal purposes. Erin keeps a mileage log that shows the business purpose, her business destination, and the date of each use of the car. Her records are adequate to substantiate that 75% of the car's use is for business purposes and 25% is for personal purposes, so she may deduct 75% of her auto expenses on her Schedule C.

Statute of Limitations for Records Retention

A taxpayer should keep all relevant records as long as they may be needed for the administration of any provision of the Internal Revenue Code. As a practical matter, this means a taxpayer must retain relevant records until the statute of limitations for each tax return expires. The responsibility to prove entries, deductions, and statements made on a taxpayer's tax return is known as the burden of proof. The taxpayers must meet their burden of proof by having the information and receipts for the expenses and deductions taken on the return.

For assessment of tax owed, this period is generally three years from the date a return was due or is filed, whichever is later.

For filing a claim for credit or refund, the period to make the claim is generally three years from the date the return was filed, or two years from the date the tax was paid, whichever is later.

If the return was filed prior to the original due date, the three-year statute of limitations starts as of the original due date of the return. If the return was filed on extension, the three-year period starts when the return was received by the IRS.

Example: Nisha is a delinquent filer. In January 2018, she meets with an Enrolled Agent who files her delinquent tax returns, 2012 through 2016. She is owed a refund for each year. However, she will receive refunds only for tax years 2014 through 2016, because those are the years still open under the three-year time statute. The claim for refund was due on April 15, 2016, for the 2012 return, and on April 18, 2017, for the 2013 return, so both of those refunds are now outside the statute of limitations. Nisha will not receive refunds for her 2012 or her 2013 tax return.

Property Records: Records relating to the basis of property should be retained as long as they may be material to any tax return involving the property. The basis of property is material until the statute of limitations expires for the tax year an asset is sold or otherwise disposed. A taxpayer must keep these records to figure the asset's basis, as well as any depreciation, amortization, or depletion deductions.

> **Example:** Reynold sells a vacation home he has owned for eight years. He uses records relating to the purchase of the property and improvements made on it to compute the basis and his gain. He reports the sale on his 2017 tax return. He must retain the records relating to the sale until the statute of limitations for the tax return expires, usually three years from the original due date of the return.

Employment Tax Records: A business is required to retain payroll and employment tax records for at least four years after the tax becomes due or is paid, whichever is later. This rule also applies to businesses that employ other tax preparers.

> **Example:** Shantel is an EA who employs five other tax preparers in her tax preparation franchise. She is required to keep the employment tax records relating to her employees for at least four years.

Applicable employer tax records must be made available for IRS review upon request. These include:

- Employer identification numbers
- Amounts and dates of wages, annuity, and pension payments
- Amounts of tips reported
- Names, addresses, Social Security numbers, and occupations of employees
- Dates of active employment and sick leave
- Records of fringe benefits provided
- Forms W-4
- Dates and amounts of tax deposits
- and copies of all employment returns filed (this refers to payroll tax returns and applicable employment records related to wages paid, such as Forms 940 and 941)

Statute of Limitations	
Type of Record/Return	**Applicable Statute or Retention Period**
Normal tax return	Three years after a return is due or filed, whichever is later
Omitted income that exceeds 25% of the gross income shown on the return	Six years from the filing date
Fraudulent return	No limit
No return filed	No limit
A claim for credit or amended return	The later of three years from the due date of the original return or two years after tax was paid
A claim for a loss from worthless securities	Seven years
Employment and payroll tax records	The later of four years after the tax becomes due or is paid
Fixed assets, real estate	Until the statute of limitations expires for the tax year in which the asset is disposed

Other Retention Periods

Longer record retention periods may apply in some cases. For example, if a taxpayer files a claim from a loss of worthless securities, the period to retain records related to the transaction is seven years.

If a taxpayer fails to report income that exceeds 25% of the gross income shown on his return, the statute of limitations is six years from when the return is filed. The IRS has no time limit to assess tax if a taxpayer never files a return or if a taxpayer files a fraudulent return.

Tax Avoidance vs. Tax Evasion

The U.S. system of federal taxation operates on the concept of voluntary compliance; it is the taxpayer's responsibility to report all income. When a taxpayer fails to pay what officials say he owes, the IRS can collect back taxes and assess penalties. The Internal Revenue Code imposes many different kinds of penalties, ranging from civil fines to imprisonment for criminal tax evasion.

The term *tax avoidance* is not defined by the IRS, but it is commonly used to describe the legal reduction of taxable income, such as through deductions, credits, and adjustments to income. Avoidance of tax is not a criminal offense. Taxpayers have the right to reduce, avoid, or minimize their taxes by legitimate means. Most taxpayers use at least a few methods of tax avoidance in order to reduce their taxable income and therefore lower their tax liability.

> **Example:** Tamera contributes to her employer-sponsored retirement plans with pretax funds. She also uses an employer-based flexible spending account for her medical expenses, which reduces her taxable income by making all of her medical expenses pretax. She owns a home and claims a deduction for interest she pays on her mortgage. All of these strategies lower her taxable income by using legal tax avoidance.

Tax evasion, on the other hand, is an illegal practice in which individuals or businesses intentionally avoid paying their true tax liabilities. Evasion involves some affirmative act to evade or defeat a tax, or payment of tax. Examples of affirmative acts are deceit, subterfuge, camouflage, concealment, attempts to obscure events, or make things seem other than they are.

IRS auditors are trained to spot common types of deception and fraud on tax returns. These acts are known as "badges of fraud" and include deducting personal items as business expenses, the overstatement of deductions, and the understatement of income. Other common tax evasion schemes include:

- Intentional omission of income, especially cash payments;
- Claiming fictitious deductions;
- False allocation of income;
- Improper claims, credits, or exemptions; and/or
- Concealment of assets.

Although most Americans comply with their tax obligations, the U.S. government estimates that 3% of taxpayers do not file tax returns at all. Tax evasion is a felony, and those caught evading taxes are subject to criminal charges and substantial penalties.

> **Note:** For each year a taxpayer willfully does not file a tax return, the penalty can include a fine of up to $25,000 and a prison sentence of up to one year. If it can be demonstrated that the taxpayer deliberately did not file in an attempt to evade taxation, the IRS can pursue a felony conviction, which can include an additional fine of up to $100,000 ($500,000 for corporations) and a maximum prison sentence of five years (IRC §7201).

Example: Victor owns a jewelry store. For several years, he failed to report cash he received from his stores. He often accepted large cash payments from his customers but did not report the income. He also kept a separate accounting system for the cash receivables as a second set of books. In addition, Victor broke cash receipts greater than $10,000 into smaller receipts in order to evade federal cash reporting requirements. When he filed his tax report, Victor reported income of $27,000, while his actual taxable income was nearly $195,000. Victor was convicted of committing tax evasion, a felony.[38]

Penalties Imposed Upon Taxpayers

The IRS can assess penalties on individual taxpayers who fail to file, fail to pay, or both. The failure-to-file penalty is generally greater than the failure-to-pay penalty. If someone is unable to pay all the taxes he owes, he is better off filing on time and paying as much as he can, as the IRS will consider payment options with individual taxpayers.

A taxpayer will not have to pay either penalty if he shows he failed to file or pay on time because of reasonable cause and not willful neglect.

Penalties are payable upon notice and demand. They are generally assessed, collected, and paid in the same manner as taxes. The taxpayer will receive a notice that contains:

- The name of the penalty,
- The applicable code section, and
- How the penalty was computed.

Failure-to-File Penalty: The penalty for filing late is usually 5% of the unpaid taxes for each month or part of a month that a return is late, up to a maximum of 25% of the amount due. The penalty is based on the tax that is not paid by the due date, without regard to extensions.

If both the failure-to-file penalty and the failure-to-pay penalty apply in any month, the 5% failure-to-file penalty is reduced by the failure-to-pay penalty. However, if a taxpayer files his return more than 60 days after the due date or extended due date, in 2017, the minimum penalty is the smaller of $210 or 100% of the unpaid tax.

If a taxpayer is owed a refund, he will not be assessed a failure-to-file penalty.

Failure-to-Pay Penalty: If a taxpayer does not pay his taxes by the due date, he will be subject to a failure-to-pay penalty of ½ of 1% (0.5%) of unpaid taxes for each month or part of a month after the due date that the taxes are not paid. This penalty can be as much as 25% of a taxpayer's unpaid taxes. If a taxpayer fails to file a tax return and it is determined that the failure to do so is fraudulent, the maximum penalty is increased from the regular 25% penalty to 75% of the amount owed.

The failure-to-pay penalty rate increases to a full 1% per month for any tax that remains unpaid the day after a demand for immediate payment is issued, or ten days after notice of intent to levy certain assets is issued. For taxpayers who filed on time but are unable to pay their tax liabilities, the failure-to-pay penalty rate is reduced to ¼ of 1% (0.25%) per month during any month in which the taxpayer has a valid installment agreement with the IRS.[39] The taxpayer will also owe interest on the amount due. Interest accrues daily on any unpaid tax from the due date of the return until the taxpayer pays in full.

---

[38] Example is based on an actual case prosecuted by the IRS Criminal Enforcement division.
[39] Regardless of whether or not the taxpayer has the ability to pay, it is always better to file and pay what you can. The IRS will normally work with a taxpayer who makes the attempt to be compliant with their tax obligations.

The IRS may abate a taxpayer's penalties for filing and paying late if the taxpayer can show reasonable cause. There are exceptions in the law for the following situations:
- A member of the Armed Forces serving in a combat zone or contingency operation.
- A citizen or resident alien working abroad
- Victims in certain disaster situations. In those situations, the IRS has the legal authority to extend filing and payment deadlines.[40]

Note: If a taxpayer is affected by a natural disaster in a presidentially declared disaster area, and the taxpayer receives a late filing or late payment penalty notice from the IRS that has an original or extended filing payment or deposit due date that falls within the postponement period, the taxpayer should call the telephone number on the notice to have the IRS abate the penalty.

Example: Yuliana was a victim of a Hurricane Harvey that took place on September 1, 2017 in Texas. Yuliana's business was flooded and severely damaged by the storm. The President declared a major disaster in the State of Texas. The IRS postponed filing deadlines as well as deposit deadlines for employment taxes for people who were living in the affected region. Yuliana later receives a notice from the IRS because the payroll tax returns for her business are delinquent. She calls the IRS disaster hotline to request tax relief, which is granted. Yuliana will receive additional time to file her payroll returns and make any applicable tax deposits.

Accuracy-Related Penalty on Underpayments

IRC §6662 describes penalties for accuracy-related violations of underpaying income tax, including penalties for substantial understatement, substantial valuation misstatement, and negligence or disregard of rules or regulations.

This section imposes an accuracy-related penalty equal to 20% of the underpayment to which Section 6662 applies. These penalties are calculated as a flat 20% of the net understatement of tax. In addition to other penalties, if the taxpayer provides fraudulent information on his tax return, he can be subject to a criminal fraud penalty,[41] as well.

Penalty for Substantial Understatement: For individual taxpayers, an understatement is considered substantial if it is more than the *larger* of:
- 10% of the correct tax, or
- $5,000.

This means that, if the understatement shown on the return is more than 10% of the correct tax or greater than $5,000 for individuals, it is considered a "substantial" understatement. For corporate taxpayers, an understatement is considered substantial if it is more than the lesser of:

- The greater of (1) 10% of the correct tax or (2) $10,000, or
- $10,000,000.[42]

---

[40] The IRS automatically identifies taxpayers located in the covered disaster area and applies automatic filing and payment relief. But affected taxpayers who reside or have a business located outside the covered disaster area must call the IRS disaster hotline to request tax relief.

[41] IRC §6663 imposes a penalty on any portion of an underpayment attributable to fraud. This would be a separate penalty, and in addition to, any other accuracy-related penalties that were assessed against the taxpayer.

[42] IRC §6662(d)(1)(B)

If the taxpayer can show that they made a reasonable attempt to report the correct tax, or if the taxpayer's position was adequately disclosed, this penalty may not potentially apply.

> **Example:** The IRS issued an audit notice to Harvest Corporation, a family farming business. The business was audited, and a large deduction was disallowed under examination. Disallowance of the deduction created a substantial understatement of 25% of the correct tax shown on the return. However, the company included a proper disclosure statement along with the original return, disclosing their position for the deduction. Harvest Corporation was issued a notice of deficiency for $15,800, disallowing the deduction, but an accuracy-related penalty was not assessed, because the company adequately disclosed their position, even if the deduction was later disallowed.

> **Example:** Crystal is a self-employed interior designer. In 2017, Crystal's tax returns were audited by the IRS. Crystal provided her accounting records and bank statements to the IRS. However, while her documents reflected the expenses allegedly incurred by the taxpayer, the records did not show why the alleged expenses were ordinary and necessary expenses that were deductible. Crystal claimed numerous large deductions for expensive furniture, cruises, and airline trips. Crystal could not provide a reasonable explanation for the deductions she claimed on her Schedule C. The IRS issued Crystal a notice of deficiency for $42,000 and an additional accuracy-related penalty of $8,400 under section 6662(a).

Penalty for Valuation Misstatement

A valuation misstatement can be either "substantial" [IRC § 6662(e)] or "gross" [IRC § 6662(h)]. "Substantial" valuation misstatements are subject to a 20% penalty. "Gross" valuation misstatements are subject to a 40% penalty.

The substantial valuation misstatement penalty generally applies when a taxpayer incorrectly reports an asset's value or its adjusted basis on a tax return; the value or basis is overstated by at least 150% of the correct value; and which results in an underpayment of tax of at least $5,000 (the threshold is $10,000 for most C corporations).

> **Example:** Walter donated a large parcel of land to a charitable foundation. He valued the donation at $9 million on his tax return and claimed a $3 million charitable deduction. The IRS examined his return and discovered that the land was significantly overvalued. The IRS adjusted the value of the land downward to $5 million, making Walter's true charitable deduction worth only $1.5 million. Walter is assessed a gross valuation misstatement penalty for overvaluing his property in order to receive an inflated deduction and pay less tax. The penalty rate would be 20% since the overstated amount of the land was greater than 150% of the land's correct value.

However, the penalty jumps to 40% of the net understatement of tax if the taxpayer claims a value for property on a tax return that is 200% or more of the correct amount. This is known as a gross valuation misstatement.

The valuation misstatement penalty also may apply if the price or valuation for any property or service claimed on a return is substantially *less* than the correct valuation. In the previous examples, the taxpayer attempted to claim larger deductions than they were legally entitled to claim. However, there are times when a taxpayer will attempt to "undervalue" an asset in order to escape tax, as well. This happens most often with the valuation of an estate. Since an estate is taxed on the value of its assets, a lower value could result in lower tax.

Example: Gary donated a conservation easement to a charitable trust. On his federal income tax return for that year, Gary valued his donation at $900,000 and claimed a large charitable contribution deduction. For the next three years, Gary claimed a carryover of charitable contribution deductions related to the conservation easement. The IRS later audits Gary's tax returns, and determined that he didn't meet the legal requirements for his charitable contribution. Gary cannot produce a qualified appraisal of the property that he donated. The IRS deems that the actual value of Gary's donation was $45,000. The actual value of the donation was far less than what was reported, and in Gary's case, the error is more than 200% of the asset's value. The IRS disallows the deduction, and assesses a 40% penalty against Gary for the gross valuation misstatement.

Example: After a Pennsylvania woman died, her executor initially valued her estate's assets at $4.45 million when he filed Form 706, the estate tax return. The executor did not hire an appraiser to help determine the correct value, and he used cost basis for many of the decedent's assets, even those that had substantially increased in value over time. The IRS disputed the valuation, putting the estate's assets at $10.2 million. The IRS assessed a 40% "gross valuation misstatement" penalty against the estate. The executor fought this determination by appealing to the courts, and the U.S. Tax Court ultimately ruled that $7 million was the correct value of the estate. Since the correct value of the estate was over 150% of what the executor originally reported, the IRS then imposed a 20% substantial valuation misstatement penalty upon the estate, which the Tax Court upheld.

A taxpayer may avoid both the substantial understatement and the substantial overvaluation penalties if he has substantial authority for his position or the position has a reasonable basis and is adequately disclosed.

Failure to Comply with Information Reporting Requirements (§6723): If a taxpayer does not include a Social Security number or the SSN of another person where required on a return, statement, or other document, he is subject to a penalty of $50 for each failure (up to a maximum of $100,000 per calendar year). The taxpayer also faces the $50 penalty if he refuses to give the SSN to another person (such as a tax preparer) when it is required on a tax return.

Negligence and Disregard of the Rules and Regulations Penalty: IRC §6662 defines negligence as any failure to make a reasonable attempt to comply with the internal revenue laws. The penalty may be imposed on taxpayers who carelessly, recklessly, or intentionally disregard IRS rules and regulations by taking positions on their returns with little or no effort to determine whether the positions are correct, or who knowingly take positions that are incorrect.

Civil Fraud Penalty (§6663): If there is any underpayment of tax due to fraud, a penalty of 75% of the underpayment will be assessed against the taxpayer. In the case of a joint return, the penalty will apply to both spouses only if some part of the underpayment is due to the fraud of each spouse. Examples of tax fraud include:

- Filing a false tax return
- Hiding or transferring assets or income
- Claiming false deductions
- Keeping a second set of books

- Failure to deposit receipts to business accounts
- Covering up sources of receipts or deliberately omitting income

Note: Negligence or simple ignorance of the law does not constitute fraud. The IRS characterizes fraud as a deliberate action for the purpose of "deceit, subterfuge, camouflage, concealment, some attempt to color or obscure events, or make things seem other than what they are."

Criminal Fraud Penalty: In addition to being a civil offense, fraud may also be a criminal offense. A criminal offense must generally include an element of willfulness, meaning a voluntary and intentional violation of a known legal duty. If IRS examiners find evidence of criminal fraud in the course of an audit, they will refer the case to the IRS Criminal Investigation Division.

Frivolous Tax Return Penalty (§6702): A frivolous tax return is one that does not include enough information to figure the correct tax, or that contains information clearly showing that the tax reported is substantially incorrect.

A taxpayer faces a penalty of $5,000 if he files a frivolous tax return or other frivolous submissions. This penalty is in addition to any other penalties provided by law. Frivolous submissions include tax protester arguments, such as contentions that filing of a tax return or payment of income tax is voluntary; that only foreign-source income is taxable; or that a taxpayer is not a citizen of the United States and thus not subject to federal income tax.

Alteration of a Jurat

Frivolous submissions also include taxpayers who alter or strike out the preprinted language above the space provided for a signature. This declaration is called the jurat.

Alteration of the jurat is prohibited and will result in a frivolous return.

Sign Here	Under penalties of perjury, I declare that I have examined this return and accompanying schedules and statements, and to the best of my knowledge and belief, they are true, correct, and complete. Declaration of preparer (other than taxpayer) is based on all information of which preparer has any knowledge.			
Joint return? See instructions. Keep a copy for your records.	Your signature	Date	Your occupation	Daytime phone number
	Spouse's signature. If a joint return, **both** must sign.	Date	Spouse's occupation	If the IRS sent you an Identity Protection PIN, enter it here (see inst.)

Civil penalties for altering a jurat may include:
- A $5,000 penalty imposed under §6702;
- Additional penalties for failure to file a return, failure to pay tax owed, and fraudulent failure to file a return under §6651; and
- A penalty of up to $25,000 under §6673 if the taxpayer makes frivolous arguments in the U.S. Tax Court.

Example: A taxpayer files Form 1040 for the 2017 tax year. The taxpayer signs the form, but crosses out the jurat on the return and writes the word "void" across it. This return is now considered frivolous and is subject to penalties.

Trust Fund Recovery Penalty (TFRP)

As authorized by IRC §6672, the trust fund recovery penalty involves the income and Social Security taxes an employer withholds from the wages of employees. These taxes are called trust fund taxes because they are held in trust on behalf of employees until they are remitted to the government. Sometimes, business owners neglect to remit these taxes to the IRS.

A trust fund recovery penalty equal to 100% of the amount of unpaid trust fund taxes can be assessed against anyone who is considered a "responsible person" in the business. This may include corporate officers, directors, stockholders, and rank-and-file employees. The IRS has assessed the penalty against accountants, bookkeepers, and even clerical staff, if they have authority to sign checks.

A person must be both "responsible" and "willful" to be liable for an employer's failure to collect or pay trust fund taxes. This means that he knew (or should have known) that the payroll taxes were not being remitted to the IRS, and that he also had the power to correct the problem.

Example: Thelma works for Smithy Construction as a full-time bookkeeper and processes all the payroll tax forms. She also has check-signing authority, so she can pay the bills when her boss is working off-site. In 2017, her boss has a heart attack, and his wife, Sherilynn, takes over the business in his absence. Sherilynn cannot manage the business properly and Smithy Construction is unable to meet its financial commitments. Sherilynn tells Thelma to pay vendors first. The business continues to withhold payroll taxes from employee paychecks, but does not remit the amounts to the IRS. Eventually, the business declares bankruptcy. Sherilynn disappears, and Thelma is contacted by the IRS. Even though Thelma was "just an employee" the IRS can assess the trust fund recovery penalty against her because she had check-signing authority, and she knew that the business was not remitting payroll taxes to the IRS as required.

Penalties Imposed on the Tax Practitioner

Just like taxpayers, tax professionals are also subject to penalties on improperly filed or fraudulent returns. Preparer fraud typically involves the preparation and filing of false income tax returns for clients. The returns may have inflated personal or business expenses, false deductions, unallowable credits, or excessive exemptions. Preparers may also manipulate income figures to obtain fraudulent tax credits, such as the Earned Income Tax Credit, for clients who are not eligible.

Sometimes a tax preparer will prepare a fraudulent return without the taxpayer being aware of the fraud. A preparer's clients may or may not know about the fraudulent items on their tax returns. Fraud may benefit preparers financially by:

- Diverting a portion of taxpayers' refunds for their own personal benefit,
- Increasing clientele by developing a reputation for obtaining large refunds; and/or
- Charging inflated fees for return preparation.

Example: Silvester is a tax preparer. In 2017, he prepares a return for his client, Rosalie. He gives Rosalie a complete copy of the return, and she goes home. After Rosalie leaves his office, Silvester adds fraudulent credits to her return, then adds his personal bank account to Rosalie's Form 8888, funneling a portion of the refund to himself.[43] Silvester has committed tax fraud.

---

[43] Example based on an actual criminal case. Criminal Case No. 14CR3658-JM.

In the case of a tax professional who has committed tax fraud, or filed fraudulent returns, the IRS' Criminal Investigation Division works closely with the US Justice Department to prosecute the tax professionals who commit financial fraud.

Penalties for Substantial Understatement

If a tax return preparer willfully understates a client's tax liability, he is subject to penalties. Under IRS regulations, understatement of liability means:

- Understating net tax payable
- Overstating the net amount creditable or refundable

Under IRC §6694, there are two specific penalties when a tax preparer understates a taxpayer's liability. The first penalty (§6694(a)) is for a non-willful act. The second penalty, which is much harsher, is for a willful act. According to the IRS, the test is whether there was an intentional violation of the law. "Willfulness" is defined as a voluntary, intentional violation of a known legal duty.[44]

- **IRC § 6694(a) – Understatement due to unreasonable position:** If there is an understatement on a tax return due to an unreasonable position, the penalty is the greater of:
  - $1,000 per tax return, or
  - 50% of the income the preparer received (or would have received) in income for preparing the tax return with the understatement.

Note: This penalty applies when a preparer knows, or "reasonably should have known," that the position was unreasonable and would not have been sustained on its merits. Even if disclosure requirements are met, penalties may apply if the position is attributable to a tax shelter, if it is not properly substantiated, or if the taxpayer failed to keep adequate books and records to support the item or position. A preparer may be excused from the penalty if he acted in good faith and there was reasonable cause for the understatement.

- **IRC § 6694(b) – Understatement due to willful or reckless conduct:** If a tax return preparer shows negligent or willful disregard of IRS rules and regulations, and makes a willful or reckless attempt to understate tax liability, the penalty is the greater of:
  - $5,000 per tax return, or
  - 75% of the income the preparer received (or would have received) in income for preparing the tax return with the understatement.[45]

Example: Oliver is a tax preparer. He prepares a tax return for a client, but ignores $50,000 of income that the client had told him about. Oliver also reported five dependents on the return, when the client said he had only two dependents. Oliver would be subject to a §6694 penalty.

If a tax return preparer is subject to a penalty for understatement of liability and this includes a change to the Earned Income Tax Credit, the preparer may be subject to additional penalties for failure to exercise due diligence while claiming the EITC.

IRC §6694 specifies that the understatement penalty will be abated if, under final judicial decision, it is found that there is no actual understatement of liability. Sometimes this occurs when a Tax Court case is decided in favor of the taxpayer.

---

[44] Internal Revenue Manual, Part 25. Special Topics, Chapter 1. Fraud Handbook
[45] IRC Sect. 6694(B)(1)(B)

Example: In 2017, Denny was audited, and a large deduction was disallowed on his return. Cassandra is Denny's tax attorney, and she prepared the return under examination. In addition to assessing penalties against Denny himself, the IRS also assesses the § 6694(b) understatement penalty against Cassandra, his tax preparer. Denny and Cassandra both believe that the tax position on the return is correct, and Denny takes his case all the way to the Tax Court, where Cassandra represents him. The U.S. Tax Court decides in Denny's favor. The court victory allows Denny to claim the previously disallowed deduction in full. Denny's understatement penalty is abated, and Cassandra's preparer penalty is abated, as well.

Listing of Preparer Additional Penalties and Amounts

Exam Tip: Specific penalties that may be imposed on both preparers and taxpayers are frequently tested on Part 3 of the EA exam. Although it is not generally necessary to memorize the IRC section numbers, test-takers should be familiar with each of the penalties and the penalty amounts listed in this PassKey study guide.

IRC § 6695(a) – Failure to furnish copy to taxpayer: The penalty is $50 for each failure to furnish a copy of a completed return to a taxpayer. The maximum penalty is $25,500[46] a year.

IRC § 6695(b) – Failure to sign return: The penalty is $50 for each failure to sign a return. The maximum penalty imposed on any tax preparer is $25,500 a year.

IRC § 6695(c) – Failure to furnish identifying number: The penalty is $50 for each failure to furnish an identifying number (an SSN, ATIN, or ITIN, whichever applies) on a tax return. The maximum penalty is $25,500 a year.

IRC § 6695(d) – Failure to retain copy of the return (or list): The penalty is $50 for each failure to retain a copy (or list) of each completed return or claim. The maximum penalty is $25,500 a year.

IRC § 6695(e) – Failure to file correct information returns. The penalty is $50 for each failure to file correct information returns for a client (examples: Forms 1099 or other information returns). The maximum penalty is $25,500 a year.

IRC § 6695(f) – Negotiation of a taxpayer's refund check: The penalty is $510 in 2017 for a tax return preparer who endorses or negotiates any check made in respect of taxes imposed by Title 26 which is issued to a taxpayer. This penalty is adjusted for inflation.

IRC § 6695(g) – Failure to exercise due diligence in determining eligibility for EITC, AOTC, or the CTC/ACTC: The penalty in 2017 is $510 for each failure to comply with the EITC, AOTC, or CTC due diligence requirements. This penalty is adjusted for inflation.

IRC § 6700 – Promoting abusive tax shelters: The penalty is for a promoter of an abusive tax shelter is $1,000 for each organization or sale of an abusive plan or arrangement (or, if lesser, 100% of the income derived from the activity).

IRC § 6701 – Penalties for aiding and abetting understatement of tax liability: The penalty is $1,000 ($10,000 if relating to a corporation's tax return) for aiding and abetting in an understatement of a tax liability. Any preparer subject to the penalty shall be penalized only once for documents relating to the same taxpayer for a single tax period or event.

---

[46] These penalties are now adjusted for inflation every year.

IRC § 6713 – (Civil penalty) Disclosure or use of information by preparers of returns: The penalty is $250 for each unauthorized disclosure or use of information furnished for, or in connection with, the preparation of a return. The maximum penalty is $10,000 a year.

IRC § 7216 – (Criminal provision) Disclosure or use of information by preparers of returns: Those found guilty of knowingly or recklessly disclosing information furnished in connection with a tax return or using such information for any purpose other than preparing or assisting in the preparation of such return. Upon conviction, a fine of up to $1,000, imprisonment for not more than 1 year, or both (along with the costs of prosecution).

IRC § 7206 – Fraud and false statements: Those found guilty of felony tax fraud, upon conviction, may be subject to a fine of up to $100,000 ($500,000 in the case of a corporation), jail time of up to 3 years, or both (together with the costs of prosecution).

IRC § 7207 – Filing a fraudulent return, statement, or other document: Any preparer who willfully files a false statement or document with the IRS may be convicted of a misdemeanor. And, upon conviction, a fine of up to $10,000 ($50,000 in the case of a corporation), plus imprisonment of not more than one year, or both.

IRC § 7407 – Action to enjoin tax return preparers: A federal district court may enjoin a tax return preparer from engaging in certain proscribed conduct, or in extreme cases, from continuing to act as a tax return preparer altogether.

IRC § 7408 – Action to enjoin specified conduct related to tax shelters and reportable transactions

A federal district court may enjoin a person from engaging in certain proscribed conduct (including any action, or failure to take action, which is in violation of Circular 230).

If a penalty is assessed against a tax preparer and he does not agree with the assessment, he may request a conference with the IRS officer or agent and explain why the penalty is not warranted. The preparer may also wait for the penalty to be assessed, pay the penalty within 30 days, and then file a claim for refund.

2017 Preparer (Most Common) Penalties Quick reference		
Type of Violation	**Penalty Per Violation**	**Calendar Year Maximum**
Failure to furnish a tax return copy to taxpayer (sec. 6695(a))	$50	$25,500
Failure to sign a taxpayer's return (sec. 6695(b))	$50	$25,500
Failure to furnish a PTIN on a return (sec. 6695(c))	$50	$25,500
Failure to retain copy or list of returns prepared (sec. 6695(d))	$50	$25,500
Failure to file correct information returns (sec. 6695(e))	$50	$25,500
Negotiation of a taxpayer's refund check (sec. 6695(f))	$510	No limit
Failure to be diligent in determining eligibility for Earned Income Tax Credit, American Opportunity Credit, or Child Tax Credit (sec. 6695(g))	$510	No limit

Other Preparer Penalties Quick Reference Guide		
IRC	Violation	Penalty
§6695	Failure to furnish a copy of return/claim for refund to taxpayer	$50 per failure/$25,500 maximum per year
	Failure to sign a return/claim for refund	$50 per failure/$25,500 maximum per year
	Failure to furnish a PTIN on a return	$50 per failure/$25,500 maximum per year
	Failure to retain a copy or list for a return/claim for refund	$50 per failure/$25,500 maximum per year
	Failure to file correct information returns	$50 per failure/$25,500 maximum per year
	Endorse, cash, or deposit a taxpayer's refund check	$510 per failure/No maximum fine
	Failure to comply with EITC, CTC, or AOTC due diligence requirements	$510 per failure/No maximum fine
§6694	Understatement due to an unreasonable position	Greater of $1,000 per return or 50% of fees derived by the preparer
	Understatement due to negligent/willful disregard	Greater of $5,000 per return or 75% of fees derived by the preparer
§6700	Sells, organizes, or promotes abusive tax shelter	Lesser of $1,000 per activity, or 100% of gross income derived from the activity
§6701	Aiding/abetting understatement of tax liability	$1,000 per individual return, $10,000 per corporate return
§6713	Unauthorized disclosure of client information (civil)	$250 per disclosure (not per return)/ $10,000 maximum per year
§7216	Unauthorized disclosure of client information (criminal)	$1,000 fine and/or up to one year in prison

1. Adele is a sole proprietor who files a Schedule C tax return. She meets with Carlos, her Enrolled Agent, and gives him a list of expenses she says she incurred for a home office, business mileage, travel, and business meals. She does not bring any receipts or other documentation to the meeting. What is Carlos required to do in order to prepare an accurate tax return for Adele?

A. Nothing further. Carlos can rely on the list of Adele's expenses without seeing any documentation.
B. Carlos must make appropriate inquiries of Adele about her list of expenses. However, he does not need to actually see any documentation if she tells him she did not retain any receipts or keep a mileage log.
C. Carlos must ask relevant and probing questions of Adele to help determine if the expenses are allowable. He must also ask if she has receipts to support the expenses.
D. Carlos must review all of Adele's receipts and her mileage log prior to preparing her tax return.

2. Basil is a tax preparer. He does not want to include his PTIN on his client's returns. What penalty does Basil face for failing to include his PTIN on a client's return?

A. No penalty, but he may receive an official censure from the IRS.
B. A fine of $50 per failure to provide his PTIN.
C. A fine of $100 per failure to provide his PTIN.
D. A fine of $400 per year.

3. All of the following statements regarding the fraud penalty are correct except:

A. If there is any underpayment of tax due to fraud, a penalty of 75% of the underpayment will be assessed against the taxpayer.
B. The fraud penalty on a joint return will automatically apply to each spouse.
C. IRS examiners who find strong evidence of fraud may refer the case to the IRS Criminal Investigation Division for possible criminal prosecution.
D. Negligence or simple ignorance of the law does not constitute fraud.

4. What percentage of tax must a taxpayer pay if he is guilty of a substantial understatement penalty?

A. 5% of the net understatement of tax.
B. 10% of the net understatement of tax.
C. 20% of the net understatement of tax.
D. 25% of the net understatement of tax.

5. Which penalty is greater: the failure-to-file penalty or the failure-to-pay penalty?

A. The failure-to-file penalty.
B. The failure-to-pay penalty.
C. Both penalties are equal.
D. It depends on the taxpayer's individual facts and circumstances.

6. Siobhan hires a friend, Gustav, to prepare her income tax returns. Gustav has prepared returns for several years, but is not a CPA, an attorney, or an Enrolled Agent. Although he knows that Siobhan is single and childless, he prepares her tax return based on the head of household filing status with two qualifying children so that Siobhan may qualify for the Earned Income Tax Credit, and thus a larger refund. Siobhan reviews a copy of the tax return and signs it. Gustav also signs the return and submits it to the IRS for processing. If the IRS detects the fraudulent credit, which of the two, if either, will face potential penalties?

A. Gustav only.
B. Siobhan only.
C. Both Gustav and Siobhan.
D. Neither. Since Gustav is not a CPA, attorney, or Enrolled Agent, he is not subject to penalties for paid tax return penalties. Siobhan is not responsible for any penalties because she relied upon Gustav's professional advice in preparing her return.

7. Which of the following statements is correct?

A. Tax avoidance and tax evasion are always illegal.
B. Taxpayers who commit fraud are subject to civil penalties only.
C. The IRS will assess a failure-to-file penalty or a failure-to-pay penalty, but never both.
D. A felony conviction against a taxpayer who deliberately failed to file taxes could mean a fine of up to $100,000 and a prison sentence of up to five years.

8. What is the penalty a preparer faces for understating income on a tax return due to an unreasonable position that is not adequately disclosed (non-willful)?

A. $1,000 per tax return or 50% of the income the preparer received in fees for preparing the tax return with the understatement.
B. $5,000 per tax return.
C. 50% of the understatement.
D. No penalty, if the preparer failed to adequately disclose the position on the return.

9. All of the following statements about the trust fund recovery penalty are correct except:

A. The penalty is equal to 100% of the amount that was not properly paid.
B. The IRS primarily targets employees for this penalty.
C. The penalty involves payroll taxes withheld from the wages of employees.
D. The penalty can be assessed against anyone who is considered a responsible person and has failed to remit trust fund taxes to the U.S. government.

10. What is the penalty for a taxpayer who has filed a return determined to be frivolous?

A. $600, plus any other penalty provided by law.
B. $1,000, plus any other penalty provided by law.
C. $5,000, plus any other penalty provided by law.
D. $10,000, plus any other penalty provided by law.

11. Which of the following statements is not correct?

A. If no other provisions apply, the statute of limitations for an IRS examination of a return is three years after the return was filed or the return was due, whichever is later.
B. If more than 25% of gross income has been omitted from the tax return, the statute of limitations is six years after the return was filed.
C. If a fraudulent return is filed, the statute of limitations is seven years.
D. If a tax return is not filed at all, there is no statute of limitations.

12. What is not considered a "badge of fraud" by the IRS?

A. Sloppy recordkeeping.
B. Taking improper credits.
C. All-cash businesses.
D. Deductions for foreign travel.

13. If there is substantial unreported income (over 25%), the IRS may audit tax returns for up to _____ after the filing date.

A. Three years.
B. Four years.
C. Six years.
D. Indefinitely.

14. Accuracy-related penalties in IRC §6662 are imposed for substantial understatement of income tax and also for:

A. Substantial misstatement of the value of assets.
B. Substantial overstatement of income tax.
C. Preparer fraud related to the Earned Income Tax Credit.
D. Negligence while representing a business entity.

15. What is the minimum penalty for failing to file a tax return more than 60 days late (assuming the taxpayer is not owed a refund)?

A. 100% of the unpaid tax.
B. A fee of $135 or 90% of the unpaid tax, whichever is greater.
C. The smaller of $210 or 100% of the unpaid tax.
D. A minimum of 25% of a taxpayer's unpaid tax.

16. Colleen owns a business and has never filed a tax return. How long should she keep her records?

A. Three years if she owes additional tax.
B. Seven years if she files a claim for a loss from worthless securities.
C. For an unlimited period of time if she does not file a return.
D. Ten years.

17. What penalty does a tax return preparer face if he cashes a client's tax refund check?

A. Nothing. This is acceptable so long as the client has given written permission to do so.
B. A fine of $50 for each violation.
C. A fine of $100 for each violation.
D. A fine of $510 for each violation.

18. An Enrolled Agent (EA) can be sanctioned under Circular 230 in each of the following ways EXCEPT:

A. Monetary penalty
B. Imprisonment
C. Censure
D. Disbarment

1. The answer is C. To prepare an accurate Schedule C return, a tax return preparer can generally rely in good faith, without verification, on information a client provides. However, a preparer cannot ignore the implications of the information. Carlos must make reasonable inquiries if the information appears to be incorrect, inconsistent, or incomplete. Since Adele may not fully understand the tax laws and may incorrectly believe she can claim deductions for non-qualifying expenses, Carlos must ask probing and relevant questions to help determine if the expenses are allowable. He must also ask if Adele has receipts to support the expenses, and further instruct her to keep the receipts in case the IRS requests supporting documentation.

2. The answer is B. Basil may receive a penalty of $50 per failure. IRC §6695 lists the penalties that may be assessed when it comes to the preparation of tax returns for other persons. The penalty is $50 for each violation of the following:

- Failure to furnish a copy of a return or claim to a taxpayer
- Failure to sign a return or claim for refund
- Failure to furnish an identifying number (PTIN) on a return
- Failure to retain a copy or list of a return or claim
- Failure to file correct information returns

3. The answer is B. The fraud penalty on a joint return does not automatically apply to a spouse unless some part of the underpayment is due to the fraud committed by that spouse.

4. The answer is C. The substantial understatement penalty is calculated as a flat 20% of the net understatement of tax. A taxpayer may also face additional fraud-related penalties if he has provided false information on his tax return.

5. The answer is A. The penalty for filing late (or not filing at all) is usually 5% of the unpaid taxes for each month that a return is late. The penalty for not paying taxes by the due date is less: ½ of 1% (0.5%). The IRS advises that if someone is unable to pay all the taxes he owes, he is better off filing on time and paying as much as he can.

6. The answer is C. The taxpayer is ultimately responsible for the accuracy of her own return. However, a tax return preparer, whether officially licensed or not, also signs a tax return attesting to its accuracy under penalties of perjury. Both Gustav and Siobhan could face penalties and other legal action in relation to the fraudulently claimed Earned Income Credit.

7. The answer is D. This is the maximum penalty and prison sentence in a tax evasion case. The other statements are false. Tax avoidance is not illegal. Taxpayers who commit fraud are subject to criminal penalties as well as civil. The IRS may assess both failure-to-file and failure-to-pay penalties.

8. The answer is A. A preparer faces an understatement penalty of $1,000 per tax return or 50% of the income the preparer received in fees for preparing the tax return with the understatement. If the position is adequately disclosed on the return, the penalty generally will not apply.

9. The answer is B. The trust fund recovery penalty is levied against employers, or other responsible persons, who have failed to pay the appropriate payroll taxes to the U.S. government.

10. The answer is C. Any taxpayer who files a return found to be frivolous may be fined $5,000, in addition to any other penalties provided by law. This penalty may be doubled on a joint return.

11. The answer is C. If a fraudulent tax return is filed, there is no statute of limitations. Under federal law, a tax return is fraudulent if the taxpayer files it knowing that the return either omits taxable income or claims one or more deductions that are not allowable.

12. The answer is D. IRS auditors are trained to spot common types of deception and attempts to defraud on tax returns. These acts are known as badges of fraud and include deducting personal items as business expenses, the overstatement of deductions, and the understatement of income. Simply having deductions for foreign travel is not an indication of potential illegal behavior on the part of a taxpayer.

13. The answer is C. In most cases, tax returns can be audited for up to three years after filing. However, the IRS may audit for up to six years if there is substantial unreported income (over 25%).

14. The answer is A. Accuracy-related penalties in IRC §6662 are imposed for substantial understatement of income tax and also for a substantial misstatement of the value of assets. IRC §6662 imposes penalties on taxpayers who misstate the value of assets in order to reap tax benefits. The penalty is 20% of the net understatement of tax for assets incorrectly valued at 150% or more than the correct amount of valuation or adjusted basis. The penalty increases to 40% of the net understatement of tax for assets incorrectly valued at 200% or more than the correct amount of valuation or adjusted basis.

15. The answer is C. In 2017, the minimum penalty for filing a tax return more than 60 days late is now the smaller of $210 or 100% of the unpaid tax.

16. The answer is C. A taxpayer must keep records as long as they are needed for the administration of any provision of the IRC. Taxpayers must keep records that support an item of income or deduction on a tax return until the statute of limitations for that return runs out. If a tax return is not filed, there is no time limit.

17. The answer is D. It is illegal for tax return preparers to negotiate or cash a taxpayer's refund check. A preparer faces a fine of $510 for each violation.

18. The answer is B. An Enrolled Agent can be sanctioned under Circular 230 in various ways, but imprisonment would be a consequence of criminal activity and would not fall under the jurisdiction of Circular 230.

Unit 8: Practitioner Misconduct

More Reading:
Publication 947, *Practice Before the IRS and Power of Attorney*

The IRS's Office of Professional Responsibility (OPR) is responsible for interpreting and applying the provisions of Circular 230 to ensure that tax professionals follow the law. The office's oversight generally covers all individuals who interact with federal tax administration, whether in person, orally, in writing, or by the preparation and submission of documents.

The following are subject to Circular 230 jurisdiction, and thus to OPR oversight:

- State licensed attorneys and CPAs who interact with federal tax administration at any level and capacity.
- Enrolled agents, enrolled retirement plan agents, and enrolled actuaries.
- Persons providing appraisals used in connection with tax matters (such as valuing estate and gift assets).
- Unlicensed individuals who represent taxpayers before the IRS examination division, IRS customer service, and Taxpayer Advocate Service in connection with returns they prepared and signed.
- Licensed and unlicensed individuals who give written advice that has the potential for tax avoidance or evasion.
- Any person submitting a power of attorney in connection with limited representation or special authorization to practice before the IRS in a specific matter before the agency.

The OPR has authority in matters related to practitioner standards and exclusive authority in matters involving discipline and sanctions. This authority includes:

- Receiving and processing referrals regarding allegations of misconduct under Circular 230 and initiating disciplinary proceedings against individuals or entities relating to allegations or findings of practitioner misconduct consistent with the applicable disciplinary rules under Circular 230.
- Making final determinations on appeals regarding practitioner eligibility or suitability decisions and recommending and imposing sanctions for violations under Circular 230.
- Making determinations on whether to appeal administrative law judge decisions and reviewing and determining petitions from practitioners seeking reinstatement to practice.

Four Categories of Practitioner Misconduct

There are four broad categories of practitioner misconduct, all of which may be reasons for the OPR to initiate disciplinary action against a tax professional:

- **Misconduct while representing a taxpayer**
- **Misconduct related to the practitioner's own return**
- **Giving a false opinion knowingly, recklessly, or through gross incompetence**
- **Misconduct not directly involving IRS representation (such as conviction of a criminal act)**

Circular 230, §10.51 outlines many instances in which the OPR might sanction a practitioner for incompetence or disreputable conduct. Types of disreputable conduct include, but are not limited to:

- Conviction of any criminal offense under federal tax laws.
- Conviction of any criminal offense involving dishonesty or breach of trust.

- Conviction of any felony under federal or state law in which the conduct renders the practitioner unfit to practice before the IRS.
- Giving false or misleading information, or participating in any way in the giving of false or misleading information to the Department of the Treasury.
- Soliciting employment as prohibited under Circular 230 or making false or misleading representations with intent to deceive a client.
- Willfully failing to file a federal tax return, or willfully evading any assessment or payment of any federal tax.
- Willfully assisting a client in violating any federal tax law, or knowingly counseling a client to evade federal taxes.
- Misappropriating funds received from a client for purposes of payment of taxes.
- Attempting to influence any IRS officer by the use of threats, false accusations, duress, coercion, or bribery.
- Disbarment or suspension from practice as a CPA, actuary or attorney.[47]
- Knowingly aiding and abetting another person to practice before the IRS during a period of suspension, disbarment, or ineligibility of such other person.
- Contemptuous conduct in connection with practice before the IRS, including the use of abusive language, knowingly making false accusations or statements, or circulating or publishing malicious or libelous matter.
- Willfully disclosing or using private tax return information.
- Willfully failing to sign a tax return.
- Willfully failing to e-file a return.
- Willfully signing a tax return without a valid PTIN.
- Willfully representing a taxpayer before the IRS without appropriate authorization.

Example: Mirabella is an Enrolled Agent with a tax preparation business. In 2017, she was convicted of forgery because she forged her father's signature on several checks and cashed them. Although this was a case unrelated to her tax preparation firm, Mirabella is guilty of disreputable conduct because she was convicted of any criminal offense involving dishonesty or breach of trust. The IRS can disbar her and strip her of her enrollment.

In addition, the most recent Circular 230 revision expands part of §10.51 that prohibits "giving a false opinion, knowingly, recklessly, or through gross incompetence." False opinions include those that reflect or result from:

- A knowing misstatement of fact or law.
- An assertion of a position known to be unwarranted under existing law.
- Counseling or assisting in conduct known to be illegal or fraudulent.
- Concealing matters required by law to be revealed.
- Consciously disregarding information indicating that material facts expressed in the opinion or offering material are false or misleading.

---

[47] For example, an attorney who is disbarred and loses his license at the state level would also be disbarred by the OPR at the federal level and be unable to represent taxpayers before the IRS.

The IRS will consider a practitioner's pattern of conduct to assess whether it reflects gross incompetence, meaning "gross indifference, preparation which is grossly inadequate under the circumstances, and a consistent failure to perform obligations to the client."

Some examples of other tax preparer misconduct include fee disputes and bad behavior such as physical threats against a client or former client.

Referrals to the Office of Professional Responsibility (OPR)

Most disciplinary cases opened by the Office of Professional Responsibility (OPR) result from internal and external referrals. OPR relies heavily on referrals involving tax practitioner misconduct from several sources including IRS employees, taxpayers, tax practitioners, law enforcement agencies, and U.S. state licensing authorities. An IRS employee who believes a practitioner has violated any provision in Circular 230 is required to file a written report to the OPR. Referrals are also mandatory following the assessment of penalties for violations of §6694(b) (a willful attempt to understate the liability for tax).

A referral must also be made when there are penalties or sanctions imposed that relate to the promotion of abusive tax shelters (§6700), or aiding and abetting the understatement of a tax liability (§6701(a)).

The OPR says other common reasons for referral include:
- Inaccurate or unreasonable entries/omissions on tax returns
- A lack of due diligence exercised by the practitioner
- Cashing, diverting, or splitting a taxpayer's refund by electronic or other means
- Patterns of misconduct involving multiple years, multiple clients, or unprofessional conduct demonstrated to multiple IRS employees
- Potential conflict of interest situations, such as representation of both spouses who have a joint liability

A taxpayer may file a complaint against a tax return preparer by using Form 14157 and submitting it to the Return Preparer Office, which will undertake an initial investigation before referring a case to the OPR. The form allows identification of complaints within the following categories: theft of refund, e-file issues, preparer misconduct, PTIN issues, false documents, employment taxes, and other issues.

Anonymous complaints are allowed. However, if a taxpayer chooses to submit his name and other personal information when he files a complaint, the information will not be shared with the individual or business being reported.

Disciplinary Sanctions

The OPR may impose a wide range of sanctions upon practitioners and other preparers who are subject to Circular 230 jurisdiction:

Reprimand: A reprimand is the least severe sanction. It is a private letter from the director of the OPR, stating the practitioner has committed some kind of misconduct under Circular 230. Although the issuance of a reprimand is kept private, it stays on a practitioner's record.

Censure: Censure is a public reprimand, with the practitioner's name published in the Internal Revenue Bulletin. The facts of the case that triggered the censure are not published. Unlike disbarment or suspension, censure generally does not prevent a practitioner from representing taxpayers before the IRS. However, in certain situations, a censure may place conditions on a practitioner's future representations in order to promote high standards of conduct.

Suspension from Practice before the IRS: An individual who is suspended is not eligible to represent taxpayers before the IRS during the term of the suspension. Suspensions may be imposed for a period of one to 60 months (five years).

Disbarment from Practice before the IRS: An individual who is disbarred is not eligible to represent taxpayers before the IRS. Disbarment lasts a minimum of five years, and Circular 230 requires the practitioner to demonstrate that he has regained fitness to practice before the IRS before he may be reinstated. As a result of suspension or disbarment, the practitioner will have the matter that caused the disbarment or suspension published in the Internal Revenue Bulletin.

Monetary Penalty: A monetary penalty may be imposed on an individual or a firm, or both, and can be in addition to any censure, suspension, or disbarment. The amount of the penalty may be up to the gross income derived, or to be derived, from the conduct that triggered the penalty.

> **Example:** Maynard is a CPA whose personal tax returns were audited by the IRS. The audit found he was improperly claiming personal expenses as business deductions and he had not timely filed his own tax returns. Even though no misconduct was discovered that related to his clients, Maynard was suspended from practice by the OPR for a period of three years. The Internal Revenue Bulletin listed his name, length of time of the suspension, and personal tax compliance issues as the reasons for the disciplinary action.

The Official Complaint Process

The OPR's response to an official complaint about a tax preparer or other referral about possible misconduct will vary depending upon the seriousness of the allegation. The OPR will first investigate whether a violation has occurred, whether the violation is one that calls into question a practitioner's fitness to continue to practice, and if so, what an appropriate sanction might be.

When it has identified a violation following its preliminary investigation, the OPR will send a "Pre-Allegation Notice" to the practitioner regarding the alleged conduct. The notice gives the practitioner an opportunity to provide evidence or documentation in the case. The OPR will then determine the appropriate level of discipline warranted for the violation and try to reach an agreement with the practitioner on a sanction. If an agreement cannot be reached, the OPR will draft a complaint and refer the case to the Office of Chief Counsel, General Legal Services (GLS). The practitioner will have one final opportunity to resolve the matter before a formal disciplinary hearing.

When a formal complaint is issued against a practitioner, the complaint must:

- Name the respondent.
- Provide a clear and concise description of the facts.
- Be signed by the director of the OPR.
- Describe the type of sanction.

If suspension is sought, the duration must be specified. The complaint may be served to the practitioner in one of the following ways: certified mail; first-class mail if returned undelivered by certified mail; private delivery service; in person; or by leaving the complaint at the office of the practitioner. Electronic delivery, such as email, is not a valid means of serving a complaint.

The complaint must specify a date by which the practitioner is required to respond, which must be at least 30 days after it is served. Within ten days of serving the complaint, copies of the evidence against the practitioner must also be served.

When a practitioner responds to a complaint, he is expected to specifically admit or deny each allegation, or state that he does not have enough information to know whether it is true or false.

He cannot deny a material allegation in the complaint when he knows it to be true. If the practitioner fails to respond to a complaint, it constitutes an admission of guilt and sanctions may be imposed without a hearing.

After a practitioner responds to a complaint, a hearing will be scheduled for an administrative law judge to hear the evidence and decide whether the OPR has proven its case.

> **Note:** To prevail in a disciplinary action involving suspension or disbarment, the OPR must prove by "clear and convincing evidence" that the practitioner willfully violated one or more provisions of Circular 230. "Willful" is defined as a voluntary, intentional violation of a known legal duty.

During a hearing, the practitioner may appear in person or be represented by an attorney or another practitioner. The OPR may be represented by a GLS attorney or by another IRS employee assigned to the case. Within 180 days of the conclusion of a hearing, the administrative law judge must enter a decision.

If there is no appeal, the decision by the administrative law judge becomes final. However, either party—the OPR or the practitioner—may appeal the judge's decision with the Treasury Appellate Authority within 30 days.

The Treasury Appellate Authority will receive briefs and render what is known as the "Final Agency Decision."

For the OPR, this decision is final, but the practitioner may contest the Final Agency Decision in a U.S. district court. The judge will review the findings from the administrative law hearing, but will only set aside the decision if it is considered arbitrary or capricious, contrary to law, or an abuse of discretion.

> **Note:** A practitioner who has been disbarred may petition the OPR for reinstatement after five years. The OPR may reinstate the practitioner if it determines that his conduct is not likely to be in violation of regulations and if granting the reinstatement is not contrary to the public interest.

> **Note:** Under a new provision in the latest revision to Circular 230, the OPR has the right to use expedited suspension procedures against a practitioner under certain circumstances. First, §10.82 allows for these procedures when an attorney or CPA has already had his license revoked for cause by any state licensing agency or board. Further, expedited procedures can be used when a practitioner has been convicted of a crime involving dishonesty or breach of trust, or when he has demonstrated a pattern of "willful disreputable conduct" by failing to comply with certain of his personal federal tax filing obligations. §10.82 gives the OPR the ability to move more quickly in sanctioning practitioners. If a practitioner fails to respond to a §10.82 complaint or does not appear at a §10.82 conference, the OPR can suspend the practitioner immediately.

Example: The OPR receives a referral from another practitioner regarding Melissa, an Enrolled Agent. After an investigation and preliminary discussions with Melissa, the OPR drafts a complaint citing violations of Circular 230. The case is referred to the Office of Chief Counsel, which sends the complaint by certified mail alleging that Melissa charged unconscionable fees, gave irresponsible advice to clients, and falsified documents. Thirty days later, Melissa offers a response in writing. The case goes before an administrative judge, who listens to evidence presented by the OPR and by Melissa's attorney. Within 180 days, the judge issues his ruling, which agrees with the OPR's recommendation that Melissa be disbarred. She chooses not to appeal and is banned from practice before the IRS.

Prohibited Actions during Suspension or Disbarment

During disbarment or suspension, a practitioner will not be allowed to practice in any capacity before the IRS (except to represent himself). A disbarred or suspended practitioner may not:

- Prepare or file documents or other correspondence with the IRS. The restriction applies regardless of whether the individual signs the documents and regardless of whether the individual personally files, or directs another person to file, documents with the IRS. However, as a result of the *Loving* case, disbarred and suspended practitioners are eligible to prepare and file tax returns for compensation.[48]
- Render written advice with respect to any entity, transaction, plan, or arrangement having the potential for tax avoidance or evasion.
- Represent a client at conferences, hearings, and meetings.
- Execute waivers, consents, or closing agreements; receive a taxpayer's refund check; or sign a tax return on behalf of a taxpayer.
- File powers of attorney with the IRS.
- Accept assistance from another person (or request assistance) or assist another person (or offer assistance) if the assistance relates to a matter constituting practice before the IRS, or enlist another person for purposes of practicing before the IRS.
- State or imply that he is eligible to practice before the IRS.

Example: Adrianne is a CPA who prepares tax returns. In 2017, she hires an Enrolled Agent named Julius. During the year, Julius comes under investigation by the Office of Professional Responsibility. Julius is later disbarred for financial fraud and loses his EA license. Adrianne must dismiss Julius as her employee. She cannot accept assistance from, or employ, a disbarred practitioner.

However, a disbarred or suspended individual is still allowed to:

- Represent himself in any matter.
- As mentioned previously, prepare tax returns for clients for compensation (due to the outcome of the *Loving* case).
- Appear before the IRS as a trustee, receiver, guardian, administrator, executor, or other fiduciary if duly qualified/authorized under the law of the relevant jurisdiction.
- Appear as a witness for a taxpayer.
- Furnish information at the request of the IRS or any of its officers or employees.

---

[48] The Office of Professional Responsibility released an official statement on this matter (OPR Statement 20052314).

- Receive IRS information pursuant to a valid tax information authorization. However, simply receiving this information does not entitle a disbarred or suspended preparer to practice before the IRS on behalf of that taxpayer.

Example: Bartlett is an attorney who was disbarred in 2017 for criminal wire fraud. Bartlett can no longer give tax advice or represent clients before the IRS. However, he is the legal guardian of his disabled adult daughter, Camilla. Bartlett is the fiduciary of Camilla's qualified disability trust. Despite the fact that he is disbarred, he may still represent his daughter (as her legal guardian) and the trust (as the trust's fiduciary) before the IRS.

1. Under Circular 230, the OPR has the right to use expedited suspension procedures against a practitioner for "willful disreputable conduct" involving which of the following transgressions?

A. Violating due diligence procedures related to the Earned Income Tax Credit.
B. Failure to use a PTIN when filing clients' federal tax returns.
C. Failure to comply with his personal federal tax filing obligations.
D. Failure to abide by IRS standards related to advertising and fees.

2. A suspended or disbarred individual may:

A. Appear before the IRS as a fiduciary.
B. File an IRS appeal request on a taxpayer's behalf.
C. Represent a client at IRS conferences, hearings, and meetings.
D. Execute a closing agreement for a client, so long as the practitioner has a valid power of attorney.

3. The OPR receives a referral about a practitioner and launches its own investigation. The OPR then determines he has violated provisions of Circular 230. Which of the following best describes the due process procedures that occur when a practitioner faces a potential sanction?

A. Notification and settlement discussions with the practitioner; formal complaint is filed; disciplinary hearing is held with an administrative law judge presiding; either the OPR or the practitioner can appeal; a final decision is rendered by the Treasury Appellate Authority; the practitioner must sue in court to contest the decision.
B. Notification and settlement discussions with the practitioner; a disciplinary hearing is held with an administrative law judge presiding; only the practitioner can appeal; a final decision is rendered by the Treasury Appellate Authority; no further appeal is granted either side.
C. A formal complaint is filed; a disciplinary hearing is held with an administrative law judge presiding; a final decision is rendered by the judge; the practitioner must sue the Treasury Appellate Authority to contest the decision.
D. A formal complaint is filed; a disciplinary hearing is held with an administrative law judge presiding; a final decision is rendered by the Treasury Appellate Authority; either the practitioner or the OPR must sue in court to contest the decision.

4. Which of the following types of disciplinary actions allow a practitioner to continue practicing before the IRS?

A. Disbarment.
B. Suspension from practice.
C. Censure.
D. All of the disciplinary actions listed above prevent a practitioner from practicing before the IRS.

5. Following disbarment, a practitioner may petition the OPR for reinstatement after a period of:

A. One year.
B. Five years.
C. Ten years.
D. Never. Disbarment is always permanent.

6. Which of the following is not listed in Circular 230 as conduct that could cause a practitioner to be censured, suspended, or disbarred?

A. Abusive language in connection with practice before the IRS.
B. Willfully failing to sign a federal tax return.
C. Conviction of a felony charge.
D. Indictment on a criminal offense charge.

7. If a practitioner has been disbarred, which of the following actions is he not allowed to do?

A. Serve as a witness at a friend's examination before the IRS.
B. Furnish information to the IRS at the request of a revenue officer.
C. Act as a representative for a client for a fee in an IRS audit.
D. Prepare his own federal tax return.

8. What is the shortest period of suspension that will be imposed upon a practitioner who has been found to violate a provision of Circular 230?

A. One month.
B. Six months.
C. One year.
D. Two years.

9. Under Treasury Department Circular No. 230, all of the following are considered to be incompetence and disreputable conduct EXCEPT:

A. Conviction of any criminal offense under the Federal tax laws.
B. Conviction of any criminal offense involving dishonesty or breach of trust.
C. Willfully disclosing tax return information with the consent of the taxpayer.
D. Willfully failing to sign a tax return prepared by the tax practitioner as required by Federal tax laws.

Unit 8: Quiz Answers

1. The answer is C. Under the §10.82, the OPR may move quicker to sanction practitioners by using expedited procedures in certain circumstances, including when a practitioner has been convicted of a crime involving dishonesty or breach of trust. The procedures are also allowed when a practitioner has demonstrated a pattern of "willful disreputable conduct" involving the following:
- Failing to file his federal income tax returns in four of the five previous tax years
- Failing to file a return required more frequently than annually (such as an employment tax return) during five of the seven previous tax periods

2. The answer is A. A disbarred practitioner may appear before the IRS as a trustee, receiver, guardian, administrator, executor, or other fiduciary, if duly qualified or authorized under the laws of the relevant jurisdiction.

3. The answer is A. A practitioner who is subject to a possible sanction has the following due process rights available. After the OPR receives a referral and investigates whether a Circular 230 violation has occurred, it notifies the practitioner and attempts to reach agreement on a sanction. If agreement cannot be reached, a formal complaint is filed, with the practitioner expected to answer the specific charges in writing. An administrative law judge then holds a hearing, with both the OPR and the practitioner (or his representative) presenting evidence. The judge has 180 days to hand down his decision on possible sanctions. At that point, either the OPR or the practitioner can appeal to the Treasury Appellate Authority, which will issue the Final Agency Decision in the matter. If the practitioner does not agree with the decision, he can sue in a U.S. district court. However, the district court judge will only reverse the decision if it is considered arbitrary or capricious, contrary to law, or an abuse of discretion.

4. The answer is C. A practitioner who is censured by the OPR is still eligible to practice before the IRS. Censure is a public reprimand. Unlike disbarment or suspension, censure does not affect an individual's eligibility to represent taxpayers before the IRS, although the OPR may subject the individual's future representation of taxpayers to conditions designed to promote high standards of conduct.

5. The answer is B. A practitioner may petition the OPR for reinstatement after a period of five years.

6. The answer is D. Circular 230 §10.51 details a large number of violations related to incompetence or disreputable conduct for which a practitioner may face sanctions from the OPR. The statute specifically cites "conviction" of criminal offense or felony charges, rather than merely an indictment on criminal offense or felony charges. Circular 230 also does not specify that conviction of misdemeanor charges is a sanctionable offense. However, the statute warns that practitioners may be sanctioned for offenses that are not specifically listed.

7. The answer is C. A practitioner who has been disbarred (or suspended) may not represent a client in front of the IRS, sign a tax return on behalf of a taxpayer, file powers of attorney with the IRS, or any number of other actions that are considered practice before the IRS. The other actions listed are allowed, even for a practitioner who has been disbarred or suspended.

8. The answer is A. The OPR can suspend a practitioner who has violated the rules and regulations of Circular 230 for a period of one month to 60 months.

9. The answer is C. Willfully disclosing tax return information with the consent of the taxpayer would not be considered disreputable conduct.

Unit 9: Tax Payments & IRS Collections

More Reading:
Publication 594, *The Collection Process*
Publication 1035, *Extending the Tax Assessment Period*
Publication 971, *Innocent Spouse Relief*
Publication 556, *Examination of Returns, Appeal Rights, and Claims for Refund*
Publication 1660, *Collection Appeal Rights*

Approved Methods of Payment

Taxpayers generally have several options to make payments owed on their tax returns or for estimated taxes. The following methods of payments are currently accepted by the IRS:

1. **Direct debit** (note: this is not the same thing as "Direct Pay")
2. **Credit card**
3. **Personal check, cashier's check, or money order**
4. **Installment agreement requests**
5. **Electronic Federal Tax Payment System (EFTPS)**
6. **Electronic funds withdrawal**
7. **Federal Tax Application (same-day wire transfer)**
8. **Direct Pay**

Payments do not have to be sent at the same time an electronic return is transmitted. For example, the return may be transmitted in January, and the taxpayer may mail a payment by check at a later date. As long as the payment is mailed by the due date of the return, it will be considered timely.

On all checks or money orders, the preparer should write the taxpayer's daytime phone number, EIN, TIN, or SSN; the type of tax return; and the tax year to which the payment applies.[49] The check or money order should be made payable to "United States Treasury."

Note: Recently, the IRS launched a free web-based payment option, Direct Pay. It allows individual taxpayers with a valid Social Security number to make IRS payments directly from their checking or savings accounts. Taxpayers may pay their tax bill or make an estimated tax payment using the service, and will receive instant confirmation that their payment was submitted.

Tax Refunds

Taxpayers have a number of options related to their tax refunds. They may:

- Apply a refund to next year's estimated tax.
- Receive the refund as a direct deposit.
- Receive the refund as a paper check.
- Split the refund, with a portion applied to next year's estimated tax and the remainder received as direct deposit or a paper check, or split the refund between three different accounts.
- Use the refund (or part of it) to purchase U.S. Series I Savings Bonds. Taxpayers can purchase up to $5,000 in bonds for themselves or others.

---

[49] Per Form 1040-V instructions.

The direct deposit option is the fastest way to receive refunds. Refunds may be designated for direct deposit to qualified accounts in the taxpayer's name. Qualified accounts include savings, checking, share draft, or retirement accounts (for example, IRA or money market accounts).

Direct deposits cannot be made to regular credit card accounts, but can be made to prepaid debit cards. Qualified accounts must be in financial institutions within the United States. The number of refunds electronically deposited into a single account is limited to three. A preparer is required to accept any direct deposit election to a qualified account at an eligible financial institution designated by the taxpayer. A preparer may not charge a separate fee for direct deposit.

A preparer must advise the taxpayer that a direct deposit election cannot be rescinded once a return is filed. In addition, changes cannot be made to routing numbers of financial institutions or to the taxpayer's account numbers after the IRS has accepted the return. A preparer should verify account and routing numbers with the taxpayer each year.

> **Example:** Karla filed her tax return on January 20, 2018. She e-filed and chose direct deposit for her refund. Three days later, her purse was stolen and she had to close her bank account to prevent fraud. The direct deposit information cannot be changed on her return after it has been e-filed. The IRS will attempt to deposit her tax refund, but once the bank declines her deposit, her refund will default to a paper check.

Tax Payment Options

If a taxpayer owes a balance after filing a return, the IRS will send him a bill for the amount due, including any penalties and interest, which must be paid within 30 days. If he agrees with the information on the bill but is unable to pay the full amount, he is advised to pay as much as he can, and contact the IRS immediately to explain his situation. For taxpayers who are unable to pay the tax they owe, options include extensions of time to pay, installment agreements, and offers in compromise.

Extension of Time for Payment (Form 1127): A taxpayer should file Form 1127, *Application for Extension of Time for Payment of Tax Due to Hardship,* by the due date of his return, or by the due date for the amount determined as a deficiency. The types of taxes covered by Form 1127 include income taxes, self-employment taxes, and gift taxes.

The term "undue hardship" does not mean a taxpayer will simply be inconvenienced by paying the tax. Rather, for the IRS to grant a Form 1127 request, a taxpayer must show he will sustain a substantial financial loss if he pays tax on the date it is due. In the request for extension, a taxpayer must:

- Enter the date he proposes to pay the tax,
- Provide a detailed explanation of the undue hardship that would result if he paid the tax on or before the due date, and
- Provide supporting documentation, including a statement of assets and liabilities and an itemized list of income and expenses for each of the three months prior to the due date of the tax.

The IRS generally will not grant an extension of more than six months to pay the tax shown on a return. An extension to pay an amount determined as a deficiency is generally limited to 18 months from the date payment is due, but an extension to pay a deficiency will not be granted at all if the deficiency is due to negligence, intentional disregard of rules and regulations, or fraud with intent to evade tax.

Example: Hugo had unexpected hospital expenses in the prior year, which depleted his savings. To pay the $8,500 he owes in taxes, he would have to sell his car at a sacrifice price. Doing so would create an undue hardship because he would not have reliable transportation, which could cause him to lose his job. Prior to the April 17, 2018 tax deadline, Hugo files Form 1127 to request an extension of time to pay tax owed because of an undue hardship. He provides a full explanation of his financial difficulties as well as the other required documentation.

Electronic Federal Tax Payment System (EFTPS)

Taxpayers can use the Electronic Federal Tax Payment System (EFTPS) for any type of IRS payment. Taxpayers and businesses enroll in EFTPS by using an online application.

Businesses and individuals can pay all their federal taxes using EFTPS. Individuals can pay their quarterly estimated taxes, and they can make payments weekly, monthly, or quarterly. Businesses can schedule payments up to 120 days in advance of their tax due date.

Individuals can schedule payments up to 365 days in advance of their tax due date. Domestic corporations must deposit all income tax payments by the due date of the return.

Installment Agreements

Installment agreements are arrangements in which the IRS allows taxpayers to pay liabilities over time. Before applying for any installment agreement, the taxpayer (or business) must file all required tax returns.

A taxpayer who files electronically may apply for an installment agreement once the return is processed and the tax is assessed. Taxpayers must either submit Form 9465, *Installment Agreement Request*, or apply online if they qualify.

The IRS charges a one-time user fee to set up an installment agreement. An agreement will be granted only if it provides for full payment of the taxpayer's account. This means the taxpayer must agree to pay the full balance due; he cannot use an installment agreement to negotiate a lower tax liability. During the term of the installment agreement, penalties and interest continue to accrue. Future refunds are applied to the tax debt until it is paid in full.

Equal monthly payments are specified in the agreement, but the taxpayer may choose to pay more than the required monthly amount. The maximum period of time to pay is up to 72 months. Taxpayers may pay a variety of ways, including by check, credit card, payroll deduction, or direct debit.

Qualified taxpayers who owe $25,000 or less may have their Notice of Federal Tax Lien withdrawn after entering into a direct debit installment agreement.

A taxpayer who owes $10,000 or less in tax cannot be turned down for an installment agreement, assuming that all of the following apply:

- The taxpayer (and spouse, if married) has timely filed all income tax returns and paid all tax due during the past five years;
- The IRS has determined the taxpayer cannot pay the tax owed in full when it is due;
- The taxpayer agrees to pay the full amount he owes within three years; and
- The taxpayer has not entered into an installment agreement with the IRS in the prior five years.

Applying for an Installment Agreement Online: Individuals must owe $50,000 or less in combined individual income tax, penalties and interest, and have filed all required returns in order to apply for an installment agreement online. In the case of a business taxpayer with a payroll tax liability, the business must owe $25,000 or less in payroll taxes and must have filed all required returns.

Direct Debit requirement: For individuals, balances over $25,000 must be paid by direct debit. For businesses, balances over $10,000 must be paid by direct debit.

Installment Agreements (Fees and Current Costs)	Increased Fee as of Jan 1, 2017
Regular installment agreement	$225
Regular installment agreement with direct debit (DDIA)	$107
Online payment agreement (regular installment agreement)	$149
Online payment agreement (Direct debit installment agreement (DDIA))	$31
Restructured/reinstated installment agreement	$89
Restructured/reinstated low-income installment agreement	$43

Example: Glenda owes $36,000 in taxes and is not able to pay the balance due. She is under the $50,000 threshold, so she is eligible to apply for an installment agreement online. She applies online, and her installment agreement is approved by the IRS. Glenda has $500 deducted from her checking account every month via direct debit. Under the terms of the agreement, she must pay the entire amount within 72 months.

If a taxpayer owes more than $50,000, he may still qualify for an installment agreement, but Form 433-A or Form 433-F, *Collection Information Statement*, must be submitted along with the installment agreement request. The IRS generally will not take collection actions:

- When an installment agreement is being considered.
- While an installment agreement is in effect.
- For 30 days after an agreement request is rejected.
- During the period the IRS evaluates an appeal of a rejected or terminated agreement.

If a taxpayer fails to make a payment on an installment agreement, an automatic 30-day notice is generated. The IRS typically charges a fee for reinstating an installment agreement that has gone into default.

IRS Collection Process

The IRS has wide powers when it comes to collecting unpaid taxes. If a taxpayer does not pay in full when filing his tax return, he will receive a bill from an IRS service center. The first notice explains the balance due and demands payment in full. It will include the amount of the unpaid tax balance plus any penalties and interest calculated from the date the tax was due.

This first notice starts the collection process, which continues until the taxpayer's account is satisfied or until the IRS may no longer legally collect the tax, such as when the collection period has expired. The date that the IRS is no longer allowed to collect the tax is called the collection statute expiration date (CSED). But this "CSED" period can be extended for a variety of reasons. The ten-year collection period can be suspended in the following cases:

- While the IRS and the Office of Appeals consider a request for an installment agreement or an offer in compromise
- From the date a taxpayer requests a collection due process (CDP) hearing
- While the taxpayer is residing outside the United States
- For tax periods included in a bankruptcy

The amount of time the suspension is in effect will be added to the time remaining in the ten-year period. For example, if the ten-year period is suspended for six months, the time left in the period the IRS has to collect will increase by six months. If a taxpayer is delinquent filing their return, the date of assessment is the date the return is filed, not the date on which the return was due. The IRS is required to notify the taxpayer that he may refuse to extend the statute of limitations.

Installment agreements do not extend the collection statute. In other words, if a taxpayer requests an installment agreement, the amount of time that the IRS has to legally collect the debt does not increase.

Bankruptcy

A filing in bankruptcy court immediately stops all assessment and collection of tax. This is called an *automatic stay*, and it remains in effect until the bankruptcy court lifts the stay or discharges liabilities, meaning they are eliminated or no longer legally enforceable. Income tax debt that may be forgiven in bankruptcy must meet the following conditions:

- The tax debt must be related to a return that was due at least three years before the taxpayer filed for bankruptcy.
- The tax return must have been filed at least two years ago.
- The tax assessment must be at least 240 days old.

The taxpayer cannot be guilty of tax evasion, and the tax return cannot be fraudulent or frivolous.

Taxpayer's Ability to Pay

When there is a delinquent tax liability or when the taxpayer makes a request for an installment agreement or an offer in compromise, the IRS may use a variety of methods to assess the taxpayer's ability to pay. The IRS may consider the taxpayer's general financial health, including factors such as cash flow and assets, lawsuits against the taxpayer, garnishments, and whether the taxpayer has filed bankruptcy. Third party research, such as property assessments, asset values, and state and local tax information, may also be used.

Collection Financial Standards: The IRS *Collection Financial Standards* are used to evaluate a taxpayer's ability to pay a delinquent tax liability. These standards help determine allowable living expenses that are necessary to provide for a taxpayer's (and his family's) health and welfare and/or production of income while his tax debt is being repaid.

Allowances for housing, utilities, and transportation vary by location, while standard amounts are allowed nationwide for food, clothing, out-of-pocket health care expenses, and other items. In most cases, the taxpayer is allowed the amount actually spent, or the local standard, whichever is less. For the items based on national standards, a taxpayer is allowed the total amounts applicable for his family size, without regard to the amounts actually spent. Generally, the number of persons for whom necessary living expenses are allowed is the same as the number of exemptions on the taxpayer's most recent income tax return.

The IRS uses these standards for taxpayers who do not qualify for streamlined installment agreements, which require little financial analysis or substantiation of expenses. If a taxpayer believes he needs a higher amount for basic living expenses than the *Collection Financial Standards* allow, he must provide documentation to explain why.

Collection Information Statements: The information described above regarding allowable living expenses may be used to prepare a *Collection Information Statement*, using Form 433-A, Form 433-B, or Form 433-F. This statement also contains detailed financial information about the taxpayer's income, his bank and retirement accounts, real estate and other assets, and his outstanding debts. Further, it may include information concerning the taxpayer's obligations for court-ordered payments, such as child support and alimony, since the taxpayer will generally have little flexibility regarding these obligations.

"Currently Not Collectible" Status: The IRS can declare a taxpayer to be *currently not collectible* if the agency has received evidence that a taxpayer has no ability to pay his tax debts. Generally, this action is taken only when other options, such as an offer in compromise, are not feasible because the taxpayer's financial situation is so bad he cannot even afford to make monthly payments.

Before this status will be declared, the IRS requires the taxpayer to submit Form 433-F in order to demonstrate that after paying necessary living expenses, he has no money left to make monthly payments to the IRS. Further, he must prove he has no assets that could be liquidated or sold to make a lump sum payment to the IRS.

Once a taxpayer is placed into currently not collectible status (also known as *Status 53),* the IRS must stop all collection activities, such as levies. A taxpayer is generally granted this status for at least one year, or until his income increases. While in currently not collectible status, penalties and interest continue to be added to the tax debt.

IRS Enforcement to Collect Unpaid Taxes

Congress has given the IRS broad powers to compel taxpayers to produce information it requires to determine tax liability or to collect tax. The IRS is permitted to do the following:

- Examine any books, papers, records, or other data;
- Summon a taxpayer or any other person, requiring the person to appear, to produce books and records, and to give testimony under oath; and
- Take testimony under oath.

These powers are most commonly used in connection with collection proceedings, such as when a taxpayer refuses to provide information voluntarily, and in IRS audits, referred to as *examinations.*[50]

IRS enforcement actions to collect unpaid taxes may include the following:

- Issuing a notice of levy on salary and other income, bank accounts, or property (legally seizing property to satisfy the tax debt)
- Filing a Notice of Federal Tax Lien

---

[50] Even though the IRS uses the term "examination" rather than "audit" the terms mean essentially the same thing.

- Issuing a summons to secure information to prepare unfiled tax returns or determine the taxpayer's ability to pay. IRS employees will prepare *substitute returns* when taxpayers do not file voluntarily [51]
- Applying future federal tax refunds to any prior amount due
- Offsetting a taxpayer's refund.

Under the Federal government's Treasury Offset Program ("TOP") there is generally no limit on the period during which an offset may be initiated or taken, meaning debts that are years, or even decades, old may be repaid by a refund offset. Debts may include past-due federal income tax, other federal debts such as student loans, state income tax, child and spousal support payments, and state unemployment compensation debt. A state income tax refund may also be applied to a taxpayer's federal tax liability.

> **Example:** Franklin has been expecting a $2,000 refund from his federal tax return. However, Franklin has past due child support payments and debt from a delinquent student loan totaling $3,000. The IRS notifies Franklin that the entire $2,000 he had been anticipating as a refund will be used to offset these debts.

Federal Tax Lien

A federal tax lien is a legal claim against a taxpayer's property, including property that the taxpayer acquires after the lien is filed. By filing a Notice of Federal Tax Lien, the IRS establishes its interest in the taxpayer's property as a creditor and as security for his tax debt, and publicly notifies the taxpayer's other creditors of its claim.

A Notice of Federal Tax Lien may be filed only after:
- The IRS assesses the taxpayer's liability,
- The IRS sends a notice and demand for payment, and
- The taxpayer neglects to pay the debt.

Once these requirements are met, a lien is created for the amount of the taxpayer's debt. The lien attaches to all the taxpayer's property, such as a house or car, and to all the taxpayer's rights to property (such as accounts receivable, in the case of a business).

Under the IRS's Fresh Start program, the filing threshold for the amount taxpayers can owe before a Notice of Federal Tax Lien is issued has been increased from $5,000 to $10,000 in most cases.

Once a lien is filed, the IRS generally cannot release it until the taxes are paid in full or until the government may no longer legally collect the tax.

Notice of Levy

An IRS seizure is the legal act of confiscating a taxpayer's property to satisfy a tax debt, as authorized by an earlier filed tax lien. If a tax lien is the IRS's authorization to act by seizing property, then the IRS levy is the actual act of seizure. A levy allows the IRS to confiscate and sell property, which may include cars, boats, or real estate. The IRS may also levy wages, bank accounts, Social Security benefits, and retirement income.

---

[51] These substitute returns generally do not give credit for deductions and exemptions a taxpayer may be entitled to receive. Even if the IRS has already filed a substitute return, a taxpayer may still file his own return. The IRS will generally adjust the taxpayer's account to reflect the correct figures after they receive the filed returns from the taxpayer.

There are special rules regarding IRS seizures. The IRS generally must wait at least 30 days from the date of the notice of intent to levy before it can make a seizure. However, if the IRS has determined that collection of tax is in jeopardy, it may immediately seize property without the normal waiting period. Typically, the IRS may not seize property in the following circumstances:

- When there is a pending installment agreement
- While a taxpayer's appeal is pending
- During the consideration of an offer in compromise
- During a bankruptcy (unless the seizure is authorized by the bankruptcy court)
- If the taxpayer's liability is $5,000 or less in a seizure of real property
- While innocent spouse claims are pending

The IRS may not seize a main home without prior approval from the IRS district director or assistant district director; judicial approval is also generally required for seizure of a main home.

Further, the following items are exempt from IRS levy:

- Wearing apparel and school books.
- Fuel, provisions (food), furniture, personal effects in the taxpayer's household, arms for personal use, or livestock, up to $9,200 in value for tax year 2017 (this amount increases to $9,380 in 2018).
- Books and tools necessary for the trade, business, or profession of the taxpayer, up to $4,600 in value for tax year 2017[52] (this amount increases to $4,690 in 2018).
- Undelivered mail.
- Unemployment benefits and amounts payable under the Job Training Partnership Act.
- Workers' compensation, including amounts payable to dependents.
- Certain annuity or pension payments, but only if payable by the Army, Navy, Air Force, Coast Guard, or under the Railroad Retirement Act or Railroad Unemployment Insurance Act. Traditional and Roth IRAs are not exempt from levy.
- Judgments for the support of minor children (child support).
- Certain public assistance and welfare payments, and amounts payable for Supplemental Security Income for the aged, blind, and disabled under the Social Security Act. Regular Social Security payments are not exempt from levy.

If an IRS levy creates an immediate economic hardship, it may be released. A levy release does not mean the taxpayer is exempt from paying the balance due.

IRS Summons

If a taxpayer or other witness refuses to comply with requests for IRS records or other information, the IRS has the power to issue a summons. An IRS examiner may issue an administrative summons to the taxpayer (or other third parties). An administrative summons directs the person summoned to appear before the examiner and testify or produce information. IRC §7602 authorizes the IRS to issue summonses for the following purposes:

- To ascertain the correctness of any return,
- To prepare a return where none has been made,
- To determine the liability of a person for internal revenue tax,

---

[52] Rev. Proc. 2016-55

- To determine the liability at law or in equity of a transferee or fiduciary of a person in respect of any internal revenue tax,
- To collect any internal revenue tax liability, or
- To inquire into any civil or criminal offense connected with the administration or enforcement of the internal revenue law.

A summons should require only that the witness appears on a given date to give testimony or produce existing books, paper, and records that "may be relevant or material." A summons cannot require a witness to prepare or create documents, including tax returns, which do not exist. A summons cannot be issued solely to harass a taxpayer or to pressure him into settling a dispute.

The IRS must follow precise procedures in serving a summons upon a taxpayer or third party. The summons must be delivered in person to the taxpayer or left at his last known residence. Third-party recordkeepers may also be served by certified or registered mail.

When a summons is served in person to a taxpayer or left at his home, the person serving the summons must sign a *certificate of service*. This certificate must include the date and time the summons was served, the manner in which it was served (such as the address and whether it was left with a person), the server's title, and the server's signature. The certificate of service certifies that the taxpayer has been properly served. The server must also sign a *certificate of notice* when he serves a summons on a third-party record keeper.

An individual has the right to contest a summons based on various technical, procedural, or Constitutional grounds. However, if a taxpayer or other witness fails to respond to a summons within the prescribed period, the IRS may seek judicial enforcement through a U.S. district court.

Taxpayer Collection Appeal Rights

A taxpayer may appeal an IRS collection action to the IRS Office of Appeals. The Office of Appeals is separate from and independent of the IRS Collection offices that initiate collection actions. The IRS ensures the independence of the Appeals office through a strict policy prohibiting *ex parte* communication with the IRS Collection office about the accuracy of the facts or the merits of each case.

> **Definition:** An **ex parte communication** is one that takes place between any IRS Appeals employee and employees of other IRS functions, without the taxpayer or his representative being given a chance to participate in the communication, whether it is written, on the phone, or in person.

The two main ways that taxpayers use to appeal an IRS collection action are collection due process and the collection appeals program. The first method is a Collection Due Process hearing, or CDP hearing. The second avenue is the Collection Appeals Program, or CAP. There are drawbacks and benefits to both of these appeals options.

Collection Due Process Hearings (CDP)

A taxpayer who wants to protest an IRS collection notice may complete Form 12153, *Request for a Collection Due Process or Equivalent Hearing,* and submit it to the address listed on the IRS notice. CDP procedures are available to taxpayers who have received any of the following notices:
- Final Notice of Intent to Levy and Notice of Your Right to a Hearing
- Notice of Jeopardy Levy and Right of Appeal
- Notice of Levy on Your State Tax Refund – Notice of Your Right to a Hearing

- Post Levy Collection Due Process (CDP) Notice

A collection notice will be mailed, given to the taxpayer, or left at his home or office. A taxpayer has 30 days from the date of a notice to request a CDP hearing. Before the hearing, the taxpayer may attempt to work out a solution with the Collection office that sent the notice. If the issue cannot be resolved, the case will be forwarded to Appeals for the taxpayer (or his representative) to schedule a conference with an Appeals officer. The conference may be by telephone, correspondence, or face-to-face for taxpayers who qualify.

Many taxpayers ignore IRS notices until they receive a final notice or a notice of intent to levy. Often, by the time this happens, it is too late to help the taxpayer solve these issues, and the IRS has already begun the collection process in earnest.

Issues that may be discussed during a collection due process hearing include:

- Whether or not the taxpayer paid all the tax owed
- Whether the IRS assessed tax and sent the levy notice when the taxpayer was in bankruptcy
- Whether the IRS made a procedural error in the assessment
- Whether the time to collect the tax (the statute of limitations) has expired
- Whether the taxpayer wishes to discuss collection options
- Whether the taxpayer wishes to make a spousal defense (innocent spouse relief)

In a CDP hearing, a taxpayer may request specific action regarding a lien against his property. For example, he may request a *lien withdrawal* on the grounds the IRS filed the Notice of Federal Tax Lien prematurely or did not follow established procedures. Alternatively, he may request a *lien discharge* that removes a federal tax lien from a specific property.

Example: The IRS placed a federal tax lien on Elwood's vacation condo in Florida. Elwood's attorney attends a CDP hearing and asks that the lien be discharged so Elwood may sell the condo and use the sales proceeds to pay the tax he owes. The IRS Appeals officer agrees and releases the lien so that the property may be sold. Elwood uses the proceeds from the sale to pay his delinquent tax debt.

After a CDP hearing, the Appeals officer will issue a written determination letter. If the taxpayer disagrees with the determination, he can request judicial review by petitioning the U.S. Tax Court. The petition must be made within the time period specified in the Appeals' determination letter. The taxpayer cannot raise any issues with the Tax Court that he did not already raise during the appeals hearing.

If a taxpayer timely files a CDP hearing request, no collection action can be taken until a final determination is made following the hearing or a subsequent appeal to the Tax Court.

Equivalent Hearing: If a taxpayer misses the deadline for requesting a CDP hearing and still wants to meet with Appeals, he may request an equivalent hearing. A taxpayer must file Form 12153, *Request for a Collection Due Process or Equivalent Hearing*, by sending it to the address on the lien or levy notice.

Note: Unlike a CDP hearing, an equivalent hearing will not prohibit levy or suspend the 10-year period for collection. Also, unlike a CDP hearing, a taxpayer cannot go to court to appeal the IRS's decision following an equivalent hearing.

Collection Appeals Program (CAP)

The collection appeals program (CAP) is generally quicker than a CDP hearing and available for a broader range of collection actions. CAP is available in the following instances:

- Before or after the IRS files a Notice of Federal Tax Lien
- Before or after the IRS levies or seizes a taxpayer's property
- After the termination of an installment agreement
- After the rejection of an installment agreement

To appeal an installment agreement that has been rejected or that the IRS is proposing to be modified or terminated, the taxpayer should appeal by completing Form 9423, *Collection Appeal Request*. The form should be submitted within 30 days to the IRS office or revenue officer who took the action regarding the installment agreement.

Example: Walter applied for an installment agreement in 2017. Later that year, he was a victim of bank fraud and his bank account was drained suddenly without his knowledge. It took Walter several months to correct the problem. In the meantime, he received notification that his installment agreement had been rescinded. Walter wants to appeal the cancellation of his installment agreement. He files Form 9423, *Collection Appeal Request*. He will explain his circumstances to an IRS employee and request a reinstatement of his installment agreement.

Example: Danton was paying his tax debt under an installment agreement and missed a few payments. The IRS sent a notice that the installment agreement was cancelled and he must now pay the full outstanding balance. Danton can appeal the termination of the installment agreement by requesting an Appeal under the Collection Appeals program (CAP).

Form 9423, *Collection Appeal Request,* is also used in the cases of liens, levies, and seizures. Generally, the taxpayer would first try to resolve the disagreement by telephone with an IRS employee, manager, or revenue officer. If the issue cannot be resolved, the taxpayer would submit a written request for Appeals consideration by completing Form 9423. The taxpayer must explain why he disagrees with the collection action and how he proposes to resolve his tax problem.

In the appeals hearing, a taxpayer may represent himself, or he may appoint a qualified representative (attorney, CPA, EA, spouse, or a family member). In the case of a business, the entity may be represented by a regular full-time employee, a general partner, or a bona fide officer.

Once the IRS makes a determination under CAP, it is binding on both the taxpayer and the IRS. The determination is final and cannot be appealed to the Tax Court.

Abatement of Penalties and Interest

In certain cases, the IRS will waive or abate penalties and interest assessed a taxpayer.

Penalties: A taxpayer may qualify for penalty relief in the following circumstances:

- When the penalty is incurred due to a major disaster or emergency affecting a large number of taxpayers in a given geographical area. Relief is often provided in the form of extensions of time to file or pay.
- When the penalty is due to an IRS computation or assessment error.
- When the penalty is incurred as a result of the taxpayer relying on advice of a tax advisor. This generally involves accuracy-related penalties and is limited to issues that are considered highly technical or complicated.
- When the penalty is incurred as the result of erroneous written advice provided by an IRS employee.

Penalty relief may also be provided due to *reasonable cause*. This is when a taxpayer has established that, despite the "exercise of ordinary business care and prudence," he was assessed a penalty due to circumstances beyond his control.

Under a special program, the IRS will use the reasonable cause standard to consider abatement of a taxpayer's first-time penalty charge on a one-time basis. This penalty relief is only available for failure to file, failure to pay, and failure to deposit penalties. The IRS will consider this relief option only if the taxpayer has filed all returns and paid, or arranged to pay, all tax currently due.

Interest: Reasonable cause is not allowed as the basis for abatement of interest. Interest may be abated or waived in the following instances:

- When it is excessive, barred by statute, or erroneously or illegally assessed
- When it is assessed on an erroneous refund
- When it was incurred on an account while the taxpayer was in a combat zone or in a declared disaster area.

Further, the IRS will waive interest that is the result of certain errors or delays caused by an IRS employee. The IRS will abate the interest only if there was an unreasonable error or delay in performing a managerial or ministerial act (defined below). The taxpayer cannot have caused any significant aspect of the error or delay. The interest can be abated only if it relates to taxes for which a notice of deficiency is required, which includes income taxes and estate and gift taxes.

Definition: A **"managerial"** act is an administrative act that occurs during the processing of the taxpayer's case involving the temporary or permanent loss of records or the exercise of judgment or discretion relating to management of personnel.
Example: A revenue agent is examining Catrina's tax return. During the course of the examination, the agent is sent to an extended training course. The agent's supervisor decides not to reassign the case, so the examination is unreasonably delayed until the agent returns. Interest caused by the delay can be abated since the decision to send the agent to the training class and the decision not to reassign the case are both managerial acts.
Definition: A **"ministerial"** act is a procedural or mechanical act that does not involve the exercise of judgment or discretion and that occurs during the processing of the taxpayer's case.
Example: Bryant moves to another state before the IRS selects his tax return for examination. Notice of the examination was sent to his old address and then forwarded to his new address. When Bryant gets the letter, he responds with a request that the examination be transferred to the area office closest to his new address. The examination group manager approves his request. However, the original examination manager forgets about the transfer and fails to transfer the file for six months. The transfer is a ministerial act. The IRS can reduce the interest Bryant owes because of the unreasonable delay in transferring the case.

A taxpayer may request an abatement of interest on Form 843, *Claim for Refund and Request for Abatement*. The taxpayer should file the claim with the IRS service center where the examination was affected by the error or delay. If a request for abatement of interest is denied, an appeal can be made to the IRS Appeals office or the U.S. Tax Court. When a portion of interest is abated, the IRS must recalculate the amount of remaining interest the taxpayer owes.

Seeking Relief from Joint Liability

Married taxpayers often file jointly because of benefits this filing status affords. In the case of a joint return, both taxpayers are liable for the tax and any interest or penalties, even if they later separate or divorce. *Joint and several liability* means that each taxpayer is legally responsible for the entire liability. This is true even if only one spouse earned all the income, or if a divorce decree states that a former spouse is or is not responsible for any amounts due on previously filed joint returns.

In some cases, however, a spouse who filed joint returns can receive relief from joint and several liability:

Innocent Spouse Relief: Provides relief from additional tax if a spouse or former spouse failed to report income or claimed improper deductions.

Separation of Liability Relief: Provides for the allocation of additional tax owed between the taxpayer and his spouse or former spouse because an item was not reported properly on a joint return. The tax allocated to the taxpayer is the amount for which he is responsible.

Equitable Relief: May apply when a taxpayer does not qualify for innocent spouse relief or separation of liability relief for items not reported properly on a joint return and generally attributable to the taxpayer's spouse. A taxpayer may also qualify for equitable relief if the correct amount of tax is reported on his joint return but the tax remains unpaid.

Requesting Innocent Spouse Relief

The taxpayer must meet all of the following conditions in order to qualify for innocent spouse relief:

- The taxpayer filed a joint return that has an understatement of tax directly related to his spouse's erroneous items.
- The taxpayer establishes that, at the time he signed the joint return, he did not know and had no reason to know that there was an understatement of tax.
- Taking into account all the facts and circumstances, it would be unfair for the IRS to hold the taxpayer liable for the understatement.

In order to apply for innocent spouse relief, a taxpayer must submit Form 8857, *Request for Innocent Spouse Relief*, and sign it under penalty of perjury.

A request for innocent spouse relief will be denied if the IRS proves that property was transferred between the taxpayer and the spouse or former spouse as part of a fraudulent scheme to defraud the IRS or another third party. If a taxpayer requests innocent spouse relief, the IRS cannot enforce collection action while the request is pending, but interest and penalties continue to accrue.

> **Example:** Bettie and Christian are married and file jointly. At the time Bettie signed their joint return, she was unaware her husband had a gambling problem. The IRS examined their return and determined that Christian's unreported gambling winnings were $25,000. Christian kept the gambling proceeds for himself and hid the bank statements from his wife. Bettie was able to prove that she did not know about, and had no reason to know about, the additional $25,000 because Christian had concealed his gambling winnings. The understatement of tax due to the $25,000 qualifies for innocent spouse relief.

Requesting Separation of Liability Relief

To qualify for separation of liability relief, the taxpayer must have filed a joint return and be no longer married (including a taxpayer who is widowed), legally separated, or living apart for the 12 months prior to the filing of a claim. Living apart does not include a spouse who is only temporarily absent from the household, in which case the taxpayer would not qualify for separation of liability relief.

The spouse or former spouse who is applying for separation of liability relief must not have known about the understatement of tax at the time of signing the return. An exception is made for spousal abuse or domestic violence, if the taxpayer had been afraid that failing to sign the return could result in harm or retaliation.

> **Example:** Charlotte and Darwin have lived apart since 2014 and divorced in 2017. In the tax year before they separated, they filed a joint return showing Charlotte's wages of $35,000 and Darwin's self-employment income of $15,000. In an audit, the IRS found that Darwin failed to report $25,000 of self-employment income, which resulted in a $7,500 understatement of tax. Since she is now divorced from Darwin, Charlotte filed Form 8857 to request relief by separation of liability. However, the IRS was able to prove that Charlotte knew about the $25,000 of additional income because it was deposited into their joint bank account and she had full ownership and use of the funds. She is not eligible for separation of liability relief, and the IRS denies her request.

Requesting Equitable Relief

A taxpayer who does not qualify for innocent spouse relief or separation of liability relief may qualify for equitable relief. The taxpayer must establish, based upon all the facts and circumstances, that it would be unfair to hold him liable for the understatement or underpayment of tax.

The IRS considers a taxpayer's current marital status, whether there is a legal obligation under a divorce decree to pay the tax, and whether he would suffer significant economic hardship if relief were not granted.

> **Example:** Brittany and Antwon were married in 2015 and filed a joint return that showed they owed $12,000 in unpaid income tax. Brittany had $7,000 of her own money and she took out a loan to pay the remaining $5,000. Brittany gave Antwon the money to pay their full $12,000 liability. Without telling Brittany, Antwon gambled away the entire $12,000 rather than paying their tax liability. The couple divorced in 2017. Brittany did not know at the time she signed the return that the tax would not be paid. These facts indicate to the IRS that it may be unfair to hold Brittany liable for the underpayment. Brittany's request for equitable relief is granted.

The following factors weigh in favor of equitable relief:
- Abuse by the spouse or former spouse
- Poor mental or physical health on the date the taxpayer signed the return or requested relief

The IRS has expanded the amount of time to request equitable relief. A taxpayer seeking relief from a balance due has up to ten years to file a request, the same period the IRS has to collect the tax. If the taxpayer is making a claim for a refund, he must file his request within the statute of limitations for refunds. More time may be allowed for taxpayers who are physically or mentally unable to manage their financial affairs or who live in federally-declared disaster areas.

Injured Spouse Claims

Innocent spouse relief should not be confused with an injured spouse claim. A taxpayer may qualify as an injured spouse if he filed a joint return and his share of the refund was applied against past due amounts owed by his spouse.

An injured spouse may be entitled to recoup only his share of a tax refund. When a joint return is filed and the refund is used to pay one spouse's past-due federal tax, state income tax, child support, spousal support, or federal nontax debt (such as a delinquent student loan), the other spouse may be considered an injured spouse. The injured spouse can request his share of the refund using Form 8379, *Injured Spouse Allocation*.

> **Example:** Andrea and Cesar marry and file jointly in 2017. Unknown to Andrea, Cesar has unpaid child support and delinquent student loan debt. Their entire refund is retained to pay Cesar's outstanding debts. Andrea may qualify for injured spouse treatment and recoup her share of the tax refund. The IRS will keep Cesar's share of the refund to pay his delinquent debts.

Offer in Compromise Program

An offer in compromise (OIC) is an agreement between a taxpayer and the IRS that settles the taxpayer's tax liabilities for less than the full amount owed. Generally, the IRS will accept an offer if it represents the most the agency can expect to collect within a reasonable period of time. Absent special circumstances, an offer will not be accepted if the IRS believes that the liability can be paid in full as a lump sum or through a payment agreement. The IRS will consider each taxpayer's unique set of facts and circumstances in determining whether to grant an OIC, including his ability to pay, income, expenses, and asset equity.

To apply for an OIC on grounds of "doubt as to collectability" or "exceptional circumstances," a taxpayer must submit an application fee and initial nonrefundable payment along with Form 656, *Offer in Compromise*. Fees may be waived for low-income taxpayers. There is no fee or initial payment required to apply for an OIC on grounds of doubt as to liability and Form 656-L is used instead.

The taxpayer may appeal a rejected offer in compromise within 30 days. As part of its Fresh Start initiative, the IRS has expanded and streamlined the OIC program. The agency has more flexibility when analyzing a taxpayer's ability to pay, which makes the program available to a larger group of taxpayers. Taxpayers can use the OIC pre-qualifier tool at www.irs.gov to see if they may be eligible for an OIC. An offer in compromise can be applied to all taxes, including interest and penalties. A taxpayer may submit an OIC on three grounds:

Doubt as to Collectability
Doubt exists that the taxpayer could ever pay the full amount of tax liability owed within the remainder of the statutory period for collection.
Example: Constance owes $80,000 for unpaid tax liabilities and agrees that the tax she owes is correct. Constance is terminally ill and cannot work. She does not own any property and does not have the ability to fully pay the liability now or through monthly installment payments.
Doubt as to Liability
A legitimate doubt exists that the assessed tax liability is correct.
Example: Darla was vice president of a corporation from 2006 to 2016. In late 2017, the corporation accrued unpaid payroll taxes and she was assessed a trust fund recovery penalty. However, before January 2017, Darla had resigned from the corporation, prior to any of these delinquent payroll taxes accruing. Since there is legitimate doubt that the assessed tax liability is correct, she may apply for an OIC under doubt as to liability.

Exceptional Circumstances (Effective Tax Administration)
There is no doubt that the tax is correct and there is potential to collect the full amount of the tax owed, but an exceptional circumstance exists. A taxpayer must demonstrate that the collection of the tax would create serious economic hardship or would be unfair.
Example: Valerie and Walter Smith have sufficient assets to satisfy their tax liability. However, they provide full-time care to their dependent child, who has a serious chronic illness. The unpaid taxes were a result of the Smiths providing necessary medical care for their sick child. They will need to continue to use their assets to provide for basic living expenses and ongoing care for the child. There is no doubt that the tax is correct, but to pay the tax would endanger the life of their child and would create a serious hardship.

Unit 9: Study Questions

(Test yourself and then check the correct answers at the end of this chapter.)

1. What recourse does a taxpayer have if he misses the deadline to request a collection due process hearing with IRS Appeals?

A. None. He must pay the contested tax liability or enter into some other payment arrangement.

B. He may request an equivalent hearing.

C. Since he missed his deadline, he cannot use the IRS Appeals system. He must instead contest his liability in the U.S. Tax Court or sue for a refund in the U.S. court system.

D. There is no deadline to request a collection due process hearing, so he may pursue his case through IRS Appeals without any issue.

2. The statute of limitations on collection activity can be suspended in certain instances. The ten-year collection period may be suspended in each of the following instances except:

A. While the IRS and the Office of Appeals consider a request for an installment agreement or an offer in compromise.

B. From the date a taxpayer requests a collection due process (CDP) hearing.

C. While the taxpayer is in prison.

D. While the taxpayer lives outside the United States.

3. A taxpayer may qualify as an injured spouse if:

A. He files a joint return and his share of the refund is applied against past due amounts owed by a spouse.

B. He files a joint return and fails to report income.

C. He files a separate return and has the refund offset by past due student loan obligations.

D. He files for bankruptcy protection.

4. If the IRS rejects an offer in compromise, a taxpayer may appeal within:

A. 30 days.

B. 60 days.

C. 90 days.

D. There is no time limit to appeal an offer in compromise.

5. A levy allows the IRS to:

A. Publicly notify a taxpayer's creditors of a claim against his property.

B. Confiscate and sell property to satisfy a tax debt.

C. Collect tax beyond the statute of limitations.

D. Sell property on behalf of the taxpayer.

6. Belinda and Neil file jointly. They report $15,000 of income, but Belinda knows that Neil is not reporting $3,000 of dividends. The income is not hers, and she has no access to it since it is in Neil's bank account. She signs the joint return. The return is later chosen for examination, and penalties are assessed. Does Belinda qualify for innocent spouse relief?

A. Yes, because she can file for divorce later.
B. Yes, because she had no control over the income.
C. No, but she is eligible for injured spouse relief.
D. No, because she knew about the understated income.

7. Art owes $55,000 to the IRS. He would like to set up an installment agreement. Which of the following statements regarding his payment options is correct?

A. Art may qualify for an installment agreement, but a *Collection Information Statement*, Form 433-F, must be completed.
B. Art does not qualify for an installment agreement because he owes more than $50,000.
C. Art may qualify for an installment agreement, but an offer in compromise must first be completed.
D. Art must enroll in EFTPS and have automatic withdrawals in order to have his installment agreement approved.

8. Lena owes $20,000 of unpaid federal tax liabilities. She agrees she owes the tax, but she has a serious medical problem and her monthly income does not meet her necessary living expenses. She does not own any real estate and does not have the ability to fully pay the liability now or through monthly installment payments. What type of offer in compromise may she qualify for?

A. Doubt as to collectability
B. Doubt as to liability
C. Effective tax administration
D. Collection advocate procedure

9. Which statement is correct regarding the process of a taxpayer appealing an IRS collection action?

A. The decision in a collection due process (CDP) hearing is final, and a taxpayer may not appeal even if he is unhappy with the determination.
B. A disposition in the collection appeals program is typically slower than in a CDP, but the taxpayer has the right to appeal if he is unhappy with a CAP determination.
C. Innocent spouse relief may not be discussed during a CDP hearing.
D. If a taxpayer disagrees with the Appeals office determination after a CDP hearing, he can appeal to the U.S. Tax Court.

10. By law, the IRS must sign a _____ when issuing a summons to a taxpayer.

A. Temporary restraining order
B. Federal notice of levy
C. Certificate of service
D. Federal notice of lien

11. Separation of liability relief does not apply to taxpayers who are:

A. Divorced.
B. Legally separated.
C. Widowed.
D. Single (never married).

12. How does the IRS begin the process of collections?

A. With an email to the taxpayer shortly after he files his tax return.
B. With a certified letter to the taxpayer immediately after a tax return is processed and flagged for audit.
C. With a written examination notice when the taxpayer is notified of the possibility of an audit.
D. A first notice will be sent, which is a letter that explains the balance due and demands payment in full.

13. Sheila and Dale were married in 2017. They are owed a refund on their joint return, but the refund is offset against Dale's past-due child support. Does Sheila have any recourse to recover her portion of the refund?

A. No. Since they filed jointly, Sheila's portion of the refund cannot be recovered.
B. Sheila may be eligible for injured spouse relief.
C. Sheila may be eligible for innocent spouse relief.
D. Both B and C.

14. The IRS may legally seize property in which of the following circumstances?

A. If the collection of tax is in jeopardy.
B. During the consideration of an offer in compromise.
C. If the taxpayer's liability is $5,000 or less in a seizure of real property (real estate).
D. While an innocent spouse claim is pending.

15. An installment agreement allows a taxpayer to do all of the following except:

A. Pay his tax debt in equal monthly payments over a period of time.
B. Negotiate with the IRS for a lower tax liability.
C. Pay his tax debt in variety of ways, such as by check, credit card, payroll deduction, or direct debit.
D. Avoid IRS collection actions, including levies.

16. All of the following statements about the IRS statute of limitations are correct except:

A. The IRS generally has ten years following an assessment to begin proceedings to collect the tax by levy or in a court proceeding.
B. The IRS is required to notify the taxpayer that he may refuse to extend the statute of limitations.
C. The IRS does not allow the taxpayer the right to extend the statute of limitations.
D. The statute of limitations on collection activity may be suspended in certain cases.

17. All of the following property is exempt from an IRS levy except:

A. Undelivered mail.
B. Child support payments.
C. Social Security payments.
D. Unemployment benefits.

18. The IRS may not generally pursue collection enforcement action against a taxpayer who has been placed in "currently not collectible" status for a minimum of:

A. Six months.
B. One year.
C. Two years.
D. No specified time limit.

19. All of the following statements regarding IRS installment agreements are correct except:

A. During the course of the installment agreement, penalties and interest continue to accrue.
B. A taxpayer who owes $10,000 or less in taxes will be automatically approved for an installment agreement.
C. An installment agreement allows a taxpayer to pay a set amount toward a tax liability on a monthly basis.
D. An IRS levy may be served during an installment agreement.

20. Which of the following amounts is the IRS least likely to challenge when evaluating a taxpayer's offer in compromise?

A. Rent
B. Prescription drugs
C. Child support
D. Food

21. Penalties and interest continue to accrue on a taxpayer's unpaid tax liability in which of the following instances?

A. When an installment agreement is in place.
B. When a taxpayer has been declared currently not collectible.
C. When a taxpayer requests innocent spouse relief.
D. All of the above.

22. How long may the IRS offset a taxpayer's past due federal tax liability by retaining his tax refund?

A. For three years.
B. For ten years.
C. Indefinitely.
D. Never. This action is prohibited.

23. If the IRS has filed a notice of seizure, how long must it wait before actually seizing a taxpayer's nonexempt property?

A. Immediately, with the exception of a taxpayer's home, which requires judicial approval.
B. Seven days.
C. 30 days.
D. 60 days.

24. Rosalyn is receiving a federal tax refund this year. Which of the following methods is not available for her to receive her refund?

A. She may apply the refund to next year's estimated tax.
B. She may receive the refund as a direct deposit to her retirement account.
C. She may use her refund to purchase U.S. Series I Savings Bonds.
D. She may direct deposit her refund to her credit card account.

25. Jason cannot pay his tax liability because of a serious health issue. How much extra time will the IRS grant for Jason to pay his tax liability under the undue hardship extension?

A. Three months.
B. Six months.
C. One year.
D. 18 months.

26. An Enrolled Agent prepared an individual income tax return for a taxpayer with a balance due of $25,900. The taxpayer is not able to pay the entire amount upon filing and would like to set up an installment agreement. Which of the following is required before an installment agreement will be approved?

A. Since the taxpayer owes more than $25,000 the taxpayer must apply using a paper application.
B. The taxpayer must authorize the installment agreement by contacting the IRS directly.
C. The taxpayer must be in filing compliance.
D. The taxpayer must be a U.S. Citizen.

1. The answer is B. If a taxpayer still wants a hearing with the IRS Appeals office after the deadline for requesting a timely collection due process (CDP) hearing has passed, he may request an equivalent hearing. A taxpayer must file Form 12153, *Request for a Collection Due Process or Equivalent Hearing*, and send it to the address on the lien or levy notice. However, an equivalent hearing has some disadvantages for the taxpayer. Unlike a CDP hearing, an equivalent hearing will not prohibit a levy or suspend the 10-year period for collection. Also, a taxpayer is not allowed to go to court to appeal the IRS's decision following an equivalent hearing. In a CDP hearing, a taxpayer does not give up his appeal rights if he loses.

2. The answer is C. The ten-year collection period is not suspended when a taxpayer is in prison. The ten-year collection period may be suspended in the following cases:
- While the IRS considers a request for an installment agreement or an offer in compromise
- From the date a taxpayer requests a collection due process (CDP) hearing
- For tax periods included in a bankruptcy
- While the taxpayer is residing outside the United States

3. The answer is A. A taxpayer may qualify as an injured spouse if he filed a joint return and his share of the refund was applied against past due amounts owed by a spouse. The injured spouse may be entitled to recoup only his share of a tax refund.

4. The answer is A. The IRS requires a taxpayer whose offer in compromise has been rejected to file an appeal within 30 days.

5. The answer is B. A levy allows the IRS to confiscate and sell property to satisfy a tax debt. An IRS levy refers to the actual seizing of property authorized by an earlier filed tax lien. Answer A refers to a lien, which gives the IRS a legal claim to a taxpayer's property as security for his tax debt.

6. The answer is D. Belinda is not eligible for innocent spouse relief because she knew about the understated income. She signed the return knowing that the income was not included, so the IRS will not grant her relief.

7. The answer is A. If a taxpayer owes more than $50,000, he may still qualify for an installment agreement, but the taxpayer will also need to complete Form 433-F, *Collection Information Statement*.

8. The answer is A. Lena may apply for an offer in compromise under doubt as to collectability. Doubt exists that she could ever pay the full amount of tax liability owed within the remainder of the statutory period for collection.

9. The answer is D. In an appeals hearing, the taxpayer retains the right to appeal to the Tax Court, unlike in the collection appeals program (CDP), where the determination is final.

10. The answer is C. When a taxpayer is served a summons in person or it is left at his home, the person serving the summons must sign a *certificate of service*. This certificate must include the date and time the summons was served, the manner in which it was served (such as the address and whether it was left with a person), the server's title, and the server's signature. The certificate of service certifies that the taxpayer has been properly served. The server must also sign a *certificate of notice* when he serves a summons on a third-party record keeper. The IRS can use its summons authority when a taxpayer or other witness refuses to comply with IRS requests for records or other information.

11. The answer is D. To qualify for separation of liability relief, the taxpayer must have filed a joint return, meaning the taxpayer must have been married at one time. Separation of liability applies to taxpayers who are no longer married (including a taxpayer who is widowed), legally separated, or living apart for the 12 months prior to the filing of a claim.

12. The answer is D. If a taxpayer does not pay in full when filing his tax return, he will receive a bill in the mail from an IRS service center. The first notice will explain the balance due and demand payment in full. It will include the amount of the tax plus any penalties and interest added to the taxpayer's unpaid balance from the date the tax was due. The IRS will never email a taxpayer a first notice about an unpaid liability.

13. The answer is B. Sheila can file Form 8379, *Injured Spouse Allocation*, and request injured spouse relief. If married taxpayers filed a joint return and the refund was offset, an injured spouse can file Form 8379 to request the portion of the refund attributed to him or her.

14. The answer is A. The IRS may seize or levy property if the collection of tax is in jeopardy, and may do so without the normal waiting period if a jeopardy assessment has been made. Typically, the IRS may not seize property in the following circumstances:
- When there is a pending installment agreement
- While a taxpayer's appeal is pending
- During the consideration of an offer in compromise
- During a bankruptcy (unless the seizure is authorized by the bankruptcy court)
- If the taxpayer's liability is $5,000 or less, in a seizure of real property
- While innocent spouse claims are pending

15. The answer is B. An installment agreement allows a taxpayer to pay his tax liability over a period of time if he cannot pay the amount when it is due. An installment agreement cannot be used to negotiate with the IRS for a lower tax bill. During the time an installment agreement is in place, penalties and interest continue to accrue.

16. The answer is C. The taxpayer may choose to extend the statute of limitations or he may refuse to extend the statute. If a taxpayer does not file a tax return, the statute of limitations does not expire. The statute of limitations on collection activity may also be suspended in certain instances. The amount of time the suspension is in effect will be added to the time remaining in the ten-year period.

17. The answer is C. Regular Social Security payments are not exempt from IRS levy.

18. The answer is B. If the IRS has determined a taxpayer's status is currently not collectible, it is generally prohibited from pursuing all collection activities for at least one year, or until the taxpayer's income has increased.

19. The answer is D. No levies may be served during installment agreements. During the course of an installment agreement, penalties and interest continue to accrue. A taxpayer who owes less than $10,000 in taxes will automatically be approved for an installment agreement under most circumstances.

20. The answer is C. The IRS *Collection Financial Standards* are used to evaluate a taxpayer's ability to pay a delinquent tax liability. These standards help determine allowable living expenses that are necessary to provide for a taxpayer's (and his family's) health and welfare and/or production of income while his tax debt is being repaid. Allowances for housing, utilities, and transportation vary by location, while standard amounts are allowed nationwide for food, clothing, out-of-pocket health care expenses, and other items. Consideration is also given to the taxpayer's income, his bank and retirement accounts, real estate and other assets, and his outstanding debts. Further, the taxpayer may have obligations for court-ordered payments, such as child support and alimony. Since the taxpayer will have little flexibility regarding these obligations, the IRS would be unlikely to challenge amounts that are supported by evidence the taxpayer provides.

21. The answer is D. The IRS will continue to assess penalties and interest on a taxpayer's unpaid tax liability in most circumstances, including during the period when an installment agreement is in place, when a taxpayer has been declared "currently not collectible," and when a taxpayer requests innocent spouse relief.

22. The answer is C. In most cases, the IRS may use a tax refund to offset a taxpayer's federal debts indefinitely. The regular 10-year collection statute does not apply. Debts may include past-due federal income tax; other federal debts such as student loans, state income tax, and child and spousal support payments; and state unemployment compensation debt.

23. The answer is C. After the IRS has filed a notice of intent to seize, it must wait 30 days before actually seizing a taxpayer's nonexempt property. It legally cannot seize items such as clothing, food, fuel, furniture, and personal effects up to a specified, inflation-adjusted amount. Undelivered mail, books and tools of the trade needed for the taxpayer's business are also exempt, up to a certain amount. Further, the IRS cannot seize unemployment benefits, worker's compensation, child support payments, and certain disability and public assistance payments. However, most Social Security benefits and retirement fund proceeds may be seized to fulfill a taxpayer's debt obligation. Before a taxpayer's home is seized, there generally must be judicial approval.

24. The answer is D. A taxpayer may not designate a credit card account for direct deposit of their federal tax refund. However, the IRS will deposit refunds onto a prepaid debit card.

25. The answer is B. The IRS generally will not grant an extension of more than six months to pay the tax due on a return. A taxpayer may file Form 1127, *Application for Extension of Time for Payment of Tax Due to Hardship*, to explain why he cannot pay the tax. He must provide a detailed explanation of the undue hardship that would result if he paid the tax when it is due and provide adequate documentation of his financial situation.

26. The answer is C. In order to set up an installment agreement, the taxpayer must be in filing compliance (all tax returns must be filed). The taxpayer they must remain tax compliant for the entire term of the installment agreement.

Unit 10: The IRS Examination Process

More Reading:

Publication 556, *Examination of Returns, Appeal Rights, and Claims for Refund*

Publication 1, *Your Rights as a Taxpayer*

Publication 3498, *The Examination Process*

Publication 3605, *Fast Track Mediation: A Process for Prompt Resolution of Tax Issues*

Overview of the IRS Audit Process

The IRS accepts most tax returns as they are filed, but selects a small percentage for examination. An IRS examination is also commonly called an "IRS audit."

Statistics: The IRS typically audits approximately 1% of the total number of individual tax returns filed.[53] Higher income earners were audited much more frequently than those who earned less. The IRS reports the audit rate for individual returns with total income of $1 million or more was 10.80%. Returns claiming refundable credits, such as the EITC, are also audited at a higher rate than normal returns. Of all the individual returns audited, more than a third were returns with Earned Income Tax Credit claims.[54]

An IRS examination is a review of the accounts and financial information supporting an organization or individual's income tax return. An examination evaluates whether information on the return is being reported correctly and according to the tax laws, and verifies that the amount of tax reported is accurate. Due to disclosure requirements, the IRS will always notify a taxpayer about an examination by mail, but never by email.

Filing an amended return does not affect the selection process for original returns. Amended returns go through a separate screening process and may be selected for audit.

Selecting a return for examination does not necessarily suggest that the taxpayer has made an error or has been dishonest. However, a taxpayer's responsibility to provide support for entries, deductions, and statements made on a tax return is known as the *burden of proof.* The taxpayer must be able to substantiate expenses in order to deduct them. Taxpayers can usually meet this burden of proof by having the receipts for the expenses.

After an examination, if any changes to a taxpayer's return are proposed, he can disagree with the changes and appeal the IRS's determination. This is done through the appeals process. We will cover the examination process next.

Types of Audits

The three types of IRS examinations are:

- Correspondence audit, which is conducted entirely by mail,
- Office audit, which takes place at a nearby IRS field office, and
- Field examinations, which typically take place at the taxpayer's home or place of business.

---

[53] In the previous tax year, the IRS audited 0.7% of all individual income tax returns filed, and 1.1% of corporate income tax returns.

[54] Internal Revenue Service Data Book.

The IRS conducts most examinations entirely by mail. In these *correspondence audits*,[55] a taxpayer will receive a letter asking for additional information about certain items shown on the return, such as proof of income, expenses, and itemized deductions.

Correspondence audits typically occur when there is a minor issue that the IRS needs to clarify. For example, the IRS may have detected a math error or there may be a discrepancy between the tax return and the 1099 statements sent by brokers, banks, or mutual funds. Other times, the IRS simply requests evidence that a particular transaction has transpired as reported on the tax return.

Example: The IRS selects Evelyn's return for examination. Evelyn had claimed her older half-brother as a qualifying child based on his permanent disability, and she had also claimed head of household status. The IRS asks for proof of disability and residency, and Evelyn provides copies of doctors' records and additional evidence that her brother lives with her full-time. The IRS accepts Evelyn's documents and closes the case as a no-change audit. Evelyn does not have to meet with the IRS auditor, as the entire audit is conducted by mail.

In an "office audit," the IRS interviews the taxpayer and inspects the taxpayer's records at an IRS office. The issue under examination is typically not a complex one. Office audits generally involve issues with Schedule A, Schedule C (small business), or rental activity on Schedule E. Office audits usually cover a few specific issues or an uncomplicated tax matter. Taxpayers can choose to represent themselves, or have an enrolled practitioner represent them.

The least common type of audit is a field audit. Field audits are the most detailed and thorough of IRS examinations. Field audits are conducted only by IRS Revenue Agents, who are highly trained and have many years of experience. Field audits may take place at:

- The taxpayer's home or place of business
- An IRS office
- The office of the taxpayer's authorized representative

If a taxpayer is selected for a field audit, most often, the taxpayer's return will be examined in the area where he lives and where the books and records are located. But if the return can be examined more conveniently in another area, the taxpayer can request the audit to be transferred to that area.

Example: Natalia runs a marketing business, and she travels frequently in order to meet with clients. She lives in Los Angeles; however, her CPA lives in Chicago, her old hometown. In 2017, Natalia's prior year tax return is selected for examination and she chooses to have her CPA represent her. Her CPA requests that the examination be transferred to Chicago where Natalia's records are located. The IRS grants the transfer.

How Returns are Selected for Examination

The IRS examines a percentage of all federal tax returns to determine if income, expenses, and credits are being reported accurately. The IRS selects returns for examination using various methods which include random sampling, computerized screening, and comparison of information received by the IRS such as Forms W-2 and 1099 (this is also called "third-party" information).

---

[55] In the prior fiscal year, the IRS conducted 70.7% of its audits by mail. The remaining 29.3 percent were conducted as office audits or field audits. For more information, see the official IRS Data Book.

When tax returns are filed, they are compared against the norms for similar returns. The IRS selects returns for examination using a variety of methods, including:

- **Potentially Abusive/Tax Avoidance Transactions:** Some returns are selected based on information obtained by the IRS through efforts to identify promoters of and participants in abusive tax avoidance transactions.
- **Computer Scoring/DIF Score:** Returns may be chosen on the basis of computer scoring. A computer program called the Discriminant Inventory Function System (DIF) assigns a numeric score to each individual and certain corporate tax returns after they have been processed.[56]
- **Information Matching:** Some returns are examined because third party reports, such as Forms W-2 or 1099, do not match the applicable amounts reported on the tax return.
- **Related Examinations:** Returns may be selected for audit when they involve transactions with or issues related to other taxpayers, such as business partners or investors, whose returns were selected for examination.
- **Third Party Information:** Returns may be selected as a result of information received from other third-party sources or individuals. Sources may include state and local law enforcement agencies, public records, and individuals. The information is evaluated for reliability and accuracy before it is used as the basis of an examination (or a possible criminal investigation).

A taxpayer's odds of being audited increase if his income is over $200,000, he is self-employed, or his itemized deductions were much higher than other taxpayers with similar incomes.

Other issues that may draw IRS attention include taking large charitable deductions; claiming the home office deduction; claiming rental losses; deducting business meals, travel, and entertainment; claiming 100% business use of a vehicle; deducting a loss for a hobby activity; running a cash business; failing to report a foreign bank account; and engaging in currency transactions.

> **Example:** Harvey is an EA with a client, Jamila, who received an audit notice this year. Jamila's tax return was selected because she had a large number of tax credits and very little taxable income. However, her tax return was prepared correctly. Jamila had adopted four special-needs children in 2017 and was able to take the Earned Income Credit and a large Adoption Credit. Harvey provided proof of the adoptions to the examining officer, which resulted in a positive outcome for Jamila: a no-change audit.

> **Example:** Alfred embezzled money from his employer and was arrested for felony embezzlement. The case was made public, and the police shared its information with the IRS. The IRS then contacted Alfred and proposed adjustments to his tax returns, assessing additional tax, interest, and penalties for fraud for failing to report the embezzled funds as income. This is an example of third party information that can trigger an IRS criminal investigation.

Taxpayer Examination Rights and Obligations

The IRS chooses to conduct some audits face-to-face, which are known as field audits. After notification of the planned audit, the taxpayer or the taxpayer's representative must make an appointment to meet with the IRS examiner. Either before or during an initial interview, the IRS

---

[56] IRS computers automatically check tax returns and assign a Discriminant Inventory Function System (DIF) score based on the probability that the return contains errors, excessive tax deductions, or other issues. This does not necessarily mean that the return was prepared incorrectly. However, the screening is intended to identify aberrations and questionable items. If a taxpayer's return is assigned a high score under the DIF system, the return has a high probability of being chosen for audit. The IRS does not release information about how it calculates a taxpayer's DIF score.

examiner must explain the examination and collection process and the taxpayer's rights during the process. These rights include:

- A right to professional and courteous treatment by IRS employees
- A right to privacy and confidentiality about tax matters
- A right to know why the IRS is asking for information, how the IRS will use it, and what will happen if the requested information is not provided
- A right to representation, either by oneself or an authorized representative
- A right to appeal disagreements, both within the IRS and before the courts

During an examination, the IRS has the right to confirm every item on a taxpayer's return. Form 4564, *Information Document Request* (IDR), is used to request information from the taxpayer. The taxpayer must make available any documents the IRS requests, including providing access to computer files such as QuickBooks. If a taxpayer fails to produce requested documents, an examiner must determine whether to issue a summons to secure the documents.

The Taxpayer's Representative

A taxpayer may always represent himself during an examination. Alternatively, the taxpayer may use a qualified representative before the IRS. The taxpayer does not have to attend the audit if the representative has the proper power of attorney authorization and is an enrolled practitioner under Circular 230, a family member, or is an unenrolled preparer (and a participant in the IRS's AFSP program) who is providing representation solely in connection with an examination of a taxable year or period covered by a return he prepared.

Example: Kimberly is an EA. A taxpayer named Lloyd hires her to represent him before the IRS during the examination of his tax return. Lloyd does not want to attend the audit. He signs Form 2848 indicating that Kimberly is now his authorized representative for all his tax affairs. Kimberly attends the examination on Lloyd's behalf.

Example: Mitchell is a 22-year-old accounting student who is not an enrolled practitioner. The IRS is auditing his sister, Aimee. Aimee designates Mitchell as her authorized representative by signing and submitting Form 2848 to the IRS. Mitchell may practice before the IRS in this limited circumstance because of the familial relationship with the taxpayer. Mitchell has full representation rights before the IRS with regards to his sister's tax issue.

When a jointly-filed tax return is selected for examination, either spouse may meet with the IRS, or the qualified representative may meet with the IRS without either spouse present. Without an administrative summons, the IRS cannot compel a taxpayer to accompany an authorized representative to an examination interview.

Just as a taxpayer is required to do, a representative is required to produce documents the IRS requests if he has them. If he does not have the requested documents, he must disclose what he knows about them. A representative cannot mislead the government, and he cannot allow his client to do so by presenting fraudulent documents or putting forth a frivolous argument. If a representative fails to promptly submit taxpayer records, fails to keep scheduled appointments, or fails to return phone calls or written correspondence, the examiner has the right to initiate procedures to bypass the representative and deal directly with the taxpayer.

Audit Location and Procedures

IRS examiners are instructed to work out times, dates, and locations that are convenient for the taxpayer. However, the IRS retains the right to make the final determination of when, where, and how the examination will take place.

Regardless of where an examination takes place, an examiner has the right to visit the taxpayer's place of business or home to establish facts (such as information about inventory or verification of assets) that can only be accomplished by a direct visit.

The examination interview may be recorded by the taxpayer or his representative, or by the IRS, but whoever initiates the recording must notify the other party in writing ten days in advance. The taxpayer may request a copy of the IRS's recording.

If a taxpayer becomes uncomfortable during the audit and wishes to consult with a qualified representative, the IRS must suspend the interview and reschedule it.

Notice of IRS Contact of Third Parties

During the examination process, the IRS may contact third parties regarding a tax matter without the taxpayer's permission. Third parties may include neighbors, banks, employers, or employees. However, the IRS must give the taxpayer reasonable notice before contacting other persons about his individual tax matters.

The IRS must provide the taxpayer with a record of persons contacted, either on a periodic basis or upon the taxpayer's request. This requirement does not apply:

- To any pending criminal investigation.
- When providing notice would jeopardize collection of any tax liability.
- When providing notice may result in reprisal against any person.
- When the taxpayer has already authorized the contact.

Example: The IRS selects Reed's tax return for audit because it suspects unreported income related to criminal drug activity. Reed is also being investigated by the FBI. Because this is a pending criminal investigation, the IRS is not required to give Reed notice before contacting third parties about his tax matters.

Revenue Agent Reports (RAR)

When the field work portion of an examination is completed, the revenue agent must prepare a detailed written report on his findings, known as a *revenue agent report* (RAR). A RAR is supposed to clearly state the amount of adjustments to a taxpayer's return and demonstrate how the tax liability was computed. Taxpayers have the right to disagree with a RAR and may choose to contest the agent's findings.

If the taxpayer agrees with the IRS's proposed changes in the report, he may immediately sign an agreement. The taxpayer is responsible for paying interest and penalties on any additional tax. If the taxpayer pays the additional tax owed when he signs the agreement, the interest and penalties are calculated from the due date of the tax return to the date of the payment.

If the taxpayer does not pay the additional amounts when he signs the agreement, he will receive a bill that includes interest and penalties. If the taxpayer pays the amounts due within ten business days of the billing date, he will not have to pay any more interest or penalties. This period is extended to 21 calendar days if the amount due is less than $100,000.

Audit Determinations

An audit can be closed in one of three ways:

- **No Change:** An audit in which the taxpayer has substantiated all of the items being reviewed and which results in no changes.
- **Agreed:** An audit in which the IRS proposes changes and the taxpayer understands and agrees with the changes.
- **Unagreed:** An audit in which the IRS proposes changes and the taxpayer understands, but disagrees with the changes. A conference with an IRS manager may be requested for further review of the issues. In addition, the taxpayer may request fast track mediation[57] or an appeal. A taxpayer does not have to file a written protest to request fast-track mediation. The taxpayer may also choose to go to court and contest the IRS determination.

The IRS will not typically reopen a closed examination case to make an unfavorable adjustment and assess additional tax unless:

- There was fraud or misrepresentation,
- There was a substantial error based on an established IRS position existing at the time of the examination, or
- Failure to reopen the case would be a serious administrative omission.

Audit Reconsideration

In certain cases, the IRS will reevaluate the results of a prior audit if additional tax was assessed and remains unpaid or a tax credit was reversed. A taxpayer may request reconsideration if he disagrees with an earlier audit assessment, but he must provide new information, with documentation, that was not considered during the original examination. The IRS may accept a taxpayer's reconsideration request if:

- Information that is submitted has not been considered previously.
- The taxpayer filed a return after the IRS completed a substitute return for him.
- The taxpayer believes the IRS made a computational or processing error in assessing his tax.
- The tax liability remains unpaid or credits are denied.

In filing a request for reconsideration, the taxpayer must attach a copy of his examination report (Form 4549), if available, along with copies of any new documentation that supports his position.

> **Example:** Cedrick is a sole proprietor who files on Schedule C. After an IRS examination, he was assessed $1,900 of additional taxes because he had lost the file with his receipts and other documentation supporting his business deductions. Cedrick disagrees with the findings of the examination, and a couple of weeks later he finds the missing file, which includes his original receipts. Cedrick requests an audit reconsideration due to the new documentation.

---

[57] Fast Track Mediation (FTM) lets taxpayers resolve disputes at the earliest possible stage in the collection process. Once a FTM application is accepted, the goal is resolution within 40 days. With FTM, a trained mediator from the IRS Office of Appeals is assigned to help you and IRS Collection reach an agreement on the disputed issue(s).

The IRS will not accept an audit reconsideration request if:

- The taxpayer previously agreed to pay the amount of tax owed by signing a closing agreement or compromise agreement.
- The amount of tax owed is the result of final partnership item adjustments related to a TEFRA partnership examination.
- The U.S. Tax Court, or another court, has issued a final determination on the tax liability.

The IRS will typically make a decision on an audit reconsideration within 30 days. The IRS is under no obligation to approve a request to reopen an audit. However, the taxpayer retains the right to appeal an IRS assessment.

Repeat Examinations

The IRS tries to avoid repeat examinations of the same items, but sometimes this happens. If a taxpayer's return was audited for the same items in the previous two years and no change was proposed to tax liability, the taxpayer may request the IRS discontinue the examination.

Example: Eleanor donates a large percentage of her salary to her church. For the last two years, the IRS has selected Eleanor's return for examination based on her large donations. In both instances, Eleanor was able to substantiate her donations and no change was made to her tax liability. Her tax return is selected again for the same reason in 2017. Eleanor contacts the IRS to request that the examination be discontinued, and the examining officer agrees to do so.

Example: Terrance's tax return has been selected for examination three years in a row. In 2015 and 2016, his tax return was selected to verify compliance with the EITC requirements. There was no change to his tax liability in either year. In 2017, Terrance's tax return is selected for audit again. This time, the IRS is questioning his education deductions. Terrance cannot request that the examination be discontinued because it was selected for a different reason than in the previous two examinations.

Unit 10: Study Questions

(Test yourself and then check the correct answers at the end of this chapter.)

1. Frank's tax return was chosen by the IRS for examination. He moved recently to another state, but the IRS notice says that his examination will be scheduled in the city where he used to live. Which of the following statements is correct?

A. Frank can request that his tax return examination be moved to another IRS service center since he has moved to another area.
B. Frank must schedule the examination in his former city of residence, but he can have a practitioner represent him there.
C. Frank is required to meet with the examiner at least once in person in order to move the examination to another location.
D. None of the above.

2. Only in rare circumstances will the IRS reopen a closed examination case and assess additional tax. Which of the following is not a reason that the IRS would reopen a closed audit case?

A. There was fraud or misrepresentation.
B. There was a substantial error based on an established IRS position existing at the time of the examination.
C. Failure to reopen the case would be a serious administrative omission.
D. The taxpayer filed a request for fast track mediation.

3. When a taxpayer is chosen for an IRS audit, which of the following statements is correct?

A. The taxpayer must appear before the IRS in person.
B. A taxpayer may choose to be represented by a federally-authorized practitioner and is not required to appear unless he chooses to do so.
C. An audit case may not be transferred to a different IRS office under any circumstances.
D. If a taxpayer feels that he is not being treated fairly during an IRS audit, he cannot appeal to the auditor's manager.

4. For the IRS to consider accepting a taxpayer's audit reconsideration request:

A. The taxpayer filed a return after the IRS completed a substitute return for him.
B. The taxpayer must have already paid the contested additional tax.
C. The U.S. Tax Court must have already issued a ruling in the case.
D. The taxpayer must have signed a closing agreement agreeing to pay the contested additional tax.

5. For a jointly filed tax return that has been selected for examination, which of the following statements is correct?

A. Both spouses must be present during an examination because both spouses signed the return.
B. Only one spouse must be present.
C. Each spouse must have his or her own representative.
D. Neither spouse may use a representative.

6. When do the IRS rules regarding notice of third parties not apply?

A. To any pending criminal investigation.
B. When providing notice would jeopardize collection of any tax liability.
C. When providing notice may result in reprisal against any person.
D. All of the above.

7. If a taxpayer or his representative wishes for an audit to be recorded, which of the following must he do?

A. Make a request the same day as the examination.
B. Notify the examiner ten days in advance, in writing.
C. Notify the examiner one week in advance, in writing.
D. Nothing. Examinations are automatically recorded by the IRS to ensure compliance.

8. What is a revenue agent report?

A. An agreement a taxpayer makes with the IRS after an examination.
B. A report detailing the in-person interview of a taxpayer or his representative.
C. A concluding report by a revenue agent that states the amount of adjustments to a taxpayer's return.
D. A preliminary report by a revenue agent that is made when a taxpayer's return is first flagged for audit.

9. The IRS has begun an examination of Elaine's income tax return. The IRS would like to ask her neighbors questions related to the examination. There is no pending criminal investigation into the matter, and there is no evidence that this contact will result in reprisals against the neighbors or jeopardize collection of the tax liability. Before contacting the neighbors, the IRS must:

A. Provide Elaine with reasonable notice of the contacts.
B. Make an assessment of Elaine's tax liability.
C. Ask the court for a third-party subpoena.
D. Mail Elaine a Statutory Notice of Deficiency.

10. Joshua received a notice from the IRS saying a prior year's tax return had been examined, creating a tax assessment of $2,875. Joshua disagrees with the amount of tax assessed. He could request an audit reconsideration in all of the following situations EXCEPT:

A. The full amount owed has already been paid.
B. There is new documentation for the examination that could help the taxpayer's case.
C. Joshua neither appeared for the examination nor sent information to the IRS.
D. Joshua moved and never received the examination notice.

11. Who may represent a taxpayer in an examination, assuming the proper power of attorney authorization is in place?

A. The taxpayer's sister.
B. The unenrolled preparer who prepared the tax return under audit and have completed the IRS's Annual Filing Season Program.
C. A tax attorney.
D. All of the above.

12. Cameron's federal income tax return has been under examination. After the revenue agent issues her report, Cameron must determine how to respond to its findings. Which of the following choices is not a term the IRS uses to classify an audit determination?

A. No change.
B. Agreed.
C. Acknowledged.
D. Unagreed.

1. The answer is A. If a taxpayer has moved or if his books and records are located in another area, he can request that the location of his audit be changed to another IRS service center. IRS examiners are instructed to work out times, dates, and locations that are convenient for the taxpayer. However, the IRS retains the right to make the final determination of when, where, and how the examination will take place.

2. The answer is D. Requesting fast track mediation during an examination is not a reason for the IRS to reopen a closed audit case. In general, the IRS will not reopen a closed examination case to make an unfavorable adjustment unless:

- There was fraud or misrepresentation,
- There was a substantial error based on an established IRS position existing at the time of the examination, or
- Failure to reopen the case would be a serious administrative omission.

3. The answer is B. The taxpayer is not required to be present during an IRS examination if he has provided written authorization, such as Form 2848, to a qualified representative per Circular 230.

4. The answer is A. There are times the IRS will reevaluate the results of a prior audit if additional tax was assessed and remains unpaid or a tax credit was reversed. The IRS may accept a taxpayer's reconsideration request if:

- Information that is submitted has not been considered previously.
- The taxpayer filed a return after the IRS completed a substitute return for him.
- The taxpayer believes the IRS made a computational or processing error in assessing his tax.
- The tax liability is unpaid or credits are denied.

The IRS will not accept an audit reconsideration request if the taxpayer previously agreed to pay the amount of tax owed by signing a closing agreement or compromise agreement. The IRS also will not reconsider an audit if the Tax Court, or any other court, has already issued a decision in the case.

5. The answer is B. For taxpayers who file jointly, only one spouse is required to meet with the IRS. Alternatively, the taxpayers can use a qualified representative to represent them before the IRS. They could be present along with the representative, or they could choose not to be at the meeting.

6. The answer is D. During the examination process, the IRS must give the taxpayer reasonable notice before contacting other persons about his individual tax matters. This provision does not apply:

- To any pending criminal investigation.
- When providing notice would jeopardize collection of any tax liability.
- When providing notice may result in reprisal against any person.

7. The answer is B. If a taxpayer, his representative, or the IRS examiner wishes for an audit to be recorded, he must notify the other parties in writing ten days in advance. If the IRS records the interview, the taxpayer may request a copy.

8. The answer is C. An IRS examiner files a revenue agent report (RAR) after he has completed the field work part of an examination. The report should clearly state the amount of adjustments to be made to a taxpayer's return and demonstrate how the tax liability was computed. A taxpayer may agree with the RAR and pay any additional tax owed, or he may contest the agent's findings. He may appeal to the IRS or fight the tax in court.

9. The answer is A. Pursuant to IRC §7602(c), a third-party contact is made when an IRS employee initiates contact with a person other than the taxpayer. A third party may be contacted to obtain information about a specific taxpayer's federal tax liability, including the issuance of a levy or summons to someone other than the taxpayer. The IRS does not need permission to contact third parties, but it must generally notify the taxpayer that the contact with third parties will be made.

10. The answer is A. Joshua could request an audit reconsideration in all of the following situations except if the full amount owed has already been paid.

11. The answer is D. Family members and unenrolled preparers have limited rights of representation during the examination of a taxpayer's return. The taxpayer does not have to be present at the audit interview, (assuming a power of attorney is in place) for a qualified representative. Attorneys, CPAs, and Enrolled Agents have unlimited rights of representation before all offices of the IRS, not just the examination division.

12. The answer is C. There are three types of audit determinations. In other words, an IRS audit can be closed in one of three ways:
- **No change:** An audit in which the taxpayer has substantiated all of the items being reviewed and which results in no changes.
- **Agreed:** An audit in which the IRS proposes changes and the taxpayer understands and agrees with the changes.
- **Unagreed:** An audit in which the IRS proposes changes and the taxpayer understands but disagrees with the changes. A conference with an IRS manager may be requested for further review of the issues. In addition, the taxpayer may request fast track mediation or an appeal. The taxpayer may also choose to go to court and contest the IRS determination.

Unit 11: The IRS Appeals Process

> **More Reading:**
> Publication 5, *Your Appeal Rights & How to Prepare a Protest If You Don't Agree*
> Publication 556, *Examination of Returns, Appeal Rights, and Claims for Refund*
> Publication 4227, *Overview of the Appeals Process*
> Publication 4167, *Appeals: Introduction to Alternative Dispute Resolution*

Because taxpayers often disagree with the IRS on tax matters, the IRS has a formal appeals process. The IRS Office of Appeals is independent of any other IRS office and serves as an informal administrative forum for any taxpayer who wishes to dispute an IRS determination.

IRS Appeals provides taxpayers an alternative to going to court to fight disagreements about the application of tax law. The role of Appeals is to resolve disputes on a fair and impartial basis that does not favor either the government or the taxpayer. Appeals officers are directed to give serious consideration to settlement offers by taxpayers or their representatives.[58]

The mission of the IRS Appeals Office is to resolve tax controversies without litigation. Appeals is a separate division and independent of IRS examinations and collections.

Appeal System Overview

A taxpayer has three choices when he wishes to protest an IRS determination on his taxes:

1. He may appeal either formally or informally within the IRS appeals system.
2. He may take his case directly to the U.S. Tax Court.
3. He may bypass both IRS Appeals and the Tax Court and take his case to the U.S. Court of Federal Claims or to a U.S. district court.

The contested tax does not have to be paid first if a taxpayer opts for either IRS Appeals or the Tax Court, but if the taxpayer goes directly to the Court of Federal Claims or a U.S. district court, he must pay the tax first and then sue the IRS for a refund.

An IRS appeal does not normally abate penalties and interest on the tax due. These continue to accumulate until one of two events occurs:

- The balance of the debt is paid, or
- The taxpayer wins his appeal and he is granted a no-change audit.

Reasons for an appeal must be supported by tax law. An appeal cannot be based solely on moral, religious, political, constitutional, conscientious, or similar grounds.

Appealing After an Examination

The 30-Day Letter: Within a few weeks after a taxpayer's closing conference with an IRS examiner, he will receive what is commonly called a 30-day letter. This letter includes:

- A notice explaining the taxpayer's right to appeal the proposed changes within 30 days
- A copy of the revenue agent report explaining the examiner's proposed changes
- An agreement or waiver form
- A copy of Publication 5, *Your Appeal Rights and How to Prepare a Protest If You Don't Agree*

---

[58] Internal Revenue Manual 1.2.17.7: "Appeals will ordinarily give serious consideration to an offer to settle a tax controversy on a basis which fairly reflects the relative merits of the opposing views in the light of the hazards which would exist if the case were litigated. However, no settlement will be made based upon nuisance value of the case to either party."

The taxpayer has 30 days from the date of notice to accept or appeal the proposed changes.

If the taxpayer chooses to appeal an examiner's decision through the IRS system, he can contact a local Appeals office, which is separate and independent of the IRS office that conducted the examination.

Conferences with Appeals office personnel may be conducted in person, through correspondence, or by telephone with the taxpayer or his authorized representative. Only practitioners are allowed to represent taxpayers before an IRS appeals hearing. The taxpayer does not need to attend if his representative has power of attorney authorization via a signed Form 2848 or any other properly written POA authorization.

> **Note:** An unenrolled tax return preparer may be a witness for a taxpayer at an appeals conference, but may not serve as an authorized representative for the taxpayer.

Filing a Formal Protest: A formal written protest is required in all cases to request an Appeals conference, unless the taxpayer qualifies for the small case request procedure. The protest statement must go into greater detail than the small case request. It must include the facts supporting the taxpayer's position and the law or authority that the taxpayer is relying upon in making his case. The protest is signed under penalties of perjury.

If an Enrolled Agent or other practitioner prepares and signs the protest for a taxpayer, he must substitute a declaration that states whether he knows personally that the facts in the protest and accompanying documents are true and correct.

> **Example:** Vladimir is an Enrolled Agent who represents Tracy, a sole proprietor who runs a small restaurant. The IRS audited Tracy's business return and found multiple discrepancies on her Schedule C. Tracy receives a 30-day letter stating that she owes an additional $32,000 in tax. Tracy disagrees with the amount, so Vladimir files a formal protest within 30 days with the IRS Appeals office. In the protest, Vladimir details why the proposed assessment is incorrect and the legal basis for his argument. He also submits the required practitioner declaration and a copy of Form 2848. Vladimir then schedules a conference with an Appeals officer. When they meet, they discuss the matter and reach a settlement agreeable to each party. Since the IRS has a signed Form 2848 authorizing Vladimir to be Tracy's representative, she was not required to attend the appeals hearing.

The 90-Day Letter (Notice of Deficiency)

If a taxpayer does not respond to a 30-day letter, or if he cannot reach an agreement with an Appeals officer, the IRS will send him a *Notice of Deficiency*, which is also known as the 90-day letter. A Notice of Deficiency is required by law and is used to advise the taxpayer of his appeal rights to the U.S. Tax Court.

A Notice of Deficiency must be issued before a taxpayer can go to the Tax Court. The taxpayer has 90 days (150 days if addressed to a taxpayer outside the United States) from the date of this notice to file a petition with the Tax Court.

If the taxpayer does not file the petition in time, the tax is due within ten days, and the taxpayer may not take his case to Tax Court. If the taxpayer does file a petition in time and the case is docketed before the Tax Court, his file will again go to an IRS Appeals office to see if it can be resolved before going to court. More than 90% of all tax cases are resolved before going to Tax Court.

U.S. Tax Court

The U.S. Tax Court is a federal court separate from the IRS where taxpayers may choose to contest their tax deficiencies without having to pay the disputed amount first. The court issues both regular and memorandum decisions. A regular decision is when the Tax Court rules on an issue for the first time. A memorandum decision is when the Tax Court has previously ruled on identical or similar issues. The Tax Court has jurisdiction over the following tax disputes:

- Notices of deficiency
- Review of the failure to abate interest
- Notices of transferee liability
- Adjustment of partnership items
- Administrative costs
- Worker classification (employee versus independent contractor)
- Review of certain collection actions

The Tax Court has jurisdiction over the following types of tax:

- Income tax
- Estate tax and gift tax
- Certain excise taxes
- Re-determine transferee liability
- Worker classification
- Relief from joint and several liability on a joint return
- Whistleblower awards

Any individual taxpayer may represent himself before the U.S. Tax Court. A taxpayer may choose to represent himself; this is referred to as *"pro se,"* which is a legal term meaning "for oneself" or "on one's own behalf." A taxpayer may also choose to be represented by a person admitted to practice before the Tax Court.

Note: Enrolled Agents and CPAs must be "admitted to practice" before the Tax Court by first passing a separate exam specific to this purpose. "Practice before the IRS" does not include practice before the Tax Court. Licensed attorneys are the only practitioners who are not required to pass the Tax Court exam before practicing before the court.

Note: The Tax Court has generally held that taxpayers who rely on software to justify errors on self-prepared returns are liable for the 6662 accuracy-related penalty.[59]

Tax Court Small Tax Case Procedure

Small tax case procedures (also known as S-case procedures) in the Tax Court are one avenue to resolve disputes between taxpayers and the IRS. Small tax cases are handled under simpler, less formal procedures than regular cases. Often, decisions are handled down quicker than in other courts.

Within the IRS appeals system, a taxpayer may file a "small case request" if the total amount of tax, penalties, and interest for each tax period involved are under a certain threshold (explained below). To make a small case request, the taxpayer may use Form 12203, *Request for Appeals Review*, or prepare a

---

[59] IRC 6662; IRC 6664(c); Reg. 1.6664-4(b)(1); Anyika v. Commissioner, T.C. Memo. 2011-69.

brief written statement requesting an appeals conference. He must specify why he does not agree with the proposed tax assessment.[60]

The taxpayer and the Tax Court must both agree to proceed with the small case procedure. Generally, the Tax Court will agree with the taxpayer's S-case request if the taxpayer otherwise qualifies.

However, the Tax Court's decision in a small tax case cannot be appealed by the taxpayer. The decision is final, as the IRS is not allowed to appeal either if it loses the case. In contrast, either the taxpayer or the IRS can appeal a decision in a regular, non-S case to a U.S. Court of Appeals.

Dollar limits for the Tax Court Small Case Division vary:

- For a Notice of Deficiency: $50,000 is the maximum amount, including penalties and interest, for any year before the court.
- For a Notice of Determination: $50,000 is the maximum amount for all the years combined.
- For a Notice of Deficiency related to a request for relief from joint and several liability: $50,000 is the maximum amount of spousal relief for all the years combined.
- For an IRS Notice of Determination of Worker Classification: The amount in the dispute cannot exceed $50,000 for any calendar quarter.

A decision entered in a small tax case is not treated as precedent for any other case and is not typically published.

Since the taxpayer cannot appeal a decision by the Small Tax Case Division, he must consider whether using the S-case procedure is worth the risk of not being able to contest an adverse decision in a higher court.

Delay Tactics are Prohibited

If a taxpayer unreasonably fails to pursue the internal IRS appeals system, if the case is filed primarily to cause a delay, or if the taxpayer's position is frivolous, the Tax Court may impose a penalty of up to $25,000.[61] Frivolous positions include those that contend that:

- The income tax is not valid,
- Payment of tax is voluntary,
- A person or a type of income is not subject to tax, or
- Espouse other arguments that the courts have previously rejected as baseless.

The Tax Court may also impose sanctions of up to $25,000 on those who misuse their right to a court review of IRS collection procedures merely to stall their tax payments. This rule is targeted at taxpayers who do not have a legitimate complaint and are instead using the Tax Court simply to delay collection action in their case.

Other Court Appeals

The vast majority of taxpayers who use the court system appeal their disputes in the Tax Court. However, a minority of taxpayers choose to challenge the IRS in a U.S. district court or Court of Federal Claims. In this case, a taxpayer must pay the contested tax deficiency first.

If either party loses at the trial court level, the court's decision may be appealed to a higher court.

---

[60] Employee retirement plans (Form 5500), exempt organizations, S corporations, and partnerships are not eligible for small case requests.

[61] The IRS makes public the names and cases of taxpayers who have been assessed these §6673 penalties by the Tax Court. The cases are published on the IRS website as well as in the Tax Court Historical Opinion area.

Example: The IRS issues Cassandra a notice of deficiency in the amount of $45,000. Cassandra disagrees with the assessment and does not wish to contest the tax through the IRS Appeals office or the Tax Court. Instead, she wants to go straight to a U.S. district court. She must first pay the contested liability and then sue the IRS for a refund.

Note: Although Enrolled Agents and CPAs have unlimited rights of representation before all levels and officers of the IRS, they cannot represent taxpayers in disputes with the IRS before U.S. district courts, bankruptcy courts, courts of appeal, or the U.S. Supreme Court. That authority is reserved only for licensed attorneys.

Taxpayer Rights to Bring Civil Action

The government cannot ask a taxpayer to waive his right to sue the United States or a government employee for any action taken in connection with the tax laws. However, a taxpayer can waive his right to sue if:

- He knowingly and voluntarily waives that right.
- The request to waive the right is made in writing to his attorney or other federally authorized practitioner.
- The request is made in person and his attorney or other representative is present.

Burden of Proof: In most cases, the burden of proof lies with the IRS during court proceedings, assuming the taxpayer has complied with all of the following issues:

- Adhered to IRS substantiation requirements.
- Maintained adequate records.
- Cooperated with reasonable requests for information from the IRS.
- Introduced credible evidence relating to the issue.
- In the case of a trust, corporation, or partnership, the taxpayer had net worth of $7 million or less and not more than 500 employees at the time of contested tax liability.

Recovering Court Costs

A taxpayer may be able to recover the expenses he incurred to defend his position while contesting tax assessed by the IRS. Under IRC §7430, the IRS is compelled to pay "reasonable litigation and administrative" costs incurred by a taxpayer in most administrative proceedings before the IRS and in court proceedings before most U.S. federal courts.

To recover court costs, the following general requirements must be met:

- The costs must be incurred in an administrative or court proceeding brought by or against the United States.
- The taxpayer must be the prevailing party.
- The taxpayer must have exhausted all administrative remedies within the IRS.
- The costs must be reasonable. They must have been incurred as a result of assessment, collection, or refund of tax, interest, or penalty imposed pursuant to the Internal Revenue Code.
- The taxpayer must not have unreasonably delayed any IRS proceeding.

Example: Aurora is a registered nurse. During an examination, she disagreed with an IRS assessment that disallowed educational expenses she had claimed while pursuing an MBA degree for health professionals. After receiving a notice of deficiency, she took her case to the Tax Court and won. Aurora may be able to recover attorney fees and other court costs she incurred in her fight with the IRS.

The taxpayer will not be treated as the prevailing party if the IRS establishes that its position was substantially justified. In order to request the recovery of litigation costs from the IRS, the taxpayer must meet certain net worth requirements:

- For individuals, net worth cannot exceed $2 million as of the filing date of the petition for review. Spouses filing a joint return are treated as separate individuals.
- For estates, net worth cannot exceed $2 million as of the date of the decedent's death.
- For exempt organizations and certain cooperatives, the entity cannot have more than 500 employees as of the filing date of the petition for review.
- For all other taxpayers, net worth cannot exceed $7 million, and the entity must not have more than 500 employees as of the filing date of the petition for review.

(Test yourself and then check the correct answers at the end of this chapter.)

1. An Enrolled Agent may NOT represent a taxpayer in a dispute before:

A. An IRS revenue agent.
B. An IRS revenue officer.
C. A U.S. district court judge.
D. The IRS appeals office.

2. The Statutory Notice of Deficiency is also known as:

A. A 30-day letter because the taxpayer generally has 30 days from the date of the notice to file a petition with the Tax Court.
B. A 90-day letter because the taxpayer generally has 90 days from the date of the notice to file a petition with the Tax Court.
C. An Information Document Request because the taxpayer is asked for information to support his position regarding his tax liability.
D. A federal tax lien.

3. Which of the following statements is correct about an IRS appeal?

A. An appeal does not abate the interest on a tax liability. Interest continues to accrue.
B. A taxpayer must pay the disputed tax before filing an appeal with the IRS.
C. The IRS is prohibited from filing a federal tax lien if the taxpayer is outside the U.S.
D. Taxpayers who disagree with the IRS changes may not appeal to the U.S. Tax Court.

4. Aaron wants to appeal the findings of an examination, but his tax return was prepared by an unenrolled preparer. Aaron does not wish to be present during the appeals process. What are his options?

A. Aaron must have a family member represent him.
B. Aaron may represent himself or hire a practitioner (CPA, attorney, or EA) to represent him at the appeals level.
C. Aaron may be represented by the unenrolled preparer, so long as the unenrolled preparer is the one who prepared the tax return at issue.
D. Aaron may ask an IRS employee to represent him at IRS Appeals.

5. If a taxpayer wishes to challenge the IRS in a district court, the taxpayer must:

A. First attempt to resolve the contested tax with the IRS Appeals office.
B. Pay the contested liability first and then sue the IRS for a refund.
C. Pay a retainer to the IRS for a refund.
D. Go first to the U.S. Tax Court before appealing to a U.S. district court.

6. Which of the following best states the purpose of the IRS Office of Appeals?

A. To help the taxpayer and the government settle their tax dispute and reach an equitable settlement.
B. To advocate for the taxpayer in connection with the taxpayer's disagreement with the collection or examination divisions of the IRS.
C. To advocate for the government and convince the taxpayer to pay his fair share before he pursues his case through the court system.
D. To look at the facts and circumstances of each case, and then take a side in the tax dispute.

7. Kevin and Javier are partners in a body shop business. Both had their individual returns examined and both disagreed with the IRS. Kevin decided to take his case to the IRS Appeals office. After the conference, he and the IRS still disagreed. Javier decided to bypass the Appeals office altogether and go directly to court. Which of the following statements is correct?

A. Neither may petition the Tax Court.
B. Both Kevin and Javier can take their cases to the following courts: U.S. Tax Court, U.S. Court of Federal Claims, or the U.S. District Court.
C. Only Kevin may petition the Tax Court, because he went through the IRS appeals process first.
D. Both can take their cases to the Tax Court, but not to other U.S. courts.

8. Alyssa disagrees with the IRS examiner regarding her income tax case. Her appeal rights are explained to her, and she decides to contest the tax by pursuing the case in the Tax Court. Which of the following statements is correct?

A. Alyssa must receive a Notice of Deficiency before she can go to the Tax Court.
B. Alyssa must wait for the IRS examiner to permanently close her audit case.
C. Alyssa must request a collection due process hearing before she can go to the Tax Court.
D. Alyssa cannot go to the Tax Court unless she agrees with the auditor's findings.

9. Danielle owes a substantial sum to the IRS. She files a petition with the U.S. Tax Court. Her case is later determined to be frivolous, wholly without merit, and merely to cause delay. As a repercussion to Danielle's action, the Tax Court may impose a penalty of:

A. Up to $10,000.
B. Up to $25,000.
C. Up to $50,000.
D. Up to $25,000 and one year in prison.

10. At the beginning of each examination, the IRS auditor must explain:

A. A taxpayer's appeal rights.
B. A taxpayer's right to a fair trial.
C. A taxpayer's right to remain silent.
D. A taxpayer's right to confidentiality.

11. Which of the following statements is correct regarding a taxpayer's right to appeal a tax assessment?

A. A taxpayer must first pay the contested tax before he can appeal in the U.S. Tax Court, or U.S. district or federal courts.
B. A taxpayer has the right to appeal a tax assessment on the basis of religious, political, or constitutional grounds.
C. The IRS Appeals office is an arm of the IRS Collection division.
D. A taxpayer must first pay the contested tax before he can appeal in a U.S. district or federal court.

12. Which of the following tasks can be performed by any Enrolled Agent on behalf of their client?

A. Prepare and file a suit for refund in United States District Court.
B. Prepare and sign a United States Tax Court petition to contest a notice of deficiency.
C. Prepare and sign a protest to challenge examination results in the IRS Appeals Office.
D. Prepare and file a bankruptcy petition in United States Bankruptcy Court due to unpaid tax balances.

13. If a taxpayer and the IRS fail to settle a non-docketed examination controversy in the IRS Appeals Office, the next event to occur is:

A. Issuance of a notice of deficiency
B. Issuance of notice and demand for payment
C. Return of the case to the Revenue Agent for further review
D. Referral of the case to the Taxpayer Advocate

14. The Tax Court has generally held that taxpayers who rely on software to justify errors on self-prepared returns are:

A. Not liable for the 6662 accuracy-related penalty.
B. Liable for the 6662 accuracy-related penalty.
C. Liable for 20% of the 6662 accuracy-related penalty.
D. Liable for 40% of the 6662 accuracy-related penalty.

1. The answer is C. An Enrolled Agent may represent taxpayers at all levels of the IRS, but does not have the same practice rights in the U.S. court system.

2. The answer is B. The Statutory Notice of Deficiency, or 90-day letter, gives the taxpayer 90 days to file a petition in the U.S. Tax Court challenging the proposed deficiency. However, a taxpayer is granted 150 days if the notice is addressed to a taxpayer outside the United States.

3. The answer is A. An IRS appeal does not abate the interest, which continues to accrue until the balance of the debt is paid, or until the taxpayer wins his appeal and he is granted a no-change audit. A no-change audit means the IRS has accepted the tax return as it was filed.

4. The answer is B. Aaron can appear before IRS Appeals by himself, or hire a qualified representative to appear on his behalf. If he wants to be represented by someone else, he must choose a person who is eligible to practice before the IRS. Only enrolled practitioners (attorneys, CPAs, and EAs) are allowed to represent taxpayers before an appeals hearing (unless a special exception applies, for example, an executor representing an estate or a parent representing their own minor child).

5. The answer is B. In order to appeal in district court, the taxpayer must first pay the contested liability and then sue the IRS for a refund. If either party loses at the trial court level, the court's decision may be appealed to a higher court.

6. The answer is A. The Office of Appeals helps taxpayers resolve their tax disputes with the IRS without going to Tax Court. Appeals is an independent organization within the IRS. After the applicable IRS compliance division has made its decision, Appeals reviews a case and works to settle disagreements on a basis that is fair and impartial to both the government and the taxpayer.

7. The answer is B. Both Kevin and Javier can take their cases to court. A taxpayer is not required to use the IRS appeals process. If a taxpayer and the IRS still disagree after an appeals conference or a taxpayer decides to bypass the IRS appeals system altogether, the case may be taken to the U.S. Tax Court, the U.S. Court of Federal Claims, or a U.S. district court.

8. The answer is A. A Notice of Deficiency (90-day letter) must be issued before a taxpayer can go to Tax Court. A taxpayer has 90 days from the date of the notice to respond and file a petition with the court.

9. The answer is B. Danielle may be liable for a $25,000 penalty. If a taxpayer unreasonably fails to pursue the internal IRS appeals system, if the case is filed primarily to cause a delay, or if the taxpayer's position is frivolous, the Tax Court may impose a penalty of up to $25,000.

10. The answer is A. At the beginning of each examination, the IRS auditor must explain a taxpayer's appeal rights.

11. The answer is D. A taxpayer has the right to appeal a tax assessment through the IRS Appeals office, the U.S. Tax Court, or a U.S. District Court or the Court of Federal Claims. However, if the taxpayer opts to have his appeal heard in a district or Federal Claims court, the taxpayer must first pay the contested tax and sue the IRS for a refund.

12. The answer is C. An Enrolled Agent may prepare and sign a protest to challenge examination results in the IRS Appeals Office.

13. The answer is A. If a taxpayer and the IRS fail to settle a non-docketed examination controversy in the IRS Appeals Office, the next event to occur is the issuance of a notice of deficiency. Once the notice of deficiency is issued, the taxpayer has 90 days (150 days if addressed to a taxpayer outside the United States) from the date of this notice to file a petition with the U.S. Tax Court.

14. The answer is B. The Tax Court has generally held that taxpayers who rely on software to justify errors on self-prepared returns are: liable for the 6662 accuracy-related penalty.

Unit 12: The IRS E-File Program

More Reading:

Publication 3112, *IRS e-file Application and Participation*

Publication 1345, *Handbook for Authorized IRS e-file Providers of Individual Income Tax Returns*

The IRS e-file program allows taxpayers to transmit their returns electronically. More than 84% of American taxpayers file their tax returns electronically. According to the IRS, the processing of e-file returns is not only quicker, but is also more accurate than the processing of paper returns. However, as with a paper return, the taxpayer is responsible for ensuring an e-filed return contains accurate information and is filed on time.

Paid preparers who prepare more than ten individual returns a year are required to e-file income tax returns.[62] The e-file mandate covers returns for individuals, trusts, and estates.

If that number is 11 or more for the calendar year, all preparers of a firm must e-file the returns they prepare and file. This is true even if, on an individual basis, a member prepares and files fewer than the threshold.[63]

Note: For the purposes of the e-file mandate, members of firms must count their returns *in the aggregate*. If the number of applicable income tax returns is 11 or more, then all members of the firm generally must e-file the returns they prepare and file. This is true even if an individual preparer expects to prepare and file fewer than 11 returns.

Example: Ashley is an Enrolled Agent who works as a full-time employee for AZ Tax Preparation. She also has a side business preparing tax returns from her home. Ashley specializes in fiduciary and estate tax issues and does not prepare very many individual tax returns. For the coming tax year, Ashley expects to prepare and file five Form 1041 returns (for estates and trusts) while working for the CPA firm. She also expects to prepare and file seven Form 1040 tax returns as a self-employed preparer. Since she expects to file 11 or more forms between her regular job and her side-business, Ashley is required to e-file all of the returns.

Some preparers are exempt from the e-file mandate.[64] The IRS e-file does not accept foreign preparers without social security numbers into their e-file program, so those preparers are exempt. A tax preparer may request exemption from the e-file program by submitting Form 8944, *Preparer e-file Hardship Waiver Request,* to request a waiver.

Waivers are reviewed and approved in cases where the preparer demonstrates that complying would be an undue hardship.

These exemptions are rare and considered only on a case-by-case basis.

---

[62] Individual taxpayers are not bound by this mandate. A taxpayer may always file on paper, if he chooses. The e-file mandate only applies to paid preparers. It does not apply to tax returns that are not prepared for compensation, such as a tax return that an Enrolled Agent files for a family member at no charge.

[63] Financial institutions and fiduciaries that file Forms 1041 as a trustee or fiduciary are not required to e-file and are not subject to the mandate. The e-file mandate also does not apply to payroll tax returns.

[64] A tax return preparer and a member of a recognized religious group that is conscientiously opposed to filing electronically is not required to apply for a waiver using Form 8944. Preparers who claim a religious exemption to e-filing must attach Form 8948, Preparer Explanation for Not Filing Electronically, to their clients' paper returns and check box 3.

Applying to the IRS E-File Program

To begin e-filing tax returns, a preparer must apply and be accepted as an authorized IRS e-file provider. There is no fee to apply, and the process takes up to 45 days. The first step is to create an IRS e-Services account by providing required personal information including a Social Security number, an address where confirmation of the account will be mailed, and the preparer's adjusted gross income from the current or prior tax year.

After being approved for an e-services account, an applicant begins the comprehensive process to become an *IRS e-file provider*, which is an umbrella term for anyone authorized to participate in e-file, from software developers to transmitters. A preparer who wants to e-file for clients must be approved as an *electronic return originator* (ERO). The application must also identify a firm's principals and at least one responsible official.

Each person on an e-file provider application must:

- Be a United States citizen or a legal U.S. alien lawfully admitted for permanent residence,
- Be at least 18 years of age as of the date of application, and
- Meet applicable state and local licensing and/or bonding requirements for the preparation of tax returns.

If the principal or responsible official is someone who is certified or licensed (such as an attorney, CPA, or Enrolled Agent), he must enter current professional status information. All other individuals must be fingerprinted as part of the application process.

After the application is submitted, the IRS will conduct a suitability check on the firm and on each person listed on the application as either a principal or responsible official. Suitability checks may include the following:

- A criminal background check
- A credit history check
- A tax compliance check to ensure that the applicant's personal returns are filed and paid
- A check for prior noncompliance with IRS e-file requirements

It can take up to 45 days for the IRS to approve an e-file application. When a business is accepted to participate in IRS e-file, it is assigned an electronic filing identification number (EFIN). All preparers in a firm based in the same physical location are covered by the same number.

For example, a tax preparation business with ten employee-preparers in one location would all file using the same EFIN. Each preparer would then use his own PTIN on the returns that he individually prepares.[65]

Electronic Return Originators

An ERO is an authorized IRS e-file provider who originates the electronic submission of tax returns to the IRS.

Although an ERO may engage in tax return preparation, and many do, tax preparation is a distinct and separate activity from the electronic submission of tax returns to the IRS. An ERO submits a tax return only after the taxpayer has authorized the e-file transmission. The return must be either:

- Prepared by the ERO; or

---

[65] The IRS requires firms with multiple physical locations to obtain separate EFINs for each location.

- Collected from a taxpayer who has self-prepared his own return and is asking the ERO to e-file it for him.

An ERO is required to:

- Timely submit returns.
- Submit any required supporting paper documents to the IRS.
- Provide copies to taxpayers.
- Retain records and make records available to the IRS.
- Work with the taxpayer and/or the transmitter to correct a rejected return.
- Enter the preparer's identifying information (name, address, and PTIN).
- Be diligent in recognizing fraud and abuse, reporting it to the IRS and preventing it when possible.
- Cooperate with IRS investigations by making documents available to the IRS upon request.

An ERO who originates returns that he has not prepared, but only collected, becomes an income tax return preparer when he makes substantive changes to the tax return.

A non-substantive change is a correction limited to a transposition error, misplaced entry, spelling error, or arithmetic correction. The IRS considers all other changes substantive. As such, the ERO may be required to sign the return as the preparer.

Example: Carolina is an ERO. A taxpayer brings a self-prepared tax return for Carolina to e-file. She notices gross errors on the tax return and talks with the client about the mistakes. The taxpayer agrees to correct the return, and Carolina makes the necessary adjustments on the return for a small fee. Carolina is now required to sign the return as the preparer.

Authorized Transmitters

After an ERO submits a tax return, it is sent to an authorized transmitter, which submits it to the IRS. Once received at the IRS, the return is automatically checked for errors. If it cannot be processed, it is sent back to the originating transmitter to clarify any necessary information.

After correction, the transmitter retransmits the return to the IRS. Within 48 hours of electronically sending the return, the IRS sends an acknowledgment to the transmitter stating the return is accepted for processing. This is called an electronic postmark, and it is the taxpayer's proof of filing and assurance that the IRS has the return.

Authorized e-file providers must retain a record of each electronic postmark until the end of the calendar year and provide the record to the IRS upon request. Most tax software packages automatically retain a record of the return transmission report and electronic postmark.

Example: Curley is a paid preparer and an ERO who uses Ultra TaxPro software to prepare returns. Once he has completed a tax return, he gives a copy to the client, who gives signature authorization to e-file the return by completing Form 8879. Curley transmits the return to Ultra TaxPro, which is an authorized transmitter. Ultra TaxPro then transmits the return to the IRS. Most tax practitioners use this method; all the major tax preparation software companies have e-file transmission options.

Electronic Signature Requirements

Electronically filed returns have signature requirements, just as paper tax returns do. For e-filed tax returns, both taxpayers and preparers must complete Form 8879, *IRS e-file Signature Authorization*. The

IRS has issued recent guidance clarifying that taxpayers may sign Form 8879 with an electronic signature.

Form 8879 includes a taxpayer's consent to electronic filing; a declaration that the e-filed return is true, correct, and complete; and an indication of which method of signature authorization is used on the e-filed return. The form must be retained for three years from the return due date or the IRS received date, whichever is later. Unless the IRS requests to see the form, it is not submitted.

> **Example:** Derek is an Enrolled Agent. He has a long-time client who comes to his office to consult with him about her tax return. Derek verifies her identity by inspecting her driver's license. Another long-term client lives in a different state. Derek uses an agency that provides identity verification services for this client. After confirming the identity of each client, Derek can allow each to sign Form 8879 with electronic signatures.

If an e-filed return does not have an appropriate electronic signature via a personal identification number (PIN), it will be rejected. This requirement also applies to volunteers at VITA and TCPE sites who provide free tax assistance and e-filing.

- The **self-select PIN** allows a taxpayer to electronically sign his e-filed return by selecting and entering a five-digit PIN as his signature. The IRS uses the taxpayer's prior year adjusted gross income or prior year PIN to validate the signature. The taxpayer may also authorize an ERO to enter or generate his PIN.
- The **practitioner PIN** is an 11-digit number that includes the ERO's six-digit EFIN and the preparer's five-digit self-selected PIN. The ERO uses the same practitioner PIN for the entire tax year.

Form 8453, *U.S. Individual Income Tax Transmittal for an IRS e-file Return*, is used to send any required paper forms or supporting documentation that may be needed with an e-filed return. Form 8453 must be mailed to the IRS within three business days after receiving acknowledgment that the IRS has accepted the electronically-filed return.

If the ERO is signing the tax return as a representative, Form 2848, *Power of Attorney and Declaration of Representative*, must be attached to Form 8453.

> **Example:** Dexter is an Enrolled Agent and ERO. He has power of attorney for a client, Faulkner, who is working overseas for several months. Dexter uses his practitioner PIN and signs Faulkner's tax return on his behalf. He e-files the return and then mails Form 8453 to the IRS the next day. Dexter attaches Form 2848 showing he is Faulkner's authorized representative to sign his tax return.

> **New Verification Requirements:** Practitioners who accept electronic signatures must take additional steps to authenticate the identity of the taxpayer. For in-person transactions, the preparer must inspect a valid government-issued picture ID, compare the picture to the applicant, and record the name, Social Security number, address, and date of birth. A credit check or other identity verification is optional. For remote transactions, the preparer must verify that the name, Social Security number, address, date of birth, and other personal information on record are consistent with the information provided through record checks with applicable agencies or institutions, or through credit bureaus or similar databases. The IRS has clarified that an electronic signature via remote transaction does not include handwritten signatures of Forms 8879 sent to the ERO by hand delivery, U.S. mail, private delivery service, fax, email, or an Internet website.

The verification of a client's identity[66] must be done every year; if a preparer cannot verify identity after three attempts, he must obtain a handwritten signature instead of an electronic one.

E-File Rejections

If the IRS rejects an e-filed return and the preparer cannot rectify the reason for the rejection, the preparer must inform the taxpayer of the rejection within 24 hours.

The preparer must provide the taxpayer with the IRS reject codes accompanied by an explanation. If the taxpayer chooses not to have the electronic return corrected and retransmitted to the IRS, or if the IRS cannot accept the return for processing, the taxpayer must file a paper return. The due dates for filing paper income tax returns also apply to electronic returns, however, if an e-filed return is rejected, the taxpayer does have time to rectify the problem.

Paper Returns Submitted After an E-file Rejection

Sometimes, a taxpayer cannot correct the e-filed return, and is therefore forced to file a paper return. This happens in the case of identity theft. In order to timely file, the taxpayer must file the paper return by the later of:

- The due date of the return, or
- Ten calendar days after the date the IRS gives notification that it rejected the e-filed return. This is called the *ten-day transmission perfection period*. It is additional time the IRS gives a preparer and taxpayer to correct errors in the electronic filing and resubmit a tax return without a late filing penalty.

If a taxpayer files on paper after an e-file rejection, the following information must be included:

- An explanation of why the paper return is being filed after the due date
- A copy of the rejection notification
- A brief history of actions taken to correct the electronic return

The taxpayer should write in red at the top of the first page of the paper return:

"REJECTED ELECTRONIC RETURN-(DATE)"

The date should be the date of the first e-file rejection. The paper return must be signed by the taxpayer. The PIN that was used on the rejected e-filing may not be used as the signature on the paper return. If an e-file submission is rejected, a return can be corrected within the ten-day transmission period and not be subject to a late filing penalty, but this is not the case for a late payment penalty. If a return is rejected on the due date, an electronic payment should not be transmitted with the return, because a tax payment must still be submitted or postmarked by the due date.

Rejected individual e-filed returns can be corrected and retransmitted without new signatures or authorizations if the changes do not differ from the amount on the original electronic return by more

---

[66] Although no specific technology is required, the IRS gives the following examples of acceptable electronic signature methods: a handwritten signature input onto an electronic signature pad; a handwritten signature, mark, or command input on a display screen by means of a stylus device; a digitized image of a handwritten signature that is attached to an electronic record; a typed name (e.g., typed at the end of an electronic record or typed into a signature block on a website form by a signer); a shared secret code, password, or PIN used by a person to sign the electronic record; a digital signature; or a mark captured as a scalable graphic. The new guidance also applies to Form 8878, *IRS e-file Signature Authorization for Form 4868 or Form 2350*.

than $50 to "total income" or "AGI," or more than $14 to "total tax," "federal income tax withheld," "refund," or "amount you owe."

> **Example:** Harvey is an EA who e-files a tax return for his client, Joelle, on April 17. The next day, Harvey receives an IRS notice that the return was rejected. Harvey notifies Joelle of the rejection within 24 hours. The issue cannot be corrected, so she must file a paper return. Harvey mails the return on April 19 and gives Joelle a copy. The tax return will be considered filed timely, because the paper return was filed within ten days of the rejection and the original e-filing of the return was attempted in a timely manner. If Joelle had owed tax, she would have needed to send payment by the due date.

Safeguarding IRS e-File

Authorized IRS e-file providers are responsible for helping recognize and prevent fraud and abuse in IRS e-file. The IRS has mandated six security, privacy, and business standards to which providers must adhere, including the reporting of security incidents. Providers who e-file individual income tax returns must report incidents to the IRS as soon as possible, but no later than the next business day. Any unauthorized disclosure, misuse, modification, or destruction of taxpayer information is considered a reportable security incident.

Entity Electronic Filing Requirements

Certain corporations, partnerships, and tax-exempt organizations are required to file electronically. Corporate taxpayers, including tax-exempt organizations, with $10 million or more in assets and that file at least 250 returns (information returns and others, such as Forms 1099 and W-2) are required to file electronically via magnetic media. This requirement applies regardless of whether they use a paid preparer.

> **Definition:** The term **magnetic media** means magnetic tape, tape cartridge, and diskette, as well as other media, such as electronic filing, which are specifically permitted by IRS regulations.

> **Example:** The Clements Company is a calendar-year S corporation with assets of $11 million. In 2017, the company is required to file one Form 1120S, 105 Forms W-2, 145 Forms 1099-DIV, four Forms 941, and one Form 940. Since the Clements Company is required to file 256 returns during the calendar year, it is required to file its Form 1120S electronically via magnetic media.

Partnerships with more than 100 partners are also required to use magnetic media. Partnerships with 100 or fewer partners (Schedules K-1) may voluntarily file their returns electronically, but are not required to do so. A partnership has more than 100 partners if, over the course of the taxable year, the partnership had over 100 partners on any particular day in the year, regardless of whether a partner was a partner for the entire year.

A preparer's e-file application must be current and must list all the form types (1120, 1065, 990, etc.) that he will transmit to the IRS. If the preparer does not list a certain form on his application and later attempts to transmit that form, he will receive a rejection for the return type.

> **Example:** Rosemarie is an EA. When she first applied to be an e-file provider, she only prepared individual returns. In 2017, she prepares a partnership return. However, Rosemarie forgets to update her e-file application. When she submits the partnership return online, it is rejected. Rosemarie will have to update her e-file application in order to submit partnership returns electronically.

Paper Returns

A taxpayer may choose to file a paper return that has been prepared by a paid preparer. The taxpayer must mail the return himself and include a hand-signed and dated statement documenting his choice to file on paper. A preparer is required to attach Form 8948, *Preparer Explanation for Not Filing Electronically*, to a client's paper return.

A preparer may also request a hardship waiver from the IRS to be exempt from e-filing. The IRS says it will grant waivers only in rare cases and usually not for more than one calendar year. It will deny waivers if the request is made because the preparer does not have appropriate software or simply prefers not to e-file.

Some returns are impossible to e-file for various reasons and are therefore exempt from the e-file requirement. The following *individual* tax returns cannot be processed using IRS e-file:

- Amended tax returns
- Individual tax returns with fiscal year tax periods (very rare)
- Returns containing forms or schedules that cannot be processed by IRS e-file
- Tax returns with taxpayer identification numbers within the range of 900-00-0000 through 999-99-9999 (with the exception of certain ITIN and ATIN returns)
- Returns with rare or unusual processing conditions

The IRS also may grant administrative exemptions when technology issues prevent specified preparers from filing returns electronically.

Form W-2 Requirements for E-Filing

An e-file provider is prohibited from submitting electronic returns prior to the receipt of all Forms W-2, W-2G, and 1099-R from the taxpayer. A provider also cannot advertise that he can file a tax return using only pay stubs or earning statements.

> **Example:** Kristen is a tax preparer. She advertises in her local newspaper that she will prepare a taxpayer's return "early" by using just their final earnings statement. This is prohibited.

If the taxpayer cannot provide a correct Form W-2, W-2G, or 1099R, the return may be electronically filed after Form 4852, *Substitute for Form W-2, Wage and Tax Statement*, or Form 1099-R, *Distributions from Pensions, Annuities, Retirement or Profit-Sharing Plans, IRAs, Insurance Contracts, etc.*, is completed. This is the only time information from pay stubs or leave and earnings statements is allowed.[67] The taxpayer must first make an attempt to obtain all the necessary forms from the employer. The Form 4852 should only be used as a last resort. Tax returns filed using Form 4852 cannot be e-filed. They must be filed on paper.

E-File Advertising Standards

Once accepted to participate in IRS e-file, a firm may represent itself as an "Authorized IRS e-file Provider." A practitioner must not use improper or misleading advertising in relation to IRS e-file, including promising a time frame for refunds.

Practitioners may not use the regular IRS logo (the eagle symbol) or IRS insignia in their advertising, or imply any type of relationship with the IRS. They may use the IRS e-file logo, but cannot combine the

---

[67] A leave and earning statement (LES) is a document given on a monthly basis to members of the U.S. military that documents their pay and leave status.

e-file logo with the IRS eagle symbol, the word "federal," or with other words or symbols that might suggest a special relationship with the IRS.

Advertising materials must not carry the FMS, IRS, or any other Treasury seals, but may use the IRS e-file logo. Use of any type of logo or insignia that copies of the IRS "eagle" logo is strictly prohibited.

If an e-file provider uses radio, television, Internet, signage, or other methods of advertising, the practitioner must keep a copy and provide it to the IRS upon request if any fee information is included in the advertising.

Copies of any advertising containing fee information or a fee schedule must be retained for a period of at least 36 months from the date of the last transmission or use.[68]

E-file Revocations and Sanctions

The IRS may revoke e-file privileges if a firm or individual is either:

- Prohibited or disbarred from filing returns by a court order, or
- Prohibited from filing returns by any federal or state legal action that forbids participation in e-file.

The IRS may also sanction any e-file provider who fails to comply with e-file regulations. Before sanctioning, the IRS may issue a warning letter that describes specific corrective action the provider must take.

The IRS categorizes the seriousness of infractions as Level One (the least serious), Level Two, and Level Three (the most serious). Sanctions may be a written reprimand, suspension, or expulsion from participation from IRS e-file. Suspended providers are generally not eligible to participate in e-filing for one to two years, depending on the seriousness of the infraction. If a principal or responsible official is suspended or expelled from participation in IRS e-file, every entity listed on the firm's e-file application may also be expelled.

Providers who are denied participation in IRS e-file usually have the right to an administrative review. In order to appeal, a provider must mail a written response within 30 days addressing the IRS's reason for denial or revocation and include supporting documentation. During this administrative review process, the denial of participation remains in effect.

In certain circumstances, the IRS can immediately suspend or expel an authorized IRS e-file provider without prior notice.

> **Example:** Malcom was a CPA who was convicted of felony embezzlement. He was also stripped of his license by his state accountancy board. The IRS revoked his e-file privileges without prior notice.

---

[68] Circular 230 (§ 10.30 Solicitation) states that copies of advertising that includes any mention of fees must be retained for a minimum of 36 months.

Unit 12: Study Questions

(Test yourself and then check the correct answers at the end of this chapter.)

1. Which logo may a practitioner use in his advertising?

A. The official IRS logo.
B. The IRS e-file logo.
C. The official seal of the U.S. Treasury.
D. The IRS eagle symbol.

2. Under new verification requirements, what must a preparer who accepts electronic signatures do to authenticate the identity of a client he meets with in person?

A. Inspect the client's Social Security card, or other taxpayer identification document.
B. Perform a credit check or take other identity verification measures through a third party.
C. Inspect a valid government-issued picture ID, compare the picture to the applicant, and record the name, Social Security number, address, and date of birth.
D. Both B and C.

3. The IRS may sanction providers who fail to comply with e-file regulations. It uses a specific system of categorizing how serious infractions are. Which is the most serious?

A. Level One.
B. Level Two.
C. Level Three.
D. Level Four.

4. Katie is an EA subject to the e-file mandate. She has power of attorney authority for her client, Timothy, who is paralyzed and physically unable to sign the return himself. What must she do to e-file Timothy's return?

A. Use Form 8453 and submit Form 2848, *Power of Attorney and Declaration of Representative,* as an attachment.
B. Use Form 8879 and submit Form 2848, *Power of Attorney and Declaration of Representative,* as an attachment.
C. Use the Practitioner PIN method as her signature requirement.
D. Katie is not allowed to e-file Timothy's return in this instance. She must file it on paper.

5. The IRS may excuse a preparer from the mandate to e-file in which of the following instances?

A. An administrative exemption due to technology issues.
B. An individual case of hardship documented by the preparer.
C. Lack of access to tax preparation software.
D. A preparer who does not like using a computer and prefers to fill out tax forms by hand.

6. If the IRS rejects an e-filed tax return for processing and the reason for the rejection cannot be rectified with the information already provided to the ERO, what is the ERO's responsibility at that point?

A. The ERO is not legally required to notify the taxpayer.
B. The ERO must attempt to notify the taxpayer within 24 hours and provide the taxpayer with the rejection code accompanied by an explanation.
C. The ERO is required to notify the taxpayer in writing within 72 hours.
D. The ERO is required to file the tax return on paper within 36 hours.

7. Electronic filing identification numbers (EFINs) are issued:

A. On a firm basis.
B. On a preparer basis.
C. On a client basis.
D. Only to foreign firms.

8. Tammy is an Enrolled Agent who e-files a return for her client, Rick. However, Rick's e-filed return is rejected by the IRS. They cannot resolve the rejection issue, and the return must be filed on paper. In order to timely file Rick's tax return, what is the deadline for filing a paper return?

A. The due date of the return.
B. Ten calendar days after the date the IRS rejects the e-filed return.
C. Forty-eight hours after the date the IRS rejects the e-filed return.
D. The later of either A or B.

9. Which of the following statements is correct?

A. Separate fees may be charged for direct deposits.
B. An e-file provider cannot charge a contingent fee based on a percentage of the refund on an original return.
C. An e-file provider cannot charge a fee for paper returns.
D. An e-file provider cannot charge a fee for e-filing.

10. What is the first step of the process for an individual to become an authorized e-file provider?

A. Apply for a PTIN.
B. Be fingerprinted and undergo a background check by the IRS.
C. Become a federally authorized practitioner.
D. Create an authorized e-Services account online.

11. Which of the following tax return preparers would be subject to the mandate that requires preparers to e-file their clients' returns?

A. Dean, a bookkeeper who prepares a tax return for himself.
B. RJ, an EA who only prepares payroll tax returns for her employer.
C. Scott, who files six individual tax returns and seven estate returns for compensation.
D. Chon, a CPA who files 100 returns for the Volunteer Income Tax Assistance (VITA) program.

1. The answer is B. A practitioner may use the IRS e-file logo, but may not use the IRS logo or insignia in his advertising or imply a relationship with the IRS. A practitioner may not combine the e-file logo with the IRS eagle symbol, the word "federal," or with other words or symbols that suggest a special relationship between the IRS and the practitioner. Advertising materials must not carry the IRS or other Treasury seals.

2. The answer is C. For in-person transactions, the preparer must inspect a valid government-issued picture ID, compare the picture to the applicant, and record the name, Social Security number, address, and date of birth. A credit check or other identity verification measures are optional. For remote transactions, the preparer must verify that the name, Social Security number, address, date of birth, and other personal information on record are consistent with the information provided through record checks with applicable agencies or institutions, or through credit bureaus or similar databases.

3. The answer is C. Under the IRS system of rating e-file infractions, Level One is the least serious, Level Two is moderately serious, and Level Three is the most serious. There is no Level Four infraction.

4. The answer is A. Since Katie is signing the return as Timothy's representative, she must use Form 8453, *U.S. Individual Income Tax Transmittal for an IRS e-file Return*, and also submit Form 2848, *Power of Attorney and Declaration of Representative,* as an attachment. Form 8879, *IRS e-file Signature Authorization,* is used by EROs, but only submitted to the IRS upon request.

5. The answer is B. An individual preparer's dislike of using a computer or the fact that he does not have appropriate software are not considered legitimate reasons to grant a hardship waiver. The IRS will grant e-file waivers in cases when technology makes it impossible to file electronically. E-file waivers due to hardship will also be granted, but only on a rare case-by-case basis and typically only for a single year. The preparer must submit Form 8944, *Preparer e-file Hardship Waiver Request*, to request a waiver. Waivers are reviewed and approved in cases where the preparer demonstrates that complying would be an undue hardship.

6. The answer is B. If the IRS rejects an e-filed tax return for processing and the reason for the rejection cannot be rectified, the ERO must take reasonable steps to inform the taxpayer of the rejection within 24 hours. The ERO must provide the taxpayer with the rejection code(s) accompanied by an explanation. After receiving a rejection, the ERO is not required to file a tax return on paper. The ERO and the client should attempt to correct the e-file. However, if the return continues to be rejected, the taxpayer may be forced to file on paper.

7. The answer is A. Electronic filing identification numbers (EFINs) are issued on a firm basis. All tax return preparers in a firm with the same physical location are covered by a single EFIN. Providers need an EFIN to electronically file tax returns.

8. The answer is D. In order to timely file a tax return, the taxpayer must file a paper return by the later of:
- The due date of the return, or
- Ten calendar days after the date the IRS gives notification that it rejected the e-filed return.

This is called the *Ten-Day Transmission Perfection Period*. This is not an extension of time to file; rather, this is additional time that the IRS gives a preparer and taxpayer to correct and resubmit a tax return without a late filing penalty.

9. The answer is B. Based on the current version of Circular 230, an e-file provider may not charge a contingent fee based on a percentage of the refund of an original tax return. Separate fees cannot be charged for direct deposits. However, a practitioner is allowed to charge a fee for e-filing. In 2014, in the landmark case of *Ridgely v. Lew*, the U.S. District Court issued a permanent injunction preventing the IRS from regulating contingent fee arrangements. At the time of this book's printing, the IRS has not yet made a public comment specifically about contingent fee arrangements or the outcome of the *Ridgely* case.

10. The answer is D. To become an authorized e-file provider, an individual must first register with the IRS by creating an IRS e-Services account online. The individual will need to provide personal information, including a Social Security number and an address where confirmation of the account will be mailed.

11. The answer is C. Any paid preparer who files 11 or more individual or trust returns in aggregate in a calendar year is required to e-file. There are limited exceptions, such as for returns that cannot be e-filed (returns that require paper attachments, nonresident returns, amended returns, etc.). The e-file mandate does not apply to payroll tax returns, volunteer preparers, or returns prepared under the Volunteer Income Tax Assistance (VITA) program.

Unit 13: Identity Theft and Safeguarding Taxpayer Data

More Reading:
Publication 4557, *Safeguarding Taxpayer Data*
Publication 5199, *Tax Preparer Guide to Identity Theft*
Publication 4600, *Safeguarding Taxpayer Information Quick Reference Guide for Business*

Identity Theft

Identity theft occurs when someone uses another individual's personally identifiable information, such as their name, Social Security number, or credit card number, without permission to commit fraud or other crimes. Fraudulent refunds have become a major issue, and identity theft is considered one of the biggest challenges facing the IRS. Safeguarding taxpayer data has become a top priority for the IRS.

Innocent taxpayers are victimized by tax fraud because their refunds are subsequently delayed. The taxpayer may be unaware that this has happened until they attempt to e-file their own return and discover that a return had already been filed using their SSN. The IRS may also send the taxpayer a letter saying it has identified a suspicious return using someone else's SSN.

Employment-related identity theft occurs when someone other than the valid owner of an SSN uses that SSN or other personal information for the purpose of obtaining employment. This type of fraudulent activity can affect both individuals and business entities.

If a taxpayer believes someone may have used his SSN fraudulently to file taxes, he should notify the IRS immediately. He will need to submit Form 14039, *Identity Theft Affidavit,* along with documentation to verify his identity.

Warning Signs for Individual Clients

A taxpayer's SSN can be stolen through a data breach, a computer hack or even a lost wallet. A client's SSN has been compromised when:

- A return is rejected and the IRS reject codes indicate the taxpayer's SSN already has been used.
- The client receives IRS notices regarding a tax return after all tax issues have been resolved, refund paid or account balances have been paid.
- An IRS notice indicates the client received wages from an employer unknown to them.
- The taxpayer's state or federal benefits were reduced or cancelled because the agency received information reporting an income increase or change.

Example: Sandra receives an IRS notice regarding her previous year's tax return. The notice includes a proposed adjustment for unreported wages. The IRS notice includes a transcript for wages from a company in another state where Sandra has never lived or worked. Sandra is a victim of identity theft.

Note: a tax practitioner must have a valid power of attorney (Form 2848) on file and authenticate the taxpayer's identity before any IRS employee can provide the practitioner with any taxpayer information regarding a fraud issue.

Warning Signs for Business Entities

Business identity theft (also known as corporate or commercial identity theft) happens when someone creates or uses the identifying information of a business to obtain tax benefits. Business identity thieves file fraudulent business returns to receive refundable business credits or to perpetuate individual identity theft. Business identity theft is more complex than individual identity theft. Many of the same indicators that signify simple filing or processing errors also hint at business identity theft.

Examples of when a client's EIN has been compromised include when:

- The client's business return is accepted as an amended return, but the taxpayer has not filed an original return for that year.
- The business receives IRS notices about fictitious or non-existent employees.
- Your client notices activity related to or receives IRS notices regarding a defunct, closed or dissolved business entity.

Example: Alan is the sole shareholder of a C corporation in the State of California. In 2017, he receives a notice from the IRS about a large refund for an amended return that had been filed for his corporation. Alan never filed or signed an amended return. He later discovers that his former bookkeeper, who had worked for him in a prior year, had filed the return and directed the refund to her home address, intending to illegally cash the check using stolen documents that she took from the business. Alan immediately contacts the IRS to report the fraud.

The majority of tax-related identity theft is initiated online, by using fake or "spoofed" email accounts. The IRS does not initiate contact with taxpayers by email to request personal or financial information. This includes any type of electronic communication, such as text messages and social media channels. Some of the individuals committing identity theft fraud are members of high-tech global rings engaged in organized criminal enterprises for stealing identities and profiting from that information. The U.S. Federal Trade Commission, the nation's consumer protection agency, provides guidance to businesses regarding information compromise and data theft schemes.

Authorized IRS e-file Providers must follow the six IRS mandated security, privacy, and business standards to better serve taxpayers and protect their individual income tax information that is collected, processed, and stored.[69]

Avoid Being a Victim

Be suspicious of unsolicited phone calls, visits, or email messages from individuals asking about employees or other internal information. Do not provide personal information or information about an organization, unless you are certain of a person's authority to have the information.

Do not reveal personal or financial information in an email, and do not respond to email solicitations for this information. This includes following links sent in email. Pay attention to the URL (web address) of a website. Malicious websites may look identical to a legitimate site, but the URL may use a variation in spelling or a different domain that looks or sounds similar to the genuine website.

If you are unsure whether an email request is legitimate, attempt to verify it by contacting the company directly by phone. Do not use contact information provided on a website connected to the request; instead, check previous statements for contact information. Install and maintain anti-virus software, firewalls, and email filters to reduce some of this traffic. Consider reporting attacks to the police, and file a report with the Federal Trade Commission.

---

[69] See "Safeguarding IRS e-file" in Publications 1345 for more information.

If a tax professional has a data breach where client information is compromised, the data breach must be reported to the IRS.

Phishing Attacks

Phishing attacks (also called "spear phishing" attacks) are a form of social engineering. Phishing attacks use email or malicious websites to solicit personal information by posing as a trustworthy person or organization. Phishing emails target a broad group of users in hopes of catching a few victims. For example, an attacker may send email seemingly from a reputable credit card company, bank, or other financial institution that requests account information, often suggesting that there is a problem. When users respond with the requested information, attackers can use it to gain access to the accounts.

Phishing attacks may also appear to come from other types of organizations, such as charities. Attackers often take advantage of current events and certain times of the year, such as natural disasters (i.e., Hurricane Irma and Harvey) or economic concerns (i.e., IRS scams) major political elections, and holidays in order to lure a response. Most phishing emails have a "call to action" as part of their tactics, an effort to encourage the receiver into clicking a link or opening an attachment.

Other phishing emails impersonate the IRS, or in some instances a private tax software provider. In those examples, preparers are warned that they must immediately update their account information or suffer some consequence. The link may go to a website that has been disguised to look like the login pages for IRS e-Services or a tax software provider.

> **Example:** Paul receives an email alert from his brokerage firm, attempting to warn him of an "invalid login" to his account. The email urges him to click on a link in order to re-login to his account to update his personal data and verify his identity. Paul immediately clicks on the link within the email, not realizing that the link leads to a fake or "spoofed" website. Paul enters his username and password into the fake site, and the scammer records them and is able to use them.

Protecting Clients from Phishing

There is no one action to protect your clients or your business from spear phishing. It requires a series of defensive steps. Tax professionals should consider these basic steps:

- Educate all employees about phishing in general and spear phishing in particular.
- Use strong, unique passwords. Use a phrase instead of a single word. Use different passwords for each account.
- Never take an email from a familiar source at face value; example: an email from "IRS e-Services." If it asks you to open a link or attachment, or includes a threat to close your account, think twice. Visit the e-Services website for confirmation.
- If an email contains a link, hover the mouse cursor over the link to see the web address (URL) destination. If it's not a URL you recognize or if it's an abbreviated URL, don't open it.
- Consider a verbal confirmation by phone if you receive an email from a new client sending you tax information or a client requesting last-minute changes to their refund destination.
- Use security software to help defend against malware, viruses and known phishing sites and update the software automatically.
- Use the security options that come with your tax preparation software.
- Report all suspicious tax-related phishing emails to phishing@irs.gov.

Social Engineering Attacks

In a social engineering attack,[70] an attacker uses social skills and human interaction to obtain information about an organization. An attacker may seem unassuming and respectable, possibly claiming to be a new employee, repair person, or researcher and even offering credentials to support that identity. If an attacker is not able to gather enough information from one source, he or she may contact another source within the same organization and rely on the information from the first source to add to his or her credibility. Cybercriminals will sometimes pose as company executives in order to obtain sensitive personal information, such as names, birthdates, and payroll information.

Example: Cindy is the company bookkeeper for Cape Industrial Construction. The company has 250 employees. In late January, Cindy had just completed the Form W-2s for all the employees when she received an urgent email from the company's owner. The email stated: "I want you to send me the copies of all the employees' wage and tax statement for 2017. You can send it as an attachment. Kindly prepare the lists and email them to me ASAP." Cindy immediately prepared the document and emailed it back to her boss. However, she did not realize that the email address had been "spoofed" or had a forged sender address. Cindy unknowingly sent sensitive employee information to a cybercriminal.

Stolen Identity Refund Fraud (SIRF)

Tax refund fraud involving the use of stolen identities is referred to as SIRF, for Stolen Identity Refund Fraud.

This growing type of crime occurs when thieves file fraudulent refund claims using a legitimate taxpayer's identifying information, which they have stolen. In a recent IRS report, the IRS estimated that approximately $30 billion of identity theft-related refund fraud was attempted during the tax year, and approximately $5.8 billion was paid out (since some refund fraud remained undetected, the government's actual losses were actually even greater).[71]

SIRF Enforcement: The IRS has greatly expanded its identity theft enforcement efforts, with more than 3,000 employees now assigned to work on identity-theft related issues. In fiscal year 2017, the IRS started over 1,400 criminal investigations regarding taxpayer identity theft.

Identity Theft Prevention

Every day, the theft of personal and financial information puts people at risk of identity theft. Generally, thieves try to use the stolen data as quickly as possible to:

- Sell the information to other cybercriminals.
- Withdraw money from the victim's bank account.
- Make fraudulent credit card purchases.
- File a fraudulent tax return for a refund using victims' names.

To help stop identity thieves, the IRS says it now has dozens of identity theft screening filters in place to protect tax refunds. To educate taxpayers, the IRS has added a guide to identity theft on its website. Taxpayers are advised to be on the alert for possible identity theft if they receive an IRS notice or letter stating that any of the following has occurred:

- There was more than one tax return filed by the taxpayer.

---

[70] Information provided by the U.S. Department of Homeland Security, U.S. Computer Readiness Team.
[71] Internal Revenue Service Advisory Council Public Report.

- The taxpayer has a balance due, refund offset, or has had collection actions taken against him for a year in which he did not file a tax return.
- IRS records indicate the taxpayer received wages from an unknown employer.

The IRS will never seek financial or personal information by initiating contact with taxpayers by email. Many of these so-called "phishing" scams attempt to collect taxpayer Social Security numbers by contacting taxpayers using these methods. Phone scams with callers purporting to be from the IRS also have become widespread in recent years, with more than 190,000 reports of these calls in the last three years.

Clients may also be victims of identity theft not related to tax administration if they:
- Receive bills for business lines of credit or credit cards they do not have.
- Notice that a credit report indicates credit or other open accounts they did not authorize.
- See unexplained bank account withdrawals.
- Suddenly don't get their bills or other mail.
- Find unfamiliar accounts or charges on their credit report.

Even if the taxpayer has not been a victim of tax-related identity theft, but has been a victim of another type of fraud, it is still advisable for the taxpayer to fill out IRS Form 14039, *Identity Theft Affidavit,* in order to report the potential for future fraudulent activity.

Tax practitioners can also become targets of cyber-criminals. Online providers who experience a data breach are required to contact the IRS within one business day.

If the taxpayer's SSN is compromised, the IRS recommends the following steps:
- Get a notice that information was compromised by a data breach at a company where they do business or have an account.
- Complete IRS Form 14039, *Identity Theft Affidavit*, if the taxpayer's e-file return rejects because of a duplicate filing under the client's SSN.
- The taxpayer should continue to pay their taxes and file their tax return, even if they must do so by paper.
- If the taxpayer had previously contacted the IRS and did not receive a resolution, they may contact the IRS for specialized assistance at 1-800-908-4490.
- Respond immediately to any IRS notice; call the number provided or, if instructed, go to *www.IDVerify.irs.gov*. The IRS offers an Identity Verification Service for taxpayers who receive an IRS notice regarding possible identity theft on their accounts.

IP PINs

As part of its crackdown on identity theft, the IRS is issuing an identity protection personal identification number (IP PIN) to certain taxpayers. An IP PIN is a six-digit number assigned to eligible taxpayers. A taxpayer is eligible if he:
- Reported to the IRS he has been the victim of identity theft and the IRS has resolved his case;
- Filed his federal tax return as a resident of Florida, Georgia, or the District of Columbia; or
- Received an IRS notice or letter asking him to voluntarily opt in to receive an IP PIN.

The IP PIN helps prevent the misuse of a taxpayer's Social Security number or taxpayer identification number. It is used on both paper and electronic returns. If the taxpayer attempts to file an electronic return without his IP PIN, the return will be rejected.

If the taxpayer loses his IP PIN and decides to submit a paper return, there will likely be a delay in processing, as the IRS will have to validate the taxpayer's identity.

The IP PIN is only valid for a single year. A taxpayer will receive a new IP PIN every year for three years after reporting the identity theft incident to the IRS. If a spouse also has an IP PIN, only the person whose SSN appears first on the tax return needs to input his PIN.

> **Example:** Bethany attempted to file her tax return electronically this year, but it was rejected. The IRS reject code stated that a tax return had already been filed for her. Bethany immediately contacted the IRS and reported the fraud. The IRS determined that she was a victim of refund fraud and placed an "identity theft indicator" on her account. Bethany is forced to file her return on paper this year, and the processing time for her return is increased. In December, the IRS will send her a CP01A Notice containing her IP PIN. Bethany will not be able to e-file her tax return without the IP PIN, which will help prevent refund fraud on her account in the future.

Direct Deposit Limits

IRS procedure limits the number of refunds electronically deposited into a single financial account or prepaid debit card to three. Any additional refunds will be converted to a paper refund check and mailed to the taxpayer.

The direct deposit limit is intended to prevent criminals from easily obtaining multiple tax refunds. It is also designed to protect taxpayers from unscrupulous tax preparers who obtain payment for their services by depositing part or all of their clients' refunds into their own bank accounts, an action that is prohibited under the IRC and subject to discipline under Circular 230.

Safeguarding Taxpayer Data

Since tax return preparers are required to obtain and store client information, they have an important role to play in keeping this information secure. To help prevent identity theft, the IRS suggests preparers to confirm identities and taxpayer identification numbers of taxpayers, their spouses, and dependents on the returns to be prepared. TINs include Social Security numbers (SSNs), adopted taxpayer identification numbers (ATINs), and individual taxpayer identification numbers (ITINs).

To confirm identities, the preparer can request a picture ID showing the taxpayer's name and address, and Social Security cards or other documents providing the TINs for all other individuals to be listed on the return.[72] Additional steps practitioners can take to guard against identity theft include the following:

- File clients' returns early when possible.
- E-file returns, in order to be notified of duplicate return notices more quickly.
- Let clients know that refunds may take longer in future years as additional system security steps are taken.

Since tax return preparers are at risk of having their identities, and those of their clients, stolen, they should take special precautions to safeguard their clients' sensitive information. A tax practitioner must determine the appropriate security controls for their business. Security controls are the management, operational, and technical safeguards you may use to protect the confidentiality, integrity and availability of your customers' information. Examples of security controls are:

---

[72] A later unit, (*IRS E-File*), covers new requirements to confirm clients' identities for tax preparers who e-file.

- Locking desk drawers and file cabinets.
- Locking doors to restrict access to paper and electronic files.
- Requiring passwords to restrict access to computer files
- Using encrypted flash drives and using other encrypted procedures in electronically transferring a client's information to a third party – including e-mails.
- Keeping a backup of electronic data for recovery purposes.
- Redacting or truncating SSNs and other personal information.
- Shredding paper containing taxpayer information before throwing it in the trash.
- Using couriers and certified mail to ensure that the correct person receives the correspondence.
- Installing and requiring antivirus and other security software on all of the firm's computers.
- Requiring that all outside contractors maintain the same level of security protocols as the preparer

Note: Taxpayer data is defined as any information that is obtained or used in the preparation of a tax return (i.e., income statements, bookkeeping records, information statements, tax organizers, etc.).

Safeguarding taxpayer information is a top priority for the Internal Revenue Service. The *Gramm-Leach-Bliley Act* "Safeguards Rule" requires tax preparers and others who are significantly engaged in providing financial products or services that include preparation and filing of tax returns, to ensure the security and confidentiality of their customer's records and information.[73]

An "information security incident" is an adverse event that can result in an unauthorized disclosure, misuse, modification, or destruction of sensitive taxpayer information. Information security incidents are events that give cybercriminals access to sensitive information (personally identifiable details, passwords, academic, or financial records) without permission.

Types of incidents include: theft of taxpayer information, malicious attacks, and even natural disasters such as a flood, earthquake, or fire that destroys unrecoverable information and computer systems or networks.

---

[73] The Safeguards Rule, which is a law that took effect in 2003, requires tax professionals, data processors, and financial institutions to develop, implement and maintain a comprehensive information security program for handling customer information.

(Test yourself and then check the correct answers at the end of this chapter.)

1. The maximum number of refunds that may be electronically deposited into a single financial account is:

A. One.
B. Two.
C. Three.
D. No limit.

2. Which of the following events would be considered an "information security incident"?

A. A client attempts to claim a false dependent.
B. An email containing sensitive client information is sent to incorrect recipients.
C. A taxpayer files their own tax return using online software.
D. A tax professional loses their internet access.

3. What is an IP PIN?

A. An alternative method of signing a tax return.
B. An alternative Social Security number.
C. A tax ID number for taxpayers who are ineligible for an ITIN or an SSN.
D. A six-digit number that helps prevent the misuse of a taxpayer's Social Security number.

4. Donald discovers that he is the victim of identity theft. Which IRS form should he use in order to alert the IRS to possible refund fraud on his individual tax account?

A. Form 14039
B. Form 8821
C. Form 2448
D. Form 2106

5. How long is an IP PIN valid?

A. Indefinitely.
B. An IP PIN is valid for one year.
C. An IP PIN is valid for six months.
D. An IP PIN is valid for three years.

Unit 13: Quiz Answers

1. The answer is C. To combat identity theft, new IRS procedures limit the number of refunds that may be electronically deposited into a single financial account or prepaid debit card to three. Any additional refund(s) will be converted to a paper refund check and mailed to the taxpayer.

2. The answer is B. The IRS requires tax professionals to report data breaches and other security incidents. An "information security incident" is an adverse event or the threat of an event that can result in an unauthorized disclosure, misuse, modification, or destruction of sensitive taxpayer information.

3. The answer is D. An IP PIN is a six-digit number assigned to eligible taxpayers that helps prevent the misuse of their Social Security number as part of its crackdown on identity theft, the IRS is issuing an identity protection personal identification number (IP PIN) to certain taxpayers. A taxpayer is eligible if he:
- Reported to the IRS he has been the victim of identity theft and the IRS has resolved his case;
- Filed his federal tax return as a resident of Florida, Georgia, or the District of Columbia; or
- Received an IRS notice or letter asking him to voluntarily opt in to receive an IP PIN.

4. The answer is A. Donald should fill out Form 14039, which is an identity theft affidavit. Even if the taxpayer has not been a victim of tax-related identity theft, but has been a victim of another type of fraud, it is still advisable for the taxpayer to fill out IRS Form 14039, Identity Theft Affidavit, in order to report the potential for future fraudulent activity.

5. The answer is B. An IP PIN is only valid for a single year. A taxpayer will receive a new IP PIN every year for three years after reporting the identity theft incident to the IRS. If a spouse also has an IP PIN, only the person whose SSN appears first on the tax return needs to input his PIN.

INDEX

About the Authors

Richard Gramkow, EA, MST

Richard Gramkow is an Enrolled Agent with more than eighteen years of experience in various areas of taxation. He holds a master's degree in taxation from Rutgers University and is currently a tax manager for a publicly held Fortune 500 company in the New York metropolitan area.

Christy Pinheiro, EA, ABA®

Christy Pinheiro is an Enrolled Agent and an Accredited Business Accountant. Christy was an accountant for two private CPA firms and for the State of California before going into private practice.

Kolleen Wells, EA

Kolleen Wells is an Enrolled Agent and a Certified Bookkeeper who specializes in tax preparation for individuals and small businesses. She has worked in the accounting field for many years, including positions at a CPA office and at the county assessor's office.

Joel Busch, CPA, JD

Joel Busch is a tax professor at San Jose State University, where he teaches courses at both the graduate and undergraduate levels. Previously, he was in charge of tax audits, research, and planning for one of the largest civil construction and mining companies in the United States.